GW01090469

FORRARD

FORRARD

The Story of the East Riding Yeomanry

by

PAUL MACE

with

TED WRIGHT

with a Foreword by
FIELD MARSHAL LORD CARVER
GCB, CBE, DSO, MC

LEO COOPER

First published in Great Britain in 2001 by
LEO COOPER
an imprint of
Pen & Sword Books Ltd
47 Church Street
Barnsley
South Yorkshire
S70 2AS

Copyright © Paul Mace 2001

ISBN 0 85052 800 3

A catalogue record for this book is available from the British Library.

Typeset in 10.5/12.5pt Plantin by
Phoenix Typesetting, Ilkley, West Yorkshire

Printed in England by
CPI UK

CONTENTS

MAPS

FOREWORD

by
Field Marshal Lord Carver, CGB, CBE, DSO, MC.

Paul Mace and Ted Wright's account of the experiences of the East Riding Yeomanry in the Second World War is a labour of love. It will give great pleasure to all old comrades of the Regiment and to those who have been members of, or associated with it and its successors, since 1945.

But it will also appeal to all those who are interested in learning what war, from 1939 to 1945, was like for those who fought in it. Based as it is on many first-hand accounts of men of all ranks, it paints a vivid picture of life in a Yeomanry Regiment, with its close family and regional links, both in and out of action, involving sometimes a certain tension with the regular army.

Those 224,320 British troops who were successfully evacuated from Dunkirk in May 1940 owed a great debt of gratitude, too often forgotten, to the gallant stand made by the troops acting as rearguard, who included the 1st East Riding Yeomanry at Cassel supporting 145th Infantry Brigade. Only 237 members of the Regiment returned: the rest had either become casualties or were marched off into prisoner-of-war camps. The 2nd Regiment, subject to many changes of command and role, proved themselves as adaptable as they were courageous in action in Normandy, in clearing the Channel coast as Montgomery drove his forces into Belgium, in driving the Germans northwards out of the Low Countries, and in the Ardennes. They played a key part in crossing the Rhine and helped Montgomery forward all the way to the Baltic. Those who carried the Fox as their badge and 'Forrard' as their motto have every reason to be proud of their deeds, so vividly here portrayed.

Michael Carver. FM

AUTHORS' NOTE
by
Paul Mace

This all started with the sentence in a book I was reading: "The two other regiments in the Brigade were '*absentees* from the battle'." Good heavens, I thought, he's talking about *my* Regiment. I have always understood the word "Absentee" to mean someone who has deliberately absented himself from a duty. It was the first time in decades that I had thought of the East Riding Yeomanry as *my* Regiment, and it converted me from an attitude of indifference to one of pride and loyalty.

I had been reading Max Hastings' otherwise excellent book *Overlord*. He was giving a description of the battle for Caen on that first day of the landings in Europe on 6 June 1944. Our Armoured Brigade, the 27th, with the insignia of the Sea Horse (known as the "Pregnant Prawn"), was supporting the 3rd British Infantry Division on the initial landings, with Caen as the first day's initial objective, but the "high ground about Bourguebus" beyond as General Montgomery's ultimate aspiration for the armour.

I had read more than enough. The book winged its way across the room as I hurled it into a corner. "Absentees" from the battle! Faces I remember from the past flashed before me – George Jenkin who won an MC on 7 June, Victor Ellison, the 2 i/c of the regiment, the coolest of cool gentlemen, Emmerson, my gunner, and a host of others. Absentees – that they never were.

I was so taken aback by this assessment that I contacted and joined our Old Comrades' Association and with an old friend went to France the following June to see for myself where the Regiment had landed on that day, to trace the battles they fought and to confound the slur upon the Regimental escutcheon.

I confess that some time later I picked up the book again and read the paragraph once more. After that bald sentence, Max Hastings had gone on to describe at some length the role of an Independent Armoured Brigade. At the end of this paragraph was a short sentence: "The other two regiments in the Brigade (of which the East Riding Yeomanry was one) were heavily engaged on the beaches clearing the flanks". They were in fact off the beaches and had advanced inland a short way, but that first sentence was the catalyst for what now follows.

I must therefore acknowledge my thanks to that notable author for returning me to the fold!

I went to France in June 1990 with my old friend Keith Loughlin, having spent some months researching for our few days, and on our return I wrote a report which we sent to various people concerned with the Yeomanry. One copy I sent to Victor Ellison who was the Colonel of the reformed regiment and had been President of the Old Comrades' Association. He wrote to me immediately with encouragement and enthusiasm and ignited the flame, so this story is the result.

In order to write the story of the East Riding Yeomanry, I have tried to use the descriptions of the members of the Regiment themselves. So I sent out several hundred questionnaires, visited many at their homes and went to the Old Comrades' Dinners; the response has been great. The odd negative came in, but mostly tremendous help, support and enthusiasm, stories, photographs and memories. To everyone I say "Thank You". Victor, who died in February 1991, wrote an enormous amount for me; Ted Wright sent me a great quantity of files, information and a chapter of biographical memoirs relating to his time with the Regiment. Dennis Bell, when Secretary of the OCA, loaned me the original diary of the 1st Regiment compiled by the officers taken prisoner in those terrible days of 1940. Tom Carmichael and John Dixon have lent me and given me permission to use extracts from the diaries they kept of the rearguard actions fought in May 1940. These documents and writings are of prime importance to the historian who wants to read an accurate description of a regiment at war. To me, as the writer of the regimental story, they are beyond price. Particularly, I should explain that I joined the ERY on 27 October 1944 as a callow Second Lieutenant when they had already reached s'Hertogenbosh in Holland; and "retired hurt" in January 1945. I was therefore forced to rely on others for eye-witness accounts of earlier events.

My chief "other" has been Ted Wright who has not only corrected many of my errors but has written a new Chapter 10 and other passages.

He brought to life many of the actions and duties of the members of the Regiment in their daily tasks. At the same time he has written the "Signposts", giving a global picture of other happenings at the time. His advice, help and capacious memory have been constantly available to me. My thanks to him are endless; he even taught me to grow up as a young Second Lieutenant when he was 2i/c B Squadron and I joined the Regiment.

NOTE BY TED WRIGHT

In 1989/90 Paul Mace told me that he was planning to write a history of the East Riding Yeomanry in the Second World War, and had begun to canvass old comrades for memories of their experiences. I was able to send him a long account of my own reminiscences of soldiering from 1939–1945, for the most part in the Yeomanry, which I had already put down for my family's information. This in turn led to a long period of collusion, since he was himself with the Regiment for an all-too-short spell in NW Europe in 1944–5 before being wounded in the Ardennes campaign and had little personal experience of events before and after. I was able therefore to provide much guidance on events and personalities outside his own knowledge.

For me this has been a great privilege and to some extent an easing of my own conscience, since I had at one time harboured ideas along the same lines, recognizing that people who could remember as much as I of what had gone on were becoming increasingly rare and sensing that I had some responsibility for doing something about it. As his account developed into a readable form, our collaboration has deepened and I have been able to help with the clarification of his successive drafts, unravel some of the problems of the sequence of events and fill in substantial gaps in the story where he was unable to obtain enough information from other sources. Finally I have been able to introduce him to a friend who, largely out of interest, has produced a tidy typescript and accompanying disc fit for delivery to a publisher. For me this has been most rewarding work and, on behalf of all Old Comrades, I salute Paul for his dedication to the task of compiling a readable and accurate account of the Regiment's exploits.

Ted Wright
February 2000

GLOSSARY

AA	Anti-aircraft guns: light or heavy.
A Echelon	Forward section of regimental transport carrying Ammunition, Fuel and Rations for front-line replenishment.
AP	Armour-piercing: shot or hollow-charge.
APC	Armoured Personnel Carrier: tracked or half-tracked vehicle for carrying infantry into action with protection against enemy fire.
Armour or AFVs	Armoured Fighting Vehicles usually applied to Tanks, operating in Armoured Divisions, Brigades and Regiments.
Armd BDE	Armoured Brigade (see 'Independent').
Armd Div	Armoured Division.
ARV	Armoured Recovery Vehicle, a turretless tank for battlefield recovery.
Army	Formation of two or more Corps with supporting troops.
Army Group	Largest formation in Allied Forces comprising two or more Armies – 12th US and 21st British in NW Europe campaign.
Artillery	Field, Medium (including 25 pdr) or Heavy guns, both towed and self-propelled (SP). Normally not deployed below divisional level.
A/TK, Anti-tank	Guns, towed or SP, for destroying tanks: (British) 2 Pdr, 6 Pdr, 17 Pdr.
AVRE	Specialized tanks (Armoured Vehicle Royal Engineers) equipped with bridges and devices for

	crossing obstacles or weapons for attacking reinforced strong points.
Battalion (Bn)	Standard (British) Infantry unit of about 800 of all ranks (CO – Lieutenant Colonel).
Battery	Smallest self-contained artillery unit normally of 8 guns in two troops.
B Echelon	Main body of regimental transport carrying bulk of supplies.
BESA	Belt-fed 7.62 mm machine gun for mounting in British tanks as secondary armament.
Boyes Rifle	Single shot .55" A/TK rifle issued to British Infantry and Divisional Cavalry Regiments in 1939–40. Penetrated lighter armour.
Bren	Standard .303 magazine-fed light machine gun in British Army.
Brigade (Bde)	British formation of 3 battalions of infantry or regiments of tanks (Armoured Brigade) commanded by Brigadier.
Browning	American belt-fed machine gun, .30 or .5, ground-mounted or in tanks and aircraft.
Cannon	20 or 22 mm automatic, drum-fed gun originally for aircraft mounting but adapted for ground use in Light AA role.
Capt	Captain.
Carrier	Light, open-topped, tracked vehicle for use in infantry and other units for a variety of purposes – originally Bren carrier and later the Universal Carrier. Armoured against small arms fire.
Churchill	At 38 tons the heaviest tank built by British in WW2. Originally designed as an infantry Tank. Slow but with excellent cross-country performance. Undergunned.
Christie Suspension	Special springing and balancing of the gun platform of a tank.
CO	Commanding Officer – usually refers to Battalion or Regiment.
Co-ax	A machine gun mounted in the same housing as the main armament of a tank but able to be fired independently.

Comet	The most up-to-date British tank just coming into use at the end of WW2. Could compete with the German Panther.
Company (Coy)	Infantry unit of about 100 commanded by Major or Captain. 4 to Battalion each of 4 Platoons.
Corps	Formation of two or more Divisions plus supporting arms. In 1940 the BEF consisted of three corps and in 1944 21 Army Group of I, VIII, XII and XXX British Corps and II Canadian Corps.
Cpl/LCpl	Corporal/Lance Corporal: non-commissioned rank below sergeant. Always considered, by themselves at least, as the most important ranks in the army.
Crocodile	Churchill Tank equipped as flame-thrower with towed trailer containing 400 gals of fuel.
Cromwell	Last "Cruiser" tank issued to 7th Armoured Division and Independent Armoured Brigades in 1944/5. Roughly equal to Sherman but less reliable.
Cruiser	Tanks for rapid manoeuvre; Mks I and II issued to 1 Armoured Division and fought in France after Dunkirk campaign. Undergunned and armoured – no match for Germans.
Crusader	Heavier Cruiser tank (weight 19 tons). Two Squadrons of ERY had Crusaders in 1941–2. Much used in the campaign in N Africa.
DCM	Distinguished Conduct Medal: the most prestigious decoration awarded to non-commissioned ranks in the British Army after the Victoria Cross (VC).
DD	Duplex Drive Sherman which with screen erected could swim ashore to assault beach defences. With screen lowered could act as a normal tank. A successful secret weapon. Driven by propeller in water and tracks on land (hence "Duplex").
Dingo	Armoured scout car, given this nickname by Australian troops in Western Desert.
DR	Dispatch Rider. A good motor-cycle rider who took messages from RHQ to different places and formations.

DSO	Distinguished Service Order: decoration awarded to officers of the rank of Major or above either for gallantry in action or other distinguished service.
DUKW	American wheeled amphibious truck.
"88"	German 88mm Heavy AA or A/TK gun on dual-purpose mounting, lethal to allied tanks even at very long range.
Engineers (Sappers)	Royal Engineers whose functions were primarily bridging and demolition; units of RE were attached down to divisional level.
Fitters	Qualified Mechanics in an Armoured Regiment dispersed down to Squadron level and undertaking repair work beyond the powers of a tank crew.
Flak	German abbreviation for anti-aircraft fire, commonly adopted by the British Army and extended to include verbal criticism.
Gen	General (See also Maj Gen, Lt Gen).
Gunners	Colloquial name for the Royal Artillery.
Honey	Nickname given (in N Africa) to the American Stuart Light Tank.
HE	High Explosive.
H-Hour	Time at which an assault landing is due to take place or on land an attack to cross the Start Line.
Indep	Independent; Especially of Independent Armoured Brigades usually of three Armoured Regiments and occasionally with a Motor Batallion added. They were normally Army or Corps troops and attached to Infantry formations for specific tanks.
Kangaroo	Name given to the first APCs in Normandy: Sherman tanks with the turret removed.
Laager or Leaguer	Formation adopted by tanks withdrawn from action at the fall of darkness, for rest and replenishment in the open.
LCA	Landing Craft Assault to land up to a platoon of infantry for a beach-assault.
LCI	Various forms of Landing Craft Infantry for other purposes in the assault.
LCT	Landing Craft Tank carrying up to nine Shermans

	or a mixture of other vehicles, with ramps for lowering them onto beaches.
L/Sgt	Lance Sergeant.
LSI	Large, often converted merchant ships which carried LCAs or LCIs on davits to convey infantry ashore.
LST	Landing Ship Tank: carrying follow-up armour landing them down ramps. Could beach if required.
Lt/2/Lt	Lieutenant/2nd Lieutenant.
Lt Col	Lieutenant Colonel.
Lt Gen	Lieutenant General.
LVT	Landing Vehicle Tracked or Buffalo: tracked amphibious vehicle to carry infantry, light vehicles or stores for assault landings or major river-crossings.
LAD	Light Aid Detachment – Unit of REME in Armoured Regiment, to carry out recovery and repairs to tanks beyond the capability of the regiment's Fitters and ARVs.
Maj	Major.
MG	Machine Gun: belt or drum-fed automatic gun of rifle or heavier calibre (e.g. .5 Vickers or Browning) for ground or as secondary armament in tanks etc.
MC	Military Cross: British decoration for bravery awarded to officers up to the rank of Major inclusive: not awarded posthumously.
MM	Military Medal British decoration awarded for bravery open to Ranks other than officers.
MO	Medical Officer in a regiment or battalion.
Mortar	Short-range device to fire explosive bombs with high trajectory: 2" and 3" mortars issued to infantry units; heavy (4.2") mortars in MG Battalions.
MkVI	Agile lightly armoured tank armed with .303 and .5 Vickers MGs issued to divisional cavalry regiments: phased out in 1941. With carriers was the equipment of 1st ERY in 1940.

Motor Battalion	Specialist battalion of mobile infantry (usually KRRC or Rifle Brigade) in Armoured Brigades of Armoured Divisions and some Independent Armoured Brigades. Carried (1944–5) in armoured half tracks; equivalent of German Panzer Grenadiers.
NCO	Non Commissioned Officer; Lance Corporal, Corporal, Sergeant or Staff Sergeant in British Army.
Nebelwerfer	Rocket-propelled HE assault-weapons in the German Army in multiple mountings for close support. Could produce severe effect on troops in the open, made worse by the sirens fitted which resulted in their name of "Moaning Minnies".
Oerlikon	20 mm cannon used in light AA role. Twin Oerlikons were mounted in the ERY's AA tanks for the Normandy Invasion.
Panther	German tank (PZKW5), well armoured and with 75mm guns. Equipment of SS Panzer Divisions and some others in NW Europe.
Panzer	Abbreviation of German "Panzerkampwagen" referred to tanks ("Panzers") and as prefix of armoured formations and units in German army.
Platoon (Pn)	Second smallest infantry unit of – Sections. Normally commanded by subaltern officer.
Panzerfaust	Short-range, hand-held anti-tank weapon in German army. Rocket propelled and with hollow-charge warhead could easily knock out a Sherman (lit. "Panzer-fist").
PZKW	German abbreviation for Panzerkampwagen. In Normandy the normal Panzer Divisions were equipped with the PZKW IV or the up-gunned PZKW IV Special and the SS Panzer Divisions with the PZKW V (Panther).
Q (function)	Supply service in the British Army.
QM	Quartermaster. In a regiment or battalion the Quartermaster was a commissioned officer: (thus: Lieutenant QM or Captain QM with an RQMS (WO II), RHQ an SQMS (WO III) etc.)

RAC	Royal Armoured Corps.
RAP	Regimental Aid Post. First aid station manned by the Medical Officer (MO) and Orderlies. Serious casualties would be sent back to an Advanced Dressing Station (ADS).
Regiment	Basic unit in British Armoured forces and Artillery commanded by a Lieutenant Colonel with HQ Squadron and three "Sabre" Squadrons plus RHQ troops. All found, an Armoured Regiment for the invasion had 61 main tanks (Shermans) plus Reconnaissance and AA Troops. In American and German armies a "Regiment" was the equivalent of a British Brigade.
Recce Troop	Reconnaissance Troop of 10 (or 12) Stuart Light Tanks.
RHQ	Regimental Headquarters.
RV	Rendezvous.
RSM	Regimental Sergeant Major, the senior Warrant Officer (WO I) in a regiment.
Sgt	Sergeant (see also L/Sgt).
SHAEF	Supreme Headquarters Allied Expeditionary Force, commanded by General Eisenhower.
SP	Self-propelled, applied to mobile anti-tank or other gun, usually on tracked chassis.
Sherman	Tank produced in great numbers by American motor industry and in several marks. It was a reasonably capable tank and very reliable, but no match for the German Tigers and Panthers except in its up-gunned form with 17 pdr ("Firefly"), issued one per troop in British armoured units.
SM	Sergeant Major (see also RSM, SSM, TSM).
Spandau	German MG 34 and MG 42 Machine Guns, notable for very high rate of fire,
SQMS	Squadron Quartermaster Sergeant.
SSM	Squadron Sergeant Major.
STEN	British standard 9mm submachine gun.
Stick	Of bombs or parachutists.
Stonk	Term used in British Army for artillery or mortar concentration.

Stuart	American-made light tank used for reconnaissance. Its high outline made it easy to spot and some units removed the turrets for better concealment. (See also Honey.)
SVDS	Super Velocity Discarding ("Sabot"). Special armour-piercing ammunition issued in time for the Ardennes counter-offensive. It had a very high muzzle velocity and could penetrate the armour even of the Tiger tank.
T.A.	Territorial Army.
Tank	Tracked Armoured Fighting Vehicle, usually with all-round traverse for the turret housing the main gun and a coaxial MG.
Tiger	The German PZKW VI with very thick armour and .88 mm main gun. Very dangerous to allied tanks and almost invulnerable except to 19 pdrs (guns or Firefly). Slow and unreliable, Tigers operated in Heavy Tank Battalions. The very heaviest Royal Tigers operated in the Ardennes campaign.
Troop	Small unit of three tanks (or artillery) in British Army commanded by a subaltern or, especially in 1940, by a Troop Sergeant Major (TSM; a WO III).
TSM	Troop Sergeant Major, Warrant Officer OC some troops (1940).
Typhoon	The main British ground support aircraft carrying eight 60 pdr rockets.
WO	Warrant Officer Class I, II or III. The senior ranks of Non Commissioned Officers; RSM, SSM, RQMS, SQMS.

Part I

ORIGINS

Chapter 1

ORIGINS

The story, then, is primarily the story of the East Riding Yeomanry during the Second World War. However, its beginnings were described in a letter to Edmund Scott, from Guy Wilson, the then Colonel of the Regiment: "The Regiment along with two or three others was raised in 1902 after the South African War: as you know after every war the Authorities are obsessed with what happened in that war and it was considered at the time Cavalry, and more especially highly trained Mounted Infantry, had been all-important against the Boers."

The Regiment can be traced back to 1714 and from then as a more or less continuous organization until it was disbanded in 1966. Its spirit and its successors live on in Y Squadron of the Queen's Own Yeomanry.

In 1902 the Government decided to form Yeomanry Regiments as a Volunteer Reserve and Lord Wenlock was entrusted to raise such a unit in the East Riding of Yorkshire and became its first Colonel. He chose the name "East Riding Imperial Yeomanry (Wenlock's Horse)". But the Army Council declined to approve "Wenlock's Horse" in the name, so these two words were dropped from the official title. However, the regiment was known for many years as "Wenlock's Horse" and Wenlock Barracks in Anlaby Road, Hull, still exists.

Lord Wenlock was assisted by Lieutenant Colonel Stracey-Clitheroe as CO and they held a meeting at Jarrett Street Hall, Hull, in September 1902 when it was decided to form the Yeomanry. These two worked diligently to form the HQ and the Squadrons. They were greatly helped by the first

1

regular Adjutant, Captain C. A. Calvert, and a small staff. Squadron Leaders were appointed with the responsibility of recruiting their own junior officers and senior NCOs and advertisements were inserted in local papers calling for volunteers. In effect each squadron was allocated an area in which to recruit and training took place in and around the separate squadron areas.

There had been considerable discussion as to the role of the Regiment and it was finally confirmed that it should be cavalry as opposed to mounted infantry. The uniform was designed taking cavalry into account, the regimental colours of maroon and a light Cambridge blue were approved and the regimental badge of the running fox with the motto underneath "Forrard". The Regimental March was "D'ye ken John Peel".

They had their first camp, which began on 6 June 1903, at Escrick Park and the first person to sign the Visitors' Book which still exists was J. S. Butcher of Riccall Hall, York. They were under canvas in the Park and one can still see photographs of the bell tents that had been erected in lines with grinning troopers peering from them.

The first headquarters and barracks were at Walton Street, Hull, which were used for administration and training.

Until the First World War everything was considered to be a bit of a holiday and a pleasant change from the work-a-day routine of the country-side. They went to camp for a fortnight each year in the summer, mostly they knew each other and many a friendship was cemented. Most of the officers were drawn from the professional and landed classes or large company concerns, with the junior officers being their sons or managerial staff. The NCOs were usually the foremen and the Other Ranks the work-force of the large landowners and organizations in the area. The method of recruitment was pretty feudal.

The First World War changed all this. It was as much of a shock for the Regiment as for the rest of the country. In 1915 the Yeomanry were sent to Egypt, after being warned more than once for embarkation for France. They were seen off from Southampton by the then Honorary Colonel, Lord Nunburnholme, who left a record of their departure. They landed in Egypt where they spent a considerable time becoming acclimatized with their horses to the type of desert warfare they were to face. Eventually they joined the Yeomanry Division in Palestine and were in action in 1917, fighting their way all through the various battles of Gaza until success was achieved and General Allenby's forces took Jerusalem. They were then brought back to England, converted into a machine-gun battalion and at the beginning

2

of 1918 sent to France. Here they spent the remainder of the War engaged in most of the battles of that time and distinguished themselves well, with the result that the regiment was awarded several battle honours.

*   *   *

After the end of the War the Regiment was disbanded, but was reformed in 1919 as the 26th Armoured Car Company, Royal Tank Corps, under the command of Major Raleigh Chichester-Constable. Maylin Wright recalled how the O/C used to time the exercises at about the maximum speed of the Rolls Royce armoured cars with which they were equipped. Not unnaturally several always used to end up in ditches. In the Dunkirk campaign of 1940 Major Chichester-Constable, by then a Lieutenant Colonel, commanded an ad hoc force of drafts and Line of Communication troops which fought valiantly to keep the line of retreat for the BEF open and he received the DSO.

Part II

BEF CASSEL AND POW

Chapter 2

MOBILIZATION AND
EMBARKATION FOR FRANCE

On 1 September 1939 Germany, without previous warning, invaded Poland, and Britain and France declared war on Germany two days later. Polish resistance ceased on 6 October and the country was partitioned between Germany and the Soviet Union.

In 1938, with the threat of the Second World War looming, the 26th Armoured Car Company was expanded to the status of an armoured reconnaissance regiment under the command of Lieutenant Colonel Douglas Thompson and became the 1st East Riding Yeomanry. A second line was also formed the following year as part of the doubling up of the TA and partly to accommodate the "Immatures" (under 19s) or those not considered well enough trained to join the first Regiment if and when it went overseas.

Major George Wade, who was a director of Gabriel Wade & English, a large timber firm in Hull and Squadron Leader of B Squadron in the Regiment, telephoned his clerk, Colin Brown, on 25 August and told him: "Brown, go at once to the Hull Barracks as the balloon is about to go up." Brown was a corporal in HQ Squadron of the Regiment as well as being George Wade's clerk in civilian life. He said, "I spent the next four weeks there, calling up and equipping the men of the First Regiment. I also had to make up menus and buy food stocks locally, until the NAAFI took over."

So it was that this man, who at the outbreak of war was a Corporal and finished the war some six years later with the Regiment as a Sergeant with the Recce Troop, helped bring the ERY to war even if he had to go grocery-

4

buying in the local shops to feed those who had answered the call of mobilization. Eric Barlow was one of those called up very early on; he was originally based at the Walton Street barracks and then moved with the rest of the Regiment to Helmsley.

George Wade could claim to be the only tank commander in the Regiment (and for all I know in the army) to have a Colonel as his official driver. This was because his driver was named "Colonel Gordon Appleton". "Colonel" being his given name, he used to tell this story with some pride and humour. It caused some confusion when he wanted to play a prank on a new recruit or put another soldier, who was not in the Regiment, in his place.

As men were embodied it meant that they had to be accommodated as near to the Walton Street barracks as possible. The officers, for example, spent the first four nights with the colours in the public lavatories in Walton Street. This caused a certain Second Lieutenant Victor Ellison, who considered himself at the age of 31 to be the oldest second lieutenant in the British Army, to be extremely uncomfortable and he was very glad that they managed to be billeted later in a house owned by a Colonel Kennedy, whose daughter was christened by the officers "OOB" since she put a notice outside her bedroom door "OUT OF BOUNDS". But the chaps made the best of it; and one notoriously lecherous sergeant was even reported as having been observed shafting one of the local girls through the iron railings round the fairground.

During the first four days the troops carried on with the various courses of instruction, in gunnery and driving and maintenance, as they had before the war started. They were often marched round the streets of Hull to the rendering of "John Brown's donkey went bang against the wall, and the wall came tumbling down". So, to keep up their spirits, rifles and bayonets were scraped along walls and doors of houses, to the displeasure of the local residents.

The Regiment was equipped very quickly up to the Divisional Recce establishment with Mark VIB light tanks and Bren gun carriers.

Whilst vehicles were being assembled together, the men were put to work at the Hull Fairground digging air-raid trenches. Very shortly after the digging was completed they were moved to North Yorkshire at Helmsley where training continued. But it was very cold, even for East Yorkshiremen, because there was no heating in the quarters and very little, if any, hot water. During the first weeks of November they all had "anti-typhoid" injections which made them feel very ill. They had been told by the Medical

Officer that, under no circumstances, were they to have anything alcoholic to drink. When the second jab came along, the officers, and certainly Second Lieutenant Ellison, ignored these instructions, had a good drink and felt much better for it. Whilst this training was in hand he was sent to France and attached to 4th/7th Dragoon Guards to obtain some experience of overseas. This was an old British Cavalry Regiment with Yorkshire connections and it was felt that Yeomanry Officers would benefit from being attached to a unit on active service. There was a joke going round about some of the old-style cavalry regiments that one officer was so stupid that his brother officers actually noticed it. However, Ellison soon realized that, with one exception, that was anything but true. He was made most welcome and had much admiration for all ranks. The exception was one of attitude in the shape of one Guy Cunard who would not under any circumstances be mechanized, but he did have an amazing memory for horses and horse racing, and was also, as his racing exploits later revealed, full of bravery and guts. He could reel off the name and breeder of almost every winner of all the big races and its lineage. But give him a tank and he was terrible, having no idea nor interest in how machinery worked nor anything about it.

So Ellison was thus the first member of the East Riding Yeomanry to go to France and he was there at the beginning of the winter and it was, as he wrote, "most awful". When he returned to the Regiment they were already under orders to move to Southampton for embarkation to France.

Meanwhile, they had moved south to Jelallabad Barracks at Tidworth on Salisbury Plain on 22 December, just three days before Christmas. They had all expected to have Christmas near home in Yorkshire as they consisted almost entirely of men from the East Riding; but this was not to be. The wrench was considerable, but they accepted it and as a unit went down to a bitterly cold reception. Some of the lads were, as they said themselves, lucky to be with ERY. Trooper C. Devonshire had joined to be a dispatch rider because of his love of motor bikes; he was equally lucky to be posted to the Dispatch Rider troop, but as a new rider had to go through a period of learning the intricacies of the 4-stroke engine. He also says that, in his learning days before the war, he had spent evenings riding a decrepit old Norton round the Hull fairground, which he did countless times. This was considered to be a drill and went towards the statutory number they had to complete in a year's service so they could be paid their £5 bounty. This he succeeded in doing and furthermore was immediately upgraded to join the DR Troop as an already qualified rider.

Another thing Trooper Devonshire comments upon is that, when they were issued with their kit, the first thing he received was his kitbag and water bottle and nothing else. It was some time before he received any other uniform, so, like many of the troops, he was still in civilian clothes. However, equipment gradually came through together with uniforms, so that by February 1940 when they were under orders to sail to France they were almost fully equipped.

As has been said, the winter of 1939–40 had so far been a terrible one. There was rain followed by heavy frost, all the trees encrusted with ice, many branches giving way under the additional weight. Of course there was no gritting of the roads in those days, and the fighting vehicles travelled from Salisbury Plain to Southampton on their tracks which made it an interesting and extended journey. They were by then fully up to establishment with the MkV1B light tanks and Bren Carriers. These tracked vehicles were a danger on the road and caused a few crashes by unwary drivers. They had done some cross-country training on Salisbury Plain prior to embarkation, but Corporal Harold Parnaby said that "these exercises were playing silly buggers". However, the tank crews of two troops of B Squadron spent a week at Castlemartin tank gunnery range in Pembrokeshire practising shooting with their machine guns. Parnaby remembers the mud in this South Wales location and observed that they never took off their gumboots, except when climbing onto the bunks in the huts where they had to sleep.

They embarked from Southampton in an old Isle of Man steam packet which was most uncomfortable; nearly all spent the night battened down below, but a few went on deck as they felt so ill.

It gave them time to reflect on their training and the time since they were embodied. How, for example, on 28 August 1939 a key party including the Doctor, the Quartermaster, a number of junior officers including Second Lieutenant Roger Waterhouse and twenty-three other ranks were first to be called away from home to join the Regiment. Then on 1 September the call-up telegram was received and all the rest of the officers and 105 troops reported for duty, and Corporal Brown had his work cut out finding rations and sleeping quarters!

By 3 September the Regiment was up to strength as a Divisional Cavalry regiment. Things happened quickly then with Officers being sent off on instructors' courses and Other Ranks getting to know their new vehicles, which started to arrive by train or transporter. They reflected how busy they suddenly became, although there was still a buoyant feeling as they were doing something different from their normal life. They received their carriers by courtesy of LNER from Mechanisation Limited and other private sources. They had plenty of motor bikes. They had been inspected by Major General Herbert, the Commander of 23rd Division. Then they were put on six hours' notice and the Hon Colonel, Guy Wilson, inspected them. Three officers, being under 19 years of age, were treated as "immatures" and posted to the 2nd Regiment much to their annoyance. Many of the Other Ranks who were not yet 21 were also posted to the 2nd Regiment as "immatures", but some fiddled their ages and stayed with 1 ERY.

They reflected on the move to Helmsley which was a bit of a shambles, but taught plenty of lessons and many useful tips were gained by them. Worse was the dreadful move to Tidworth just before Christmas, although the War Diary says nothing of it. In late February 1940 the first wireless sets were issued and they were posted to France, landing at Le Havre at the end of February.

Chapter 3

THE LULL BEFORE THE STORM

The British Expeditionary Force (BEF) consisting of I and II Corps, plus Line of Communication troops, was landed in France during September 1939. This small regular force was placed under command of the French and took up position along the Franco-Belgian frontier between their First and Seventh Armies. They spent the early weeks east and west of Lille strengthening existing defences with wire and 400 concrete pill boxes. The initial force of four divisions was progressively reinforced by a further six divisions, including Territorials, between November 1939 and March 1940 and a third corps was formed. Brigades were rotated in the Maginot Line fortifications further south-east in order to gain experience in contact with the enemy. Base facilities were built up in the expectation of a prolonged war in France.

On 30 November 1939 Russia invaded Finland which resisted through the winter but signed a peace treaty on 12 March 1940. On 7 April German transports sailed for Norway; Denmark surrendered two days later. Between 18 and 23 April the British and French landed forces north and south of Tromso, but were driven back and evacuated them from Namsos on 3 May. In mid-April the Navy fought two successful actions at Narvik in the north and the German garrison was besieged by British and French troops, eventually escaping through Sweden at the end of May. The Allied forces were withdrawn from Narvik in time to reinforce the defence of France.

After disembarkation at Le Havre, the Yeomanry was housed in what had been the Ship Passenger Terminal for the large transatlantic liners. They were there for three or four days whilst they waited for the vehicles to join them and had been issued with French money; so these young men from Hull, Driffield, Beverley and other parts of the East Riding had plenty of time to explore and see, for most of them, their first foreign town. One of the Troop Leaders, Lieutenant Harold Hopper, who was in peacetime a young gentleman farmer, gave his troop, No 4 of C Squadron, a chance to see the area. This gave them the opportunity to explore a red light district and find out what really went on in a Government-controlled brothel. The word soon got round that the place to make for was the "Rue de Galleons" and many made this pilgrimage. Corporal Moor, with his friends, had a look round and he said, "What a town for a Sunday afternoon; we had never dreamed that such a place existed" – a long promenade, one side on the sea and on the other submarines being built for everyone to see. Long articulated carriage trams to ride on; they got in one end and gradually worked their way through to the other. The French conductor, a nice-looking girl, took no fares from them. All the passengers were talking French so our men couldn't understand a word they said! They went into a cafe for their first meal. Dick Harvey and his friends went into a local brothel which he describes in detail in his book (*Yeoman Soldier, Prussian Farmer*). It is interesting to observe that none of the raconteurs of this time admitted to going with any of the girls whose praises they sang, but some said that their friends did. However, they all did praise the way in which these brothels were kept clean and under tight control. There is no entry of men going sick through VD in any diary I have seen.

One of the things that Corporal Moor found interesting was that they had the opportunity of a shower which was next to a laundry and that the shower was run by girls. "What a shock if you took too long, you had a slap on the backside. So we made sure it look a long time to have our showers!" Moor describes the Rue de Galleons. "Ladies at the door shouting, 'Come in boys, for a drink'. They did and were served by girls in the nude – not even shoes on – and for a day's pay they were yours. We were scared to death after our upbringing to see such behaviour." He then goes on to say that as they were out for a good time they couldn't believe what they saw. Further down the street they were called at again and again. "Come in, boys. This is where your dads came." "By the looks of that lot in there it must have been they who looked after our dads too!" he writes.

After two or three days the Regiment was moved with all its vehicles, which had at last arrived, to various villages, coming under command of the 1st Armoured Reconnaissance Brigade with Brigadier Charles Norman in command. They were billeted in a series of villages in the Doullens area. Corporal Moor has given a good description of the move. It was his troop which was left at a station in the middle of nowhere to guard in case of aircraft attack. They had travelled from Le Havre by train, stopping once or twice for relief and refreshment, but once they reached the station in the middle of nowhere the regiment gradually disappeared and all that was left was the troop of very young and disconsolate men with orders to act as the anti-aircraft unit and guard the train itself. It took many hours before a truck from B Squadron came shooting over the horizon to collect them. They had apparently been completely forgotten until their troop officer had missed them.

Second Lieutenant Ellison, with B Squadron, was in the village of Mezrolles and found the habits of the locals most satisfactory. They used to gather in the local estaminet for a morning cafe-au-rum, very warming, because the weather was cold in the extreme and it was very difficult even to keep the vehicles going. It helped to keep all ranks going, though. Ellison was billeted with a local woodcarver who did a statue of him which stood for many years after the War in the regimental showcase at the Museum of Transport in Beverley, but has recently been returned to his widow.

Training continued in not very suitable country. Soon the Yeomanry moved nearer to Paris to the village of Ivry-la-Bataille where there was a Michelin Star restaurant called the Moulin. At Ivry they had some very good band concerts and a concert party made up of men from the Regiment. It was a great help to compensate for the dull regime. Conditions were pretty hard for all ranks as training continued, schemes were held and the weather stayed awful. The men were in reasonable billets, the locals were simple peasants who performed their ablutions and toilets in any place that took their fancy, be it a field, the roadside or in a stream or river. They were not disturbed by the number of troops in the area and carried on regardless.

Throughout the remainder of February, March and April exercises continued; the weather gradually improved, life became quite pleasant and some were able to go to Paris where life became even more enjoyable. There was also a chance of some leave in England, but this was spasmodic. However, Corporal Moor said that there was a cafe in the village in which he was stationed: egg and chips was the only meal served, but they had many a happy night there and the people of the village were very good to them. He went on to say, "One lady asked me to come and see her mother and we had coffee together and they told tales of twenty years ago". As for ablutions, there was a bridge over a stream which ran through the village and on one bank they built their showers using eight four-gallon petrol tins for water supply and covered around with sacking for privacy. They soon had a complaint from the Maire and the Parish priest that the ladies of the village could see them showering. So Major Wade went with them one day and they soon found that you had to stand on the parapet at the side of the bridge to see over the screen. No more was said.

11

The tanks and carriers were parked in an old apple orchard, and after rain they soon had mud like the 1914 men had told them about. One wet night Moor was on guard in wellingtons and one of the lads started sinking in the mud so they had to pull him out with the help of a plank. He lost his wellingtons, but they did turn up a lot of rounds from the 1914 war in that orchard. Moor's troop and B Squadron had a coach trip to Vimy Ridge on Sunday 31 March which was a lovely fine day. "There were lots of locals about, all in holiday mood. One lovely girl passed us in a car, pulled up at the side of the road, up went her skirt, down came her knickers and she did what was natural. The lads did give her a shout; but she just waved, laughed, carried on and, when she was finished, dressed, jumped in the car and left!" They passed the large war cemeteries at Vimy and went into Amiens to see a Franco-British show. At no time in his diary of this time did Moor say anything about the effect the cemeteries had on either him or his mates; and they must have had the same attitude that affected all of those going to war for the first time: "It can't happen to me."

On 5 April Moor fired his Boyes anti-tank rifle for the first time. It had a kick like a mule and they thought it would stop a German tank quite easily. Here in the new village the house Moor and his troop were billeted in had a large lawn down to the river which was fast-flowing and cold, but it was so clear they could see the fish in it. There were barge ropes across the river and there was a diving stage at the end of the garden, so strong swimmers were allowed to swim between the ropes. This, he said, was grand as the weather was very hot at the end of April. They were there to do some training at tank ranges which was something they could certainly do with – training runs on the roads but no really hard tank training with a chance to fire their guns. (Just before the onslaught in Belgium he had fired only five rounds at a four-gallon petrol can, and had thrown one grenade!) Moor liked the village so much, he says in his diary, that "he could live there".

Moor had written the above experiences between 29 April and 10 May. Everything was idyllic; the troops thought they were in for a lovely war. They went about their normal, not too arduous, duties in complete ignorance of the horrors of the very near future.

Other activities were taking place. Reinforcement officers were posted to the Regiment from the RAC Depot, including Second Lieutenants John Dixon, Norman Bonner, Len Brabrook, Bill Coyte and Dupont. Dixon had originally been posted to B Squadron but almost immediately was transferred to C Squadron under Major Geoffrey Ratcliffe.

Whilst the movement of the Regiment was being planned Corporal Colin

Brown was the Squadron Leader's driver in a Morris PU on exercises. On one occasion whilst waiting for his OC he "passed the time in the local inn. I drank several glasses of a pleasantly flavoured drink, priced 3 francs (one old penny) a glass. When finally summoned I went outside and fell flat on my face beside the car. I remembered nothing until the next morning. It was never mentioned and I was not disciplined. The drink, as you may have guessed, was creme de menthe!"

Chapter 4

THE BALLOON EXPLODES

The Germans, without warning, invaded the Low Counties and France on the night 9/10 May. Their thrust in the north against Holland and Belgium had the immediate effect of drawing the French and British forces from their prepared defences on the frontier. This was a pre-arranged plan designed to shorten their line and link up with the Belgian army of seventeen divisions along the River Dyle and the Scheldt Estuary, the BEF's position being on the Dyle. The main target of the German attack, however, was on the French centre from Sedan to Namur through the supposedly impassable Forest of the Ardennes and outflanking the Maginot line to the south. They had secured crossings over the Meuse about Dinant and Sedan by 13 May.

10 May brought two things; first that the Germans had invaded Belgium early in the morning and that German aircraft had attacked a small village near Paris; second that Neville Chamberlain had resigned and Winston Churchill had been appointed Prime Minister in his place.

Corporal Moor and his friends thought the war was now in safer hands and things would be much better for England. They all heard on the wireless that an endless stream of British troops and tanks were entering Belgium and they all wondered if the ERY would really go too. German bombers had been seen over Ivry-la-Bataille on 10 May taking photographs. It was even claimed that ninety-seven German bombers had been shot down.

On 13 May the Regiment was put on full alert at 11.00 hours. The CO and the Intelligence Officer, Second Lieutenant Tom Carmichael, were summoned to Brigade Headquarters and received a warning order to move north. Second Lieutenant Ellison was posted to Brigade as Liaison Officer. Before he left he had arranged to store the Regiment's band instruments in the village together with those of the Fife and Forfar Yeomanry who were also in 1st Armoured Recce Brigade with them. These were hidden in stables near the railway at the village of Ivry-la-Bataille.

14

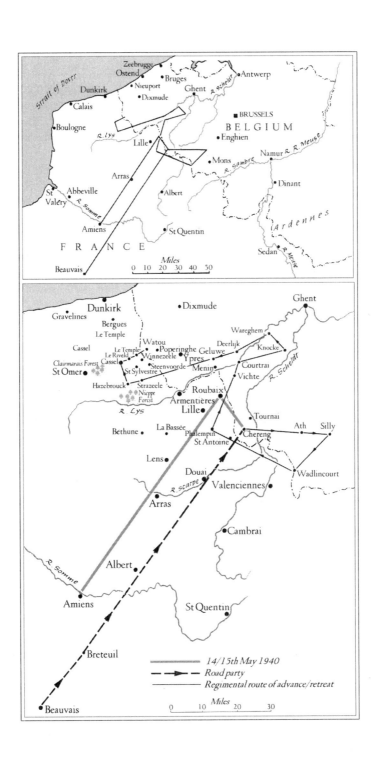

Miles
0 10 20 30 40 50

Strait of Dover

Zeebrugge
Ostend
Bruges
Nieuport
Dunkirk
Dixmude
Ghent
R. Scheldt
Antwerp

Calais
Boulogne
R. Lys
Lille
■ BRUSSELS
B E L G I U M
Enghien
Namur
R. Meuse

Arras
Mons
R. Sambre
Dinant

St Valéry
Abbeville
R. Somme
Albert
Ardennes

Amiens
St Quentin
F R A N C E
Sedan
R. Meuse

Beauvais

Dunkirk
Gravelines
Dixmude
Ghent

Bergues
Le Temple
Watou
Waregham
Deerlijk
Knocke

Cassel
Le Temple
Poperinghe
Geluwe
R. Scheldt

Le Riveld
Cassel
Winnezeele
Ypres
Courtrai

Clairmarais Forest
St Sylvestre
Steenvoorde
Menin
Vichte

St Omer
Hazebrouck
Strazeele
Roubaix

Nieppe
Forest
Armentières
Tournai
Ath
Silly

R. Lys
Lille
Chereng

Béthune
La Bassée
Phalempin
St Antoine
Wadlincourt

Lens
Douai
R. Scarpe
Valenciennes

Arras
Cambrai

Albert
St Quentin

R. Somme

Amiens

Breteuil

━━━━━ *14/15th May 1940*
━ ▶ ━ *Road party*
─────── *Regimental route of advance/retreat*

Beauvais

Miles
0   10   20   30

Once the warning order had been given, the troops spent their time cleaning guns, tuning engines and loading ammunition into tanks and carriers. With all this activity, Second Lieutenant Dixon was feeling pretty spare. He wasn't given a job to do, nor a vehicle nor a troop to command. He had even finished up in a restaurant overlooking the Seine drinking champagne cocktails provided by his Squadron Leader. He was finally ordered to join the road party. Various men were drafted in to bring the regiment up to strength. At 1100hrs on 14 May the regiment started its move to the front with a rail and a road party. The road party under Major Maylin Wright moved out in company with the Fife and Forfar Yeomanry arriving at Breteuil at 1700hrs that day enabling Second Lieutenant Carmichael and another officer to have a bath. The first train with the RHQ tanks and those of A B & C Squadrons changed under some confusion at Beuil, with the advance party arriving at Chéreng just east of Lille late that day.

The ERY finally completed their concentration at Chéreng, took over billets, organized local defence measures and just waited. That day Second Lieutenant Dixon had his first sight of an enemy aircraft, one being brought down; but the pilot's parachute had failed to open, so there was a big hole in the ground nearby. They were warned of an early move next morning.

Second Lieutenant Carmichael, the IO, and Hervé Michel, their French liaison officer, tried to drive through the streams of refugees who were in carts, on foot and in cars, all leaving the town of Ath, whilst Second Lieutenant Tom Carmichael was trying to get through it to Major Wright's A Squadron HQ, by then at Silly. This was nearly impossible, but when they did eventually arrive the Squadron Leader borrowed their car to inspect his troops' positions. Waiting to get through a road block later they were alarmed to hear the sound of tracks; and quickly dug in, but were relieved to see they were some French tanks. After more adventures they came back along the main road to Enghien. There they met up with Second Lieutenant Leslie's troop in a grisly position, sampling their first dose of whistling shells. A Squadron was holding a broad front, so it was not possible to reach all the troops, as the crowds of refugees were intermingled with retreating French troops.

The Regiment, having finally concentrated in the forward area, moved off at 0700hrs and harboured in woods north-west of Ath in Belgium. This was the first time they had met the continuous stream of refugees, plus French and Belgian troops all pouring west in a heart-rending procession. They were jamming the main roads too so it was difficult to manoeuvre the tanks and vehicles with ease. A Squadron was ordered to cover the right flank of 48 Division which was in danger of being exposed by the withdrawal of the French North African Division. Second Lieutenant Ellison saw this too and confirmed they were mainly Moroccan troops pouring back looking thoroughly dishevelled and unkempt, many of them leading dogs. Corporal Moor says, "It is four o'clock in the afternoon, our troop is behind a trench manned by Moroccans, but ordered to help if the Germans attack and also to shoot the Moroccans if they run". As Moor has said elsewhere that he never fired a shot in anger during the whole campaign, it is obvious he didn't shoot them.

C Squadron road blocks were set at night and they were warned to prepare for an 'exercise'. Second Lieutenant Dixon was aroused at 0400hrs on 17 May. Orders to move came at 0530 for the exercise and they left their concentration area at 0730hrs. The inhabitants were very excited and Dixon last saw his landlady waving a tearful farewell from the pavement. He felt really rather useless as he was still under the command of Lieutenant John Cockin, taking the place of an NCO in charge of a carrier. They passed through Tournai and arrived at some woods to the north of the town at about 1030hrs. C Squadron stayed there for the remainder of the day and by this time John realized that this was no exercise, because all day long they could hear the rumble of gunfire away to the west. Refugees on foot poured past all day, in contrast to the hundreds of cars that had gone ahead all day on the way up.

The contrast from peace to war was ruthless and young, inexperienced boys soon became hardened men. The sights were horrific, the sounds horrible. The plight of the refugees made the war seem very close and very personal. The misery that was being inflicted upon the local people, and indeed upon the Yeomanry also, sharpened the need to stop the German attack and if possible defeat them. The Regiment went to war only with Light Tanks and Bren Carriers. The MkVI tank had armour effective against little more than small arms fire and mounted coaxial machine guns in the turret, 0.5 and 0.303 Vickers which were only really useful against personnel and soft vehicles. The open-topped Bren Carrier was even more lightly armoured against small arms fire and was designed for the crew normally to fight dismounted. With a Ford V8 engine, it only had a moderate cross-country performance. But this underlines the role of an armoured reconnaissance regiment: to observe and report and to impose delay before retiring; and not therefore to get involved in serious battle unless it was forced on it. Hence, as will be seen, the ERY moved from fence to fence, wood to wood, crossing to crossing, railway line to railway line, watching the enemy, letting them make contact and then retiring. They were finally surrounded with 145 Brigade, the rearguard, at Cassel which was held while the evacuation of the main body of the BEF was completed, although there is some support for the supposition that withdrawal within the Dunkirk perimeter was unnecessarily delayed for two or three days: by then it had become too late. It is not the purpose of this account to express judgments; but I do give one as far as the armour of the BEF was concerned, consisting as it was of a few incomplete battalions of slow, fairly heavily armoured but woefully undergunned Infantry Tanks and less than a dozen Divisional Cavalry Regiments as described above. They had no towed anti-tank guns bigger than the 2pdr which had only a moderate performance against the heavier German Panzers. This emphasizes the inadequacy of the BEF's equipment throughout the campaign, a handicap which was to last for much of the Second World War. But, in spite of this inferiority, the Yeomanry did go to war and fight and by their feats of arms did all and more than was expected of them.

B Squadron were near Ath and Corporal Moor went into the by then deserted town. He was able to pick up food, bread in particular, from shops left empty and unlocked. The only other event was being gunned by a cheeky German pilot who, having made his run, flew back and waved to the troops on the ground. He didn't spoil their dinner in any event.

Once they had got up to the border and had crossed into Belgium, the fighting was fluid, information was sparse and there seemed to be little or no understanding of what was happening. The fact that there was a plan was not obvious to the troops on the ground, as one moment they were in one place and the next in another. Second Lieutenant Ellison, who was now the liaison officer between the Brigade and Lord Gort's HQ, in addition to his ERY duties, said: "It was interesting being in GHQ nearly every day and witnessing the calm that prevailed in spite of having to make ad hoc arrangements in the command structure. The ERY was put under several different commands called after the name of the General Commanding, such as 'Mac Force' among others". Ellison then goes on to say, "Of my most frightening moments, one was being machine-gunned by a low-flying aircraft down a straight road. I just managed to get into a ditch in time as the bullets were flying around me. The next was when passing through a small French town and the Luftwaffe decided to bomb it and I went with the locals into a building which was next door to a direct hit. This was my first experience of having to wait and do nothing while bombs fell all around." He then said, "The worst part of the BEF's lot was the complete air supremacy of the Germans. We seldom saw any of our planes and that did not help morale."

★   ★   ★

By 17 May the German centre, led by their Panzer Divisions, was approaching St Quentin on the Somme and only 50 miles from Amiens, and five days later had reached the Somme estuary at Abbeville. The Allies' northern armies were thus effectively cut off completely from the rest of their forces and, in the case of the BEF, from their lines of communication and supply from the Atlantic ports. The Germans were advancing northwards up the coast in their rear. An unsuccessful attempt by two British divisions with tank support to penetrate the northern flank of the German breakthrough in the area of Arras was defeated.

18 May was a day of contrasts: tragedy and horror on the one side and comparative peace and reaction on the other.

Both B and C Squadrons were supposed to be in Brigade reserve, cleaning guns and sleeping. However, Dixon's troop was sent to woods north of Wadlincourt: German bombers arrived just before they could take shelter in the woods and machine-gunned them on their way to bomb the town of Tournai. The troop shifted their positions, thinking they might be bombed again, but nothing happened. There was a CO's conference at 2300hrs and they were ordered to hold the Blatan Canal until further notice. The Germans had apparently broken through the French lines.

B Squadron were meant to cover the withdrawal of the Moroccan Division. At dusk Corporal Moor's troop drove over to the Moroccans' trenches and went on along the road into no-man's-land. They expected all hell to be let loose, but nothing happened, so the three carriers drove up and down all night making as much noise as they could until dawn, when they were withdrawn into harbour.

The previous day A Squadron had been ordered to cover the left flank of 48 Division which was exposed owing to the withdrawal of the Moroccan Division. They had, or were supposed to have had, a squadron of the Fife and Forfar Yeomanry on their right in the withdrawal of the 48th Division from Enghien to Ath. This was a wide front to cover, as the Fife and Forfars were not in position. The Squadron HQ was at Silly on the Ath road. They called for reinforcements but this request was refused. Second Lieutenant Carmichael, the IO, and the French Liaison Officer were sent out to A Squadron to inform the Squadron Leader, Major Wright, that there was to be a conference of all allied commanders at 0800hrs at the railway crossing at Enghien. These three reported at the time and place but no one else turned up. Carmichael and Hervé Michel filled in their time until the conference by visiting 2 and 3 troops of A Squadron, having to go through the Moroccan Division's withdrawal to visit them, but the withdrawal was a shambles. It was by then in full swing and at the conference they hoped to learn when the last troops were expected to pull out so that the Regiment could itself pull back. Such meagre information as could be obtained was from a patrol of the 12th Lancers. Major Wright earned praise for his energy and the excellent disposition of his squadron resulting from some well-found information. Second Lieutenant Bonner of 6 Troop placed his carrier under cover in a yard; and the crews "placed a road block", as he recalled, and dug themselves a weapon-pit and slit trench. The troop tried to make itself as comfortable as possible as they expected to stay there for a long time. It rained, of course! They had one benefit, the people on the farm were quite friendly and provided them with eggs and milk. They saw nothing during the whole day, except a local who tried to move the road block and whose papers they had to examine.

The withdrawal continued, but by 1240hrs a dispatch rider reported that the rear company of infantry were at "Dead Horse Corner", with anti-tank gunners to cover the ERY's withdrawal. Second Lieutenant Bonner wasn't quite sure where "Dead Horse Corner" was, but soon the smell of dead animals made it painfully obvious. Lieutenant Jones of 4 Troop reported that "he had seen and opened fire on what he believed to be the enemy". The OC was splendid according to his officers, sending out calm messages and making new dispositions. The IO warned the infantry and the Warrant Officer of the anti-tank guns of the proximity of the enemy and went as far as Ath with the intention of contacting the Fife and Forfar Yeomanry, but found only bridge-guards. He was unable to contact Major Wright, who was out in front with his forward troops, so tried to get back to Brigade. "We were travelling quite fast when the infantry in front seemed suddenly to scatter. There were sharp bursts of machine-gun and anti-tank fire." Second Lieutenant Carmichael and Michel were out of the vehicle fast and into the protective bank but firing died away quickly. "I peered over the bank and my heart stopped," Second Lieutenant Carmichael recorded in his diary. There were three tanks, obviously British, halted haphazardly, pale smoke issuing from one, and to his left a jubilant anti-tank gunner. "After shouting and cursing loudly at one NCO of 23 A/TK Battery, the firing stopped altogether, and I approached the deserted tanks. As if it was

20

not enough to have one's own flesh and blood destroyed, the first tank presented a picture of unparalleled horror. Second Lieutenant Phil Cockin had been thrown out of the tank and lay in the field, quite still and at peace; he must have known little of this tragedy. His operator had escaped, but his driver was unrecognizable, being head downwards with one leg trapped in the turret." He and Michel got the poor man out of the tank and laid him down, but too late; he was dead. The second tank had the driver wedged in and he could not be moved. The third tank was completely deserted, but the crew had taken cover in a wood nearby when all the firing started. It took Carmichael some time to convince the crew that he and Michel were British. The troop had one driver whose backside had been shot away. This was the action when Trooper Unwin lost his two best friends, shot and killed by our own troops. Unwin made the NCO in charge of the A/TK guns get the dead out of the tanks and sign for them, and a full report was sent in. After this Unwin said he was caught in a "gas attack", so they left their respirators for the wounded, but seemed to suffer no harm. It was probably smoke.

There had been other casualties, possibly from German fire. TSM Robson of 2 Troop had been wounded and his gunner killed by fire from a German tank. 4 Troop also had men killed and wounded from enemy fire.

A Squadron was withdrawn and travelled slowly until 0200hrs when it reached Blicquy and they lay down to sleep in the road.

In the diary that he kept as IO, and therefore very close to the CO, Second Lieutenant Carmichael said, "We then saw the beginning of another story, starting for me in the back of an 8cwt over the dustiest roads in Belgium, with the CO driving and Geoffrey (Ratcliffe) in front. Needless to say, in spite of great discomfort I slept and was dug out stiff and yawning in the shadows of a strange crossroads. The CO set off on the back of a DR and Major Ratcliffe and I set off to reconnoitre the front along the canal. One might have thought, almost expected, and certainly hoped, that bridges would be mined and that we should have this as our first line of defence." Their reconnaissance proved the theory wrong: the canal was crossable at seven or eight bridges and in addition two locks were not blown.

The task before the Squadron Leader, therefore, appeared less and less attractive as their journey along the towpath proceeded. Major Ratcliffe was heard to say, "This has foxed us". Carmichael looked up to see that the towpath, which was only just wide enough anyway, suddenly took a sharp turn towards the water between concrete walls to accommodate a bridge above.

Second Lieutenant Bonner of A Squadron said that that day they were wakened up and moved into a field under cover before daylight. They were able to have a wash in a stream and he was given command of No. 2 Tank Troop which was without their leader, Second Lieutenant Phil Cocklin, who had been killed. The tank had a large hole in the turret and was a horrible mess inside as the gunner had been killed as well. At 1000hrs they heard that the enemy were approaching the next village and B and C Squadrons needed their assistance. Out they went and kept the enemy back for a while. After about an hour they had orders to withdraw along the Tournai road with Second Lieutenant Bonner's troop acting as rearguard to the Squadron, with B and C Squadrons behind them. This was all the information he was given.

Second Lieutenant Dixon, C Squadron, said that his troop took up position on the Blaton Canal at 0100hrs, B Squadron troops doubling up with his. "No. 5 troop had the bridge at Grandéglise." His carrier was in the yard on the left. At a house just below the bridge Lieutenant John Cockin, Phil Cocklin's brother, also later killed, decided to take up a position and they upset the inhabitants very badly when he said, "We shall have to knock a hole in the wall!" It was all very eerie, but luckily there was hardly any traffic, because in the dark they were unable to distinguish the nationalities of the vehicles. By 0300hrs they were recalled nearly as far back as Wadlincourt where they bivouacked in a field and had breakfast. They were surrounded by cows all in extreme agony with swollen udders and mooing like mad. Corporal Moor took advantage of these poor animals and with his mate milked as many as he could. Trooper Unwin was also hard at work milking for his carrier crew.

Then at 0600hrs they suddenly received orders to go back to their original position but this time without B Squadron. The Troop Leader first gave Second Lieutenant Dixon a position in a house the other side of the canal, very comfortable with a good field of fire, but no sooner had they got the guns in position and barricaded up than he changed his mind and put Dixon on a bridge to the left of the main road, one that had only just been discovered. He and his men spent ages trying to work out a satisfactory position as they were rather exposed and the sun was boiling hot. Eventually he let the others go to sleep while he kept watch. This bridge was part of a deserted gasworks and it was queer to be there with hardly a soul stirring. He saw vague figures moving in the distance once or twice, but it was too far to distinguish them. Later in the morning the troop withdrew independently, but there was still no sign of the Germans, although they heard afterwards that their troop was followed at a distance by German armoured cars. On the way the troop was attacked by an enemy plane which in turn was shot down by two fighters. They crossed the river at St Antoine and at 1559hrs arrived back at Chéreng which was by then completely deserted. Long streams of vehicles kept passing through and finally at about 2000hrs the whole Regiment lined up and set off through some woods SW of Phalempin. When darkness came there was chaos: most of them had had their last sleep on 17 May and in addition to this had covered enormous mileages. Roads were thick with traffic and halts were frequent. At one halt both the driver and Second Lieutenant Dixon fell asleep, waking with a start to find the road ahead almost completely deserted. By hard driving and entire luck they caught up with the others further on. On that particular march Second Lieutenant Bonner (A Squadron) was travelling in his tank between two other tanks in his troop, when he got a message that the tank behind him had run out of petrol. "I went back with a view to taking it in tow but found when I reached the crew that they had been lucky enough to get petrol from Brigadier Norman and a passing lorry."

Chapter 5

WITHDRAWAL

Cut off from the south, the Allies began the process of withdrawal from the Dyle-Scheldt line with the BEF between the French on their right and the Belgians on their left, the French 7th Army which had advanced to the mouth of the Scheldt further to the left still. General Gort, the British C-in-C, was by then considering the possibility of retreat to the coast about Dunkirk, although there was also a school of thought which favoured an attempt to break out southwards to join up with the defences south of the River Somme. Gort's view that this was not practicable eventually prevailed. This was the period of debate on the German side whether or not the Panzer spearhead should continue its drive northwards to attack the Allies in the rear. Hitler, however, ordered them to pause and conserve their strength for the subsequent invasion of France to the south. To the dismay of the Generals in the field, the Führer's order had to be obeyed. The British garrisons at Boulogne and Calais were reinforced and after 36 hours of resistance that of Boulogne was evacuated by sea. That at Calais held out to the last after three days of vital defiance.

At last the whole Yeomanry, less stragglers, harboured in the woods SE of Phalempin; and the stragglers were all collected by 20 May. The Regiment was put on half rations, and extra food was requisitioned locally. They had two days' break for maintenance as well as rest for the crews.

During this break, on 21 May, in B Squadron, Corporal Moor and his troop had bread for the first time for a week. He had his boots off too.

A Squadron rested also and only did strict maintenance, and C did the same. On the wireless they heard that Arras and Abbeville had fallen.

Just before midnight on 22 May the Regiment was roused in the small hours of the morning and told to move at once to a position north of Lille. The orders were then changed and the actual destination was given verbally by Brigadier Norman. As the ERY moved off to the Salin–Lille road and the rendezvous beyond, Second Lieutenant Carmichael was given the task

24

of leading the Yeomanry through Lille. He lost half of it by going the wrong way, but they all met up later; Second Lieutenant Bonner's tank was unable to move as it had a serious leak in the sump and various other defects, in addition to the hole in the turret. The workshops had been working on it the previous day, but it had done no good, so he had to leave it and the crew with it and take over another.

The Yeomanry arrived at their destination and harboured in the woods NW of Vichte and the CO and the Adjutant reported to the Commander of 44th Division and received instructions to contact 133 Infantry Brigade at Knocke and 132 Infantry Brigade at Wareghem with a view to covering the withdrawal of these two brigades that night over the River Lys. B Squadron was detached to contact 132 Brigade who were under attack and prepare for a counter-attack. According to Corporal Moor, "This was the first time carriers and light tanks have covered a retreat, so we were making history!" B Squadron did a demonstration of force in the afternoon by going into the nearby town, arriving at the Square with a large church and seeing a number of Germans on motor cycles and sidecars. As soon as they saw the B Squadron carriers, the enemy drove off at high speed. (The town was in fact Knocke. Moor often had little idea of the actual name of a town or area he was in.) Once they had returned they were greatly troubled by artillery which shelled the woods all afternoon; observation being given to the enemy by a balloon which sailed serenely undisturbed in the sky in front of them. There were no casualties. At 1930 C Squadron received urgent orders to move. On coming out of the wood they encountered a very agitated Brigadier who asked frantically for Major Ratcliffe. He said the Germans had broken through our front lines and that 44th Division HQ was surrounded. The CO, however, had already received verbal reports that Divisional HQ was surrounded but on arrival found the front still intact. Second Lieutenant Dixon was one of those involved in this panic and, apart from the quite heavy shelling and desultory small-arms fire, he said there were no Germans in the actual vicinity. Second Lieutenant Dixon's troop took up a rearguard position and spread out with the rest of the Squadron to cover the withdrawal of the 44th Division, which came through gradually during the night with very little disturbance. A Squadron were holding a different line "and we in Squadron HQ were spaced along lines facing open country". It was dank, misty and cold and they had to keep a sharp lookout although they were all dead tired. They were then withdrawn and travelled through a thick mist for some way, coming into Courtrai and halting there. There was a certain amount of congestion over the bridge at Harlbeeke river. The halt enabled Second Lieutenant Bonner to buy some chocolate. This bridge was subsequently blown by the Royal Engineers. Whilst in Courtrai, they were able to obtain some bread as well. At one time during this period Corporal Harold Parnaby said, "One very moonlight night my troop followed by some of our carriers were proceeding along a country road when there was a burst of Bren gun fire from one of the carriers. We quickly dispersed into the darkness of trees and got out to investigate. The gunner involved said, 'Some bugger fired at me'. One of his mates in the same carrier, Trooper Tony Rice I seem to remember, said, 'It was me, you daft bugger, my rifle went off'." That incident showed how tense everyone was. They had no idea where the Germans were, as was the case throughout most of the hair-raising retreat. Two guns of an anti-tank battery reported to RHQ as they were lost.

★   ★   ★

By 23 May I and II British Corps were back on their old frontier defences east and west of Lille. III Corps and a French corps were in place defending key positions along the canal from La Bassée to the sea at Gravelines. Two days later General Gort finally abandoned the French Weygand plan for a breakout to the south and ordered his main reserve, still held for that purpose in the area of Arras, to move north-east to II Corps to protect the left flank against the probability of a Belgian surrender. Behind these formations the Dunkirk beachhead was being organized and manned as troops retired towards the coast. Much of these dispositions were taken on General Gort's own initiative, but his decisions were ratified by London and plans were being laid for evacuation by sea. There still remained four British Divisions in danger of being cut off in the Lille area, together with the French 1st Army; but most of this force escaped in the nick of time. On 28 May the Belgian Army surrendered.

Once 44th Division had withdrawn through them the Regiment withdrew at 0200hrs on 23 May to the village of Deerlijk some miles east of Courtrai. A Squadron and RHQ withdrew through B and C Squadrons crossing the bridge at Harelbeke. There was no sign of the Germans, however, and at 0700hrs they went back through Courtrai where the bridges were already mined and went into bivouac in some woods east of the Gheleuwe road. Some of them were able to buy some chocolate and bread as their supplies of food were running out. They managed to spend the rest of the day resting.

Corporal Moor and his troop had the biggest surprise of all. They had blown up everything they could and as they withdrew in their three carriers they seemed to be on their own. They used their land mines to blow a railway bridge over a road using hand grenades to set them off by pulling the pins out with a long wire. Later they came across a railway crossing and station. It was lovely and sunny and they had to hold the crossing for some set time.

Their carrier was on its own here and Moor didn't know what place it was, but it was near Courtrai. "We decided to push railway wagons over the line and block the road and blow up the line with our land mines. What a loud bang, as up went the lot. We slid into a dry ditch just as a long stretch of railway line dropped behind us and just missed us by a foot or so. Out we got and looked down the road. The railway wagons were stuck all right, but no Germans in sight." He goes on to say, "Looking behind us, to our great surprise we saw three girls coming towards us, all dressed up as if on holiday. We stopped them and said, 'The next thing coming down this road is the German Army. You'd better get back to where you came from.' 'Oh,' they said, 'that's all right. We're Americans. They won't touch us as we're catching the morning train to Paris.' 'Not on this line,' says we, 'we've just blown it up.' 'You cannot do that,' said the girls, 'We've got to get to Paris to get home.' 'The line has gone and there will not be any trains on this line,' we said. 'We are Americans. You cannot stop the train till we have caught it.' I'll say for those three they had guts. We must have looked awful, unshaved, unwashed, hungry and tired out. Anyway off they went from where they came from and we didn't see them any more."

The ERY were thanked by Major General Osborne commanding 44th Division for their work. The Regiment harboured with 'B' Echelon, in woods at Gheleuwe three miles north-west of Menin, for maintenance and rest. Corporal Moor was instructed to go with his Boyes anti-tank rifle to the Menin Gate and at one stage he was actually lying between the pillars and saw all the names of those who had died in the First World War, but this didn't seem to affect him at all. He saw a figure coming up the hill to the Gate on a bicycle with a bugle slung over his shoulder. He was from the fire brigade and came to sound the Last Post and Reveille, as he had done every evening at sundown since the end of the First World War. When told that the Germans were near the bugler took no notice of Moor and his companions and played those two calls beautifully. Moor *was* affected!

Going along these roads all ranks said how the German Air Force had a go at them as and when it suited them. There was no protection from our own Air Force. Moor saw a woman having a baby on the side of the road during one of the raids.

Second Lieutenant Bonner said it rained that day but they found a cafe where they had a meal of boiled eggs, bread and wine. C Squadron also found a place to buy chocolate for the troops.

The CO and Second Lieutenant Carmichael reported to Brigadier Watson, BGS III Corps, at Poperinghe. They were instructed to rejoin the 1 Armed Recce Brigade immediately at Hazebrouck; but it was agreed by GHQ through III Corps that rejoining the Brigade should be deferred until the following morning owing to the tired state of the personnel, who were, however, in good heart, and also the need for maintenance of the vehicles.

After some rest 'B' Echelon moved at 1000hrs and at 1100hrs the rest of the Regiment was ready to move. The CO was instructed on arrival at the head of the column in Hazebrouck to report to GHQ where he and Major Wright of A Squadron were informed by Colonel Wood of GHQ Staff that Hazebrouck was being attacked from the west and the south. Following verbal orders from the Staff Officer, C Squadron took up a holding position on the railway line running north to the level crossing west of Hondeghem where a junction had been made with the Fife and Forfar Yeomanry. The Regiment, when nearly at Hazebrouck, were given new orders to take up defensive positions on the Lens-La Bassée road as German tanks and armoured cars were reported to have broken through. This, in fact, proved to be false and so they went on their way to take up the original positions on the railway line north-west of Hazebrouck. "The road into the town," Second Lieutenant Dixon says, "ran dead straight and the Germans were bombing the town like mad. To be dive-bombed by Stukas was a nerve-shattering experience since, with their cranked wing shape, they could drop like a stone from the sky, position their bomb accurately and, with the howl-mechanism in operation on the dive, those on the ground were forced to scatter in terror. A great pall of smoke rose over the crater and the explosions shook the air." They passed B Squadron on the side of the road as they were going into reserve. Second Lieutenant Coyte told Second Lieutenant Dixon later that he never expected to see him again and Dixon thought that going through that lot was not making him feel very happy either. Luckily they managed to skirt the side of the town, so they were able to avoid most of the bombing. On reaching the railway, they took up positions on both sides of a level crossing where they mined the road, greatly inconvenienced by protestations from the crossing keeper who said that if the mines exploded they would break his windows.

Squadron after squadron of German aircraft flew over during the day and bombed the surrounding towns. Shortly after midday recce planes came over and proceeded to write the Regiment's positions in the sky which caused a great deal of discomfort and unease among the men and some fairly bad language was hurled at the enemy. They expected dive bombers or artillery after that, but nothing happened and at 1600hrs C Squadron was withdrawn to a farm north of St Sylvestre. Second Lieutenant Bonner, meanwhile, in A Squadron, had reached the village of Strazeele just outside of Hazebrouck and they also had to take cover because of low-flying aircraft. They simultaneously had the news that enemy tanks were approaching the town from the other side and they parked under cover waiting for enemy armour to come through, but again nothing happened. They dug in and manned weapon pits covering all approach roads.

Corporal Moor and his carriers saw some German units. They pulled up along some hedges and were told to move about quietly as it was lovely and sunny and they could easily be identified. Corporal Moor said, "We couldn't believe it. A German infantry battalion came marching across our front. What a target! A tap on my shoulder, TSM Bourne said, 'You're good on the Vickers. We don't want to start engines so we will take the Vickers machine-gun out of the tank and get it on the bank.' This we did and had belts of ammo ready for them. The Germans were now in the field in front of us singing as they went along. They had no idea we were there. 'Not yet,' says the TSM. 'Wait until half of them are past and we will get the lot.' We were all set when up comes Major Wade our Squadron Leader and says, 'Do *not* fire. I don't want them to know we have seen them.' TSM Bourne was raving mad. 'We can kill the lot, Sir.' He walked away, he was a 1914 man. Those Germans were the luckiest in the world; we could have got them all." What had not been realized, of course, was that ERY were a reconnaissance unit and this was a problem they had to face up to. They went back to their wood a somewhat disgruntled troop.

A dispatch rider, Trooper Albert Westgate, had just delivered a message from RHQ to another squadron some miles away, and was returning. "I must have lost my way somewhere," he recalls, "and I was riding around on my motor bike trying to recognize landmarks to guide me, when I saw a 15cwt truck appear round a bend on the road ahead, carrying some half-dozen men in the back and a lieutenant up front with the driver. The officer signalled me to stop, which I did, and the truck halted close to me. The officer and two or three of his men approached me, the officer carrying his revolver and the men pointing their rifles at me. I was asked where I was going and what my regiment was. I told him, but could not say where they were. He covered me with his revolver, whilst he took mine from its holster and put it in his tunic. He then told me to get in the back of the truck. I saw they were artillerymen and it crossed my mind that they were Germans in British uniforms. After driving some miles, I was relieved when the truck drove to where the Regiment was camped and the artillery officer spoke to one of my officers, eventually confirming that I was who and what I said I was. I was put back in the truck, and returned to where I had left my motor bike. On the way the officer returned my revolver and explained that they had for days been sniped at in their positions, and that they were patrolling the area to find the snipers. Apparently, whilst trying to find my way, I had wandered into a forward area and the patrol of artillerymen had suspected me of being a 'fifth columnist' in British uniform. In fact just what I had suspected them of being at one point."

The sketches on pages 31, 38, 43 and 51 were drawn from memory by Captain Tom Carmichael while in prison camp to support his diary of events in the Cassel area between 25 and 29 May 1940.

★   ★   ★

B Squadron were withdrawn from Hazebrouck on 25 May having completed their task and were relieved by 5th Oxford and Buckinghamshire Light Infantry. They slept where they could.

During the morning the whole Regiment was ordered to take up defensive positions in the St Sylvestre-Terdeghem area just east of Cassel. Here they were dispersed in woods and, where possible, got some sleep. Second Lieutenant Carmichael found some excellent farms and buildings for the squadrons to concentrate in and get some rest. Because he had lost his tank Second Lieutenant Bonner was with B Echelon. They moved into a field where there was more cover and dug slit trenches which they had to use often as many aircraft were constantly overhead and bombing them. They stayed on this field most of the day, but were moved in the evening to another near St Sylvestre. It rained to make things more uncomfortable.

A Squadron were ordered out on a patrol about 1700hrs, their objective being the Fôret de Nieppe, SSE of Hazebrouck. This was a patrol in force consisting of 3, 5 and 6 Troops, which came back with the information that the enemy advanced forces had been close to the Fôret. "They also reported that they had to liaise with a windy battery of the HAC."

Negative information was obtained from this unit and tracks of armoured vehicles were seen, but no enemy located. The CO and Major Wright set

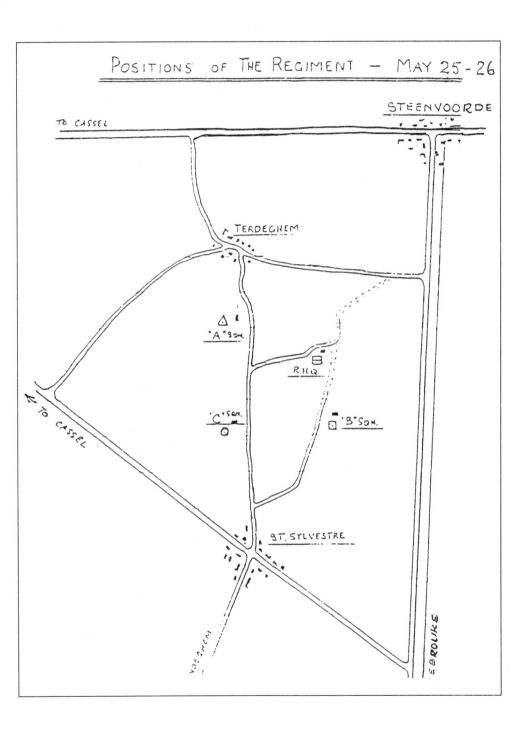

POSITIONS OF THE REGIMENT — MAY 25-26

STEENVOORDE

TO CASSEL

TERDEGHEM

"A" SQN.

R.H.Q.

"C" SQN.

"B" SQN.

TO CASSEL

ST. SYLVESTRE

EBROUKE

off to Cassel for the second time that day, to report to the Brigadier. Brigade HQ was in darkness and it was the first night for some time they had not been constantly shelled; so a sleepy Brigade Major only slowly recognized the zeal which had brought in the report so promptly.

C Squadron had been under constant air bombardment, but had received no orders to patrol.

Our tanks and carriers came through shortly afterwards and went on forward to consolidate.

★   ★   ★

After a reasonable night's sleep on 25/26 May C Squadron spent most of the time doing some much-needed maintenance. Squadron reconnaissance continued with the patrols carried out by the Fife and Forfar. At 1700hrs C Squadron was ordered to send out a patrol to the Fôret de Clairmarais north-west of the Fôret de Nieppe. The object was to locate any armoured forces of the Germans who were known to be somewhere in the region. Second Lieutenant Dixon's carrier led, but, owing to a faulty bit of map-reading which did not become apparent until later, he led the troops to a wood which was actually a small adjunct just north of the Fôret de Clairmarais. "This is the one and only time I had a map in my hand. It meant we had not come as far as we ought to have done by about 300yds and I was very shamefaced when it became apparent. As events turned out it was just as well as otherwise we would have run into the same German anti-tank nest which hit Harold Hopper." He, Second Lieutenant Hopper, who was in command of 4 Troop, C Squadron, had bumped into the enemy when he was approaching the Fôret de Nieppe and was fired on by a well-concealed anti-tank gun. Two carriers were destroyed, one Trooper being killed and three missing.

Also on patrol was 3 Troop, C Squadron. The Troop Leader, Second Lieutenant Roger Waterhouse, investigated the woods in the vicinity of Terdeghem and found short-wave wireless sets and bicycles. He had a report from the villagers that the enemy had left the village at 1400hrs. He later linked up with Second Lieutenant Hopper's troop and fired on an enemy motor cycle patrol. They thought they had inflicted some casualties.

B Squadron were lucky enough to have a reasonable sleep for a few hours, but the big guns were going at it hell for leather and creeping nearer. Some German planes had been over, so the men were herded into a ditch near a farmhouse, with the turret-manned Vickers .5 machine guns pointing skywards and with the back-up of the Bren guns on tripods.

When the German planes next came over the whole Squadron opened fire. Corporal Moor commented, "There must have been 5,000 rounds a minute going up; it moved the blighters and they didn't come back." Moor got water from a pump and started washing and shaving but never finished as they suddenly came under both shell and machine-gun fire. The Squadron as one grabbed their kit and dived for the carriers and tanks using them as cover while they dressed. They were supposed to be well behind the line at the time.

According to the Regimental Diary, the Yeomanry had a quiet day, with maintenance of vehicles, food and rest for the crews. Following his fright, Moor was due to receive a hot meal, but a shell landed next to the cook who was blown right across the road. He was OK but shocked, so the Squadron had no hot meal.

Early in the morning of 27 May the ERY was located between St Sylvestre to the west and Terdeghem to the north, with A Squadron south of Terdeghem, B Squadron half a mile north of St Sylvestre, C Squadron south-west of Terdeghem and RHQ and B Echelon in the centre.

It was reported to RHQ that the enemy had broken through at Hondeghen (south of St Sylvestre), this being part of the attack on Cassel by the enemy from the Fôret de Clairmarais.

A foot patrol from B Squadron under Second Lieutenant Chris Cousins went out to St Sylvestre and reported the enemy present in that village. Corporal Moor was one of the patrol. They had rifles and hand grenades and they were to try to get near the German tanks and lob their grenades into the tanks. They set off along a hedge in front of C Squadron who took the patrol for the enemy and started firing at them. "Our Lieutenant," Moor recalls, "ran towards them to stop them. He did just that, but got shot through the nose; you could have put a ring through it!" (as Ted Wright can confirm when they first met in November 1940). They went on and tried to head for the German tanks, but it was open ground between them and every move the patrol made a machine gun opened up.

Second Lieutenant Cousins told Moor to go back to Major Wade to report that the patrol could not get through to the Germans. He was to fire a red Very light if he wanted the patrol to go on or a green one if he wanted them to come back. "By now the German tanks knew where we were and, as soon as I started back, opened up as soon as they saw me," Moor writes. "I dived into a ditch and ran with bullets whining over like bees; the bullets went over my head until I came to a gateway. I laid there to get my breath back, thought they would have to change belts in a short while and then make a dash for it." Suddenly the firing stopped and Moor did make his dash for it.

He eventually got back with the message and, on reporting to him, was told by Major Wade that there were no Very lights. "I was told to go back and bring the troop in." His Squadron Leader's words were, "Off you go, bring them in, and there is a medal for you." Off he went; it was easier going back as the German realized they were withdrawing so held their fire. Moor only got part of the way back when he met the others returning. Second Lieutenant Cousins said to him, "I was sure they got you with all that fire!" The whole troop retired to their start line but Moor is still waiting for his medal.

At the same time as the foot patrol went out 4 Troop was ordered to block the approach road. This was a troop of carriers under TSM Arbon. They were ordered into the same area as Corporal Moor's troop, but to carry out the operation as ordered. They had just arrived at the carriers, removed the camouflage nets and started up when a solid shot hit one of them, which split open. Three of the crew were blown out and one was trapped inside. He was still alive, all but cut in half. TSM Arbon was killed with a member of the crew and one other severely wounded. On his way back to collect his troop Corporal Moor saw the lad who had been trapped in the carrier, but could do nothing for him although he was still alive.

At 1200hrs B Echelon were dispatched to woods north of Le Temple (between Le Riveld and Winnezeele on the road north-east of Cassel). Second Lieutenant Bonner, now with B Echelon, said that the leading lorry, seeking a covered way out from their original position, got stuck in the mud. "That meant," he recalled, "that all the rest of us had to take a road which gave us a run of 4 to 500 yards in the open. As soon as the first lorry made its dash it was fired at; the second was hit and set on fire; and the third had a shell pass right through it, severely injuring two men; the fourth ditched itself, its crew dismounted and ran along the road. My lorry was fifth or sixth in the column." Bonner continues, "I must say it was a most nerve-racking experience waiting to run that gauntlet of fire! I told my driver to keep his foot down and go like hell! Luckily we got through, as did most of the vehicles behind us." They kept going for a mile or so and eventually reached their rendezvous. Bonner was rather worried about Second Lieutenant Coyte, since he knew that he was in one of the carriers ahead of him. A little later a somewhat dishevelled, dirty and hot Coyte turned up on foot with his crew.

34

Others straggled in, but three hardy souls volunteered to go back in the last truck and look for any missing men. Before going they had to dump a lot of the officers' kit, leaving it in a field to make room in the back of the truck. The rest of the column moved northwards and parked in a wood and round a farm. After an hour or so the truck returned with some of B Squadron's men.

The truck which had been stuck in the mud was pulled out by Second Lieutenant Carmichael's driver Trooper Bell in their carrier. They spent a long time pulling vehicles out of the mud and getting them away. Whilst B Echelon was trying to extricate their trucks and lorries, the positions of all the squadrons were intermittently shelled all through the day. Enemy tanks and lorries were observed but out of range of our guns.

In C Squadron there was continuous firing all round them. The troops were doing as much maintenance as they could, but having to dive under cover pretty frequently. Just before 1100hrs four ambulances swept along the side road leading to St Sylvestre. About two minutes later they came racing back with the news that German tanks were just entering the village. Shells seemed to be arriving from every direction, so the Squadron Leader, Major Ratcliffe, ordered everybody out as fast as they could go. Luckily all the tracks were back on the carriers by then; so with a good deal of undignified shuffling everybody started up and shot down a track to the left which joined up with the Steenvoorde road. Troops were not properly sorted out but three complete carrier troops managed to get into a field on the side of the Steenvoorde road. They were immediately shelled and had to beat a hasty exit to a wood on the other side of the village.

Second Lieutenant Waterhouse, the senior officer of these three troops, sent out scouts to pick up what information they could about the rest of the Squadron. They came back to say that an MP told them that the Squadron's vehicles were seen moving back to Dunkirk. "We were just about to follow, when a DR from Major Ratcliffe arrived and summoned us to join him urgently on the Steenvoorde–Cassel road."

During this patrol Second Lieutenant Waterhouse recalled, "We were making our way towards Mont de Recollets, and as it was time for lunch and reasonably peaceful, we pulled off the road into the edge of a wood. Sergeant Clare went further into the wood, and on his return asked me to come and look at something. In a clearing there were about a dozen French officers seated at a table with a white cloth on it, plates knives and forks, being waited on by orderlies. They were dressed in their best uniform, their boots were polished and they all had suitcases. They informed me that the war was over and they were waiting to surrender."

The orders from Major Ratcliffe were in response to an order received by the Regiment at 1400hrs to RV on the Le Riveld–Cassel road. C Squadron were ordered to move to ground north of the Cassel–St Sylvestre road, with A Squadron to act as a rearguard, according to the War Diary. However, Second Lieutenant Carmichael said in his personal diary that A and RHQ were to move northwards past Haute Riveld. As the situation altered B and C Squadrons moved up. Corporal Moor of B Squadron said that in extricating themselves they lost several carriers and had it not been for Corporal Bob Coupland placing smoke bombs in front of their carriers most of them would have been lost. Even so Jerry was firing through the smoke, but they managed to escape, with the loss of four men and two carriers.

A rumour was going around that all British and French tanks were being brought together. Corporal Moor said, "We were moving along a road and we lost a track on the carrier going through a shelled village in the middle of the main street." They got the tools out and started to repair the track. The tools were on the window-sill of a nearby house. "We were just tightening the track when the enemy started shelling us. A shell came right through the window taking our tools with it and burst in a house on the other side of the street." However, they were ready to go, now with no tools to put away, so off they departed at full speed.

Going up this road they came to a Belgian infantry unit marching towards them. There was no room for both carrier and infantry to pass. Their Corporal, Bob Coupland, told them to be on guard as they didn't know how the Belgians would behave and they trained their guns on them. The Belgian officer shouted something and all his men jumped over a ditch and lined up on the bank letting the carriers through. "He stood his men at the salute and, as we drove past, he saluted us. He was crying."

That is how B Squadron made for Cassel.

The remaining squadrons arrived at the RV with the same sort of difficulty suffered by B.

From the RHQ point of view, Second Lieutenant Carmichael wrote that by 1400hrs on 27 May the Regiment was ready to withdraw. Then A Squadron, followed by RHQ, moved northwards. As the situation allowed, B and C Squadrons followed. The Regiment rallied on the road between Le Riveld and Recollets. RHQ found a deserted headquarters. Second Lieutenant Carmichael was amazed to see the panic in which the former occupants had left. Everything was abandoned, kit, food, valises, portable wireless and drink. Furthermore, the village shops and cafes were open but deserted, so everyone was provisioned for the next halt. They expected to go back to Le Temple as their position was deteriorating. However, this was not to be as they were ordered to take up defensive positions with the Welsh Guards and the Fife and Forfar Yeomanry, also of 1 Armoured Recce Brigade, whom they had rejoined. Vehicles had to be parked with the other two units to dig in on the Mont de Recollets, there to stand near to Mont Cassel which had been studied from their earlier position at St Sylvestre. These places had been consistently shelled and bombed. "With this in mind we had every incentive to dig and dig deeply."

Corporal Moor gave the B Squadron view. "We were all so tired, we are making for Cassel, I think. We are digging in on Mont de Recollets. The town of Cassel is in front of us. The Ox and Bucks are on Mont Cassel near us. We are all Territorials." Later he said they found some dead Welsh Guardsmen.

The weather was bad, with some heavy rain; the troops were all soaked, their slit trenches filling with water and making things worse still. German planes were flying over constantly, with no British aircraft to stop them from machine-gunning and harrying the troops all the time. However, Corporal Moor and his troop dug a deep slit trench and managed to have an hour's sleep by turn. When Moor was wakened up after his hour's sleep, he put on his tin helmet to find it full of water. It cascaded all over him, but he was so wet anyway, it didn't matter. Shells kept coming, but fell below them and did no harm. They were brought their tea by their Squadron Sergeant Major. "It tasted great!" Moor stated. More aircraft, more bombs, but they were not harmed. He made the nice observation that, "Because the main road runs past it (the Mont) and we have it well covered, the Hun will have to get us off the hill."

The firing was even heavier with "a bit of dive bombing". A French Artillery Battery firing over Mont Cassel opened up again; as they had not fired for some time, a photo reconnaissance aircraft slowly flew over the guns taking photos. "Oh hell," wrote Moor. The French gun on the left of the Battery opened up. Immediately a salvo came back, hit and destroyed it. The salvo was so accurate and fierce that the gun crew were blown up too. The next gun fired and received the same treatment, until all the guns in the battery were eliminated. There was nothing Corporal Moor nor the Regiment could do to help, but pray that the next gun would not fire, but it did and suffered the same fate as all the others.

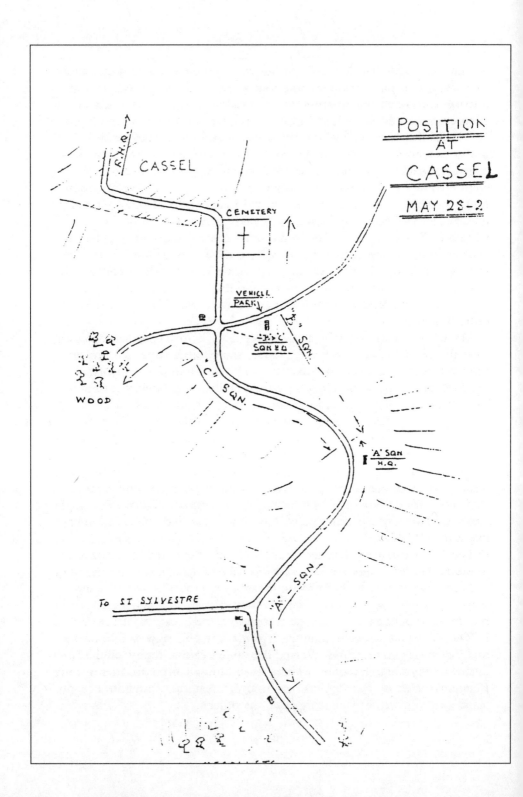

There seemed to be some firing behind them on all sides. "We kept trying to improve our gun pits, now we knew what to expect. I don't like this a bit, we are tanks, not infantry," Corporal Moor said. "One thing, it's stopped raining, so life is a little better."

C Squadron, on arriving at their position on the Steenvoorde–Cassel road, were shelled heavily and had to scatter. Second Lieutenant Dixon put his carrier behind a house and so lost contact with the rest of his troop. He went to find them on foot, met up with them and was taken to Squadron HQ on the track guard of another carrier, a bumpy and unpleasant ride, made worse by machine-gun fire. When he returned to his troop, they took up position on the side of the road and spent an uneventful afternoon, except for being fired on once or twice from the rear. In the evening they were withdrawn with the rest of the Squadron to the west of Mont de Recollets. There they were told to load up one carrier with all their weapons and ammunition and go up the side of Mont de Recollets. They had the same task as the other squadrons of digging weapon pits. They were told, "You are to defend these pits and this position to the last man and the last round." Their position was very bad as there was no field of fire, even though the ground fell away in front of them; there were trees all round at the bottom, so an attacker had plenty of cover. "It rained heavily and was most unpleasant," was Moor's comment.

★   ★   ★

By 28 May a continuous perimeter had been formed with six British divisions holding the ring from Bergues round to Nieuport on the coast, with French 16 Corps on their left from Bergues to the sea between Dunkirk and Gravelines which was already in German hands. Orders were given for retreat within this line and by 30 May it was reported that all British Divisions or the remains of them had come in. This, however, still left some rearguards outside the perimeter defending key centres such as Cassel, orders to withdraw from there not being received until 2100 hours on the night of 29/30 May by 145 Brigade and their supporting troops. It was over ten miles from Cassel to the perimeter and the countryside was largely overrun by the enemy. The ERY were the last to leave at 2400 hours and found most roads blocked; but a few Yeoman took to their feet and found their way to safety. Over 338,000 Allied troops were evacuated and landed in England of whom a third were French. General Alexander, the Corps Commander left in charge of the final phase, toured the beach in a motor-launch on the night of 2/3 June with a Naval captain and found it deserted; so operation 'Dynamo' was called off at 14.23 hours on 4 June. There is no doubt that the gallant defence of a few outlying strongpoints: the five French divisions of their First Army cut off around Lille; the garrison of Calais; and 145 Brigade group including the ERY at Cassel contributed nobly to the "miracle of Dunkirk".

All that night of 27/28 May there was constant shelling, so that the ERY, now dug in on Mont de Recollets, had little sleep. They were all tired, hungry, dirty, dazed with the constant noise but determined to hold their positions. The Welsh Guards had vanished during the night, leaving still more of their dead as evidence of their having been there.

Trooper Westlake, being a DR, had a fairly free rein as to where he went. He recalled, "I remember with a smile one incident which occurred on our way to reinforce Cassel. It was our practice if we came to an abandoned camp to rummage around to see what we could find. At one such camp I found a box of two dozen cigars in one of the huts. I put these in my side pack and didn't think any more about them until we were climbing the hill to Cassel in convoy. As we halted briefly to size up the situation and study the woods and town approaches ahead, I remembered them. During the night of 27/28 I was on the side of a road when a detachment of Welsh Guards were footslogging past us. I stood at the side of the road and gave them out to each man as they passed. 'Here you are lads, it's Christmas!' I laughed and managed to raise a few smiles."

At dawn in RHQ Second Lieutenant Carmichael and his RHQ Troop renewed their efforts with the slit trenches. After two hours' hard work, they had trenches for everyone, including the cooks. Looking out over the clearing, the trees fairly bristled with Brens. The troops were all able to have a breakfast in RHQ, but had to be ruthless with stragglers from other units who came begging for the troops' rations. There wasn't much gunfire, only the occasional burst of small arms fire, so when the sun came out everyone dried out, spirits rose and humour came to the surface. Signs appeared like "No rubbish here" which soon started a craze. Names and signs appeared outside nearly every slit trench, "Savoy", "Dodo's Den", "Orderly Room" and many more. Second Lieutenant Carmichael visited the Regimental Aid Post to have a slight wound attended to. The RAP had been made into a "Guest House" and from one of the abandoned houses the MO, Captain John Burns, had returned with an excellent wine, a glass of which revived Carmichael no end. On the way back he met Second Lieutenant Ellison on a liaison journey from GHQ. He told Carmichael some rumour about the changing situation and that soon they would be off. Carmichael wondered whether to be heartened or cynical.

During the morning two foot patrols were sent out, one by B Squadron and the other by A, to test the whereabouts and, if contacted, the strength of the enemy. He was soon located. Both patrols returned in carriers, a quick and effective way of recovering them. The two officers were able to report to the Brigadier accurately on the situation.

Second Lieutenant Bonner, having spent the night in the cab of a vehicle of B Echelon, took the A Squadron contingent who had reported to him, and he in turn reported with them to Major Wright at Squadron HQ. This was a wrecked farmhouse, and contained some gruesome sights, with others in a knocked-out lorry just outside the farm. Bonner saw how depleted the squadron was, and various troops had to be reinforced by men from B Echelon. Nine of these men were put under his command, so he had a small troop of his own. They had had nothing to eat since the afternoon of 27 May; so, after digging weapon pits all morning, Bonner made sure they had as good a late breakfast as he could muster: bully beef, biscuits and tea.

He said simply, "We were under shell-fire pretty frequently, and I would like to set down here (his diary) that the men (all TA) behaved very well indeed."

At 1400hrs the Regiment received a warning order to move north. They were to go to Bergues to hold a covering position there; but it was cancelled an hour later, to the bitter disappointment of all. They were ordered instead to move into Cassel, less A Squadron who were to maintain their position on the main road.

The Regiment was to come under command of 145 Brigade (Brigadier the Hon Nigel Somerset, a descendant of Lord Raglan, C-in-C in the Crimea) whilst the rest of 1 Armoured Recce Brigade moved off northwards. However, B Echelon were ordered to move north with them, 5 Troop, B Squadron and one carrier from Squadron HQ going as escort.

Corporal Moor was with 5 Troop under TSM Bourne. They were told they were leaving after dark. They lined up ready, guns seemed to be firing at them both in front and behind. They were told to keep driving even if they met the enemy; everything was so mixed up and confused that with any luck they might be taken as friendly.

They set off, guns firing, shells dropping and exploding all around them. They drove past some German guns in a nearby field and kept going, heading north for the coast. They eventually reached the coast and Moor was evacuated to the UK. He did see the Welsh Guards lined up on the harbour pier at Dunkirk, having left Cassel during the previous night. They also saw the Regimental Quartermaster at Dunkirk and were very surprised and angry to find him already there.

Meanwhile, the ERY less A Squadron, around 1800hrs closed into Cassel to form a strong point, while A still remained guarding and defending the road between Mont de Recollets and Cassel. The fork was shelled frequently, but the troops on the side of the road slept as if they could never be wakened. Exhaustion had asserted itself.

The ascent into Cassel was one of the last places anyone would wish to be. All round it was clear that enemy guns were ranged accurately on the road; trees shattered, two 25pounder guns destroyed having received direct hits, and the little heaps huddled under ground-sheets marking the remains of gunners and others killed. On entering the town, the Regiment saw a 3-tonner full of troops which had taken a direct hit. The result in mangled remains was sickening.

It had been raining hard so everything was cold, sodden, grey and horrible. The town of Cassel itself was in ruins from the bombing and constant shelling. Jumbled telephone wires and rubble blocked the streets; fires burnt in the shelled houses. The CO and Carmichael managed to pick their way through the debris and found Brigade HQ and went into a deep cellar to receive the Regiment's orders. They were not to evacuate and make for the coast, but "to take up positions on the ascent into Cassel". Worse orders could not have been expected by the Squadron Leaders as they awaited the CO's return.

So the squadrons dug in on the Mont de Cassel. RHQ found an unoccupied cellar and joined up with the HQ of the Ox and Bucks Light Infantry. Vehicles were moved up and RHQ Troop was treated as a mobile reserve.

A Squadron was heavily shelled, one trooper being badly wounded.

In B Squadron they were under constant mortar fire. Trooper Unwin had a knowledgeable sergeant who guessed what the Germans were doing. Unwin's troop were in a "mortar square", whereby an area was thoroughly bombed and then the fire moved on to the next area, which received the same treatment. It was only a matter of minutes before the Germans hit Unwin's troop position. The Troop Sergeant told them to get out, counting to ten and then follow him as he left. They did so at great speed and were saved as their weapon pits were badly savaged.

Corporal Harold Parnaby, also in B Squadron, watched columns of armoured German troops moving between his position at Cassel and the way north to Dunkirk. "We had been told we were heading for Dunkirk,

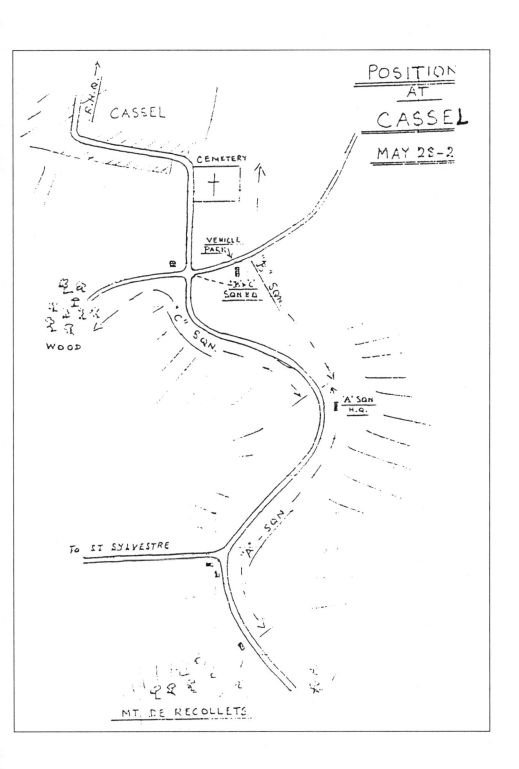

to be evacuated. My Uncle, Sergeant Major Reg Parnaby DCM, who was in HQ Squadron, said to me, 'Whatever happens, keep your chin up'. He was an old Regular soldier, who had fought in the last War where he got his decoration. He got away. I didn't." To add to their misery, it started to rain again during the night.

Second Lieutenant Dixon, in C Squadron, took up position alongside the main road which ran up to the top of the hill. Devastation was everywhere, but he found a hovel in which his troop were able to take shelter and sleep. They kept a guard in the weapon pits throughout the night. They got very wet, but were able to have a fire in the hovel, dry out and get some sleep.

★   ★   ★

29 May was a long night: noise, smoke, filthy smells and not much food to sustain the troops. There was still little or no information about the strength of the enemy around Cassel nor where their latest forward positions were.

145 Brigade under Brigadier Somerset consisted of:
2nd Battalion Gloucester Regiment
2nd Oxford and Bucks Light Infantry
1st East Riding Yeomanry
Some Royal Artillery anti-tank guns
French "75's"
plus many "odds and sods", as Carmichael put it.

As IO he was able to confirm (if that was possible) that the enemy had by-passed the opposition on both Mont de Cassel and Mont de Recollets. As the morning mists cleared they were seen to have pushed round the back of the two Monts (therefore to the north). German armoured cars were seen gingerly manoeuvring on roads to the north of the Regiment's positions. It was stated in the Regimental Diary that the enemy appeared to be surrounding the town of Cassel which continued to be heavily shelled and mortared with uncanny accuracy.

Even so, in A Squadron they manned the same positions during the day as they had held since arriving at Cassel. It had been raining all morning, so the troops were standing in trenches with water up to their ankles and their clothes were soaked. Both B and C Squadrons were in the same positions, likewise shelled, mortared and rained on continuously. Although food supplies were running out Second Lieutenant Dixon found a dump with all sorts of delicacies on which they gorged themselves.

During the morning RHQ was at the Gendarmerie, sharing it with the Ox and Bucks Light Infantry and coming under heavy fire. The CO's car was destroyed by accurate mortar fire. Lieutenant Colonel Thompson was not best pleased.

A second patrol was a more offensive operation. Second Lieutenant Nick Wilmot-Smith was put in command of a composite tank troop, consisting of two tanks of C Squadron, one from B and two dispatch riders. His orders were to protect four anti-tank guns which in turn were to clear and keep clear the road to Winnezeele to the NE of Cassel, and the crossroads to the NW of that village. This was so that the Regiment had a clear road to evacuate Cassel and Dunkirk.

Two of the anti-tank guns were placed by Major Mercer, the Battery Commander, at the crossroads at Le Temple (just south of Winnezeele) together with one of the tanks and a DR as protection. The rest of the troop went on towards Winnezeele with Wilmot-Smith's tank in the lead. About half a mile before reaching the village a German column headed by an armoured car appeared round the corner from the opposite direction. Wilmot-Smith immediately engaged the armoured car with .5 machine-gun fire (the largest gun in his tank) taking on the rest of the column and supporting infantry with his .303 co-ax. The column coming towards him turned out to consist of captured British and French vehicles loaded with British prisoners of war, escorted by the armoured car in front with three more at the rear of the column. The leading armoured car was soon disposed of, the crew moving away at a hot rate. The other armoured cars also beat a hasty retreat. Wilmot-Smith found that one British prisoner had been wounded, so the column, free of its unwanted escort, were directed to Cassel.

Wilmot-Smith and his other tank reached Winnezeele without further incident. They made a reconnaissance towards Droogland, just NE of Winnezeele, and then followed the road to Steenvoorde to the SE meeting no opposition. They came on a road-block some two hundred yards from the crossroads at Winnezeele and came under fire. The gun flash was seen and so fire was returned and there was no further response from the road-block. The remaining two anti-tank guns were moved up to the crossroads at Winnezeele.

Wilmot-Smith was able to report about an hour and five minutes after the start of the patrol that the road and village were clear of the enemy and sent back one of the DRs with the message and he then took his tanks on the northern road (i.e. towards Droogland), which was clear for about five hundred yards. He spotted some enemy light vehicles about 1,000 yards to the left of the road and also saw some infantry in the woods and garden of a nearby house, only to see an anti-tank gun being set up as well about 100 yards away. There was no cover, so he ordered his tank urgently to speed up. "I gave a fire order to 'co-ax', but changed it to the .5 which jammed!" he reported later. His tank was hit by an anti-tank shell which stopped it. He then took another hit and ordered the gunner to abandon the tank. The driver gave no reply and was thought to have been killed by the first shot.

They were then given a hot time by both enemy rifle and light machine-gun fire, but managed to get back to Winnezeele, where Major Mercer of the Anti-Tank Battery reported that there was heavy sniping.

Wilmot-Smith sent another message to RHQ reporting the loss of his tank and the position of the enemy anti-tank gun and asking for assistance. He also called up the tank left at Le Temple. As soon as it arrived with Corporal Brown in command, it was used to protect the guns at Winnezeele.

Wilmot-Smith then went on a recce to see if he could outflank the anti-tank gun that had knocked his own tank out. He took over his other tank and went cautiously along the previously reconnoitred road towards Steenvoorde. After about ¾ mile his tank too was hit. He could not identify where the shot came from so it was difficult to take effective cover. Another hit the tank, killing the driver, then a third accounting for the gunner and wounding Wilmot-Smith. He was forced to abandon the tank, took cover in a ditch, making slow progress along its bottom, when a German officer spotted him, pointing his revolver at him and forcing him to surrender. He was taken prisoner after a gallant attempt to carry out and complete the orders issued to him.

When the DR arrived at RHQ with Wilmot-Smith's message another composite tank group under Second Lieutenant Michael Lindley was sent out with orders to contact Wilmot-Smith and then make good the road to Watou NE of Droogland.

This troop set off from Mont de Recollets at 1630, consisting of three tanks. After an uneventful half hour they arrived at the outskirts of Winnezeele, where they met the two British anti-tank guns and the DR, who told him of the latest position of the enemy and when he had last seen Wilmot-Smith.

Second Lieutenant Lindley's troop then went up the road towards Steenvoorde for ¼ mile. No enemy was met, so they returned and went towards Herzeele for about five hundred yards, up to a road-block, again meeting no enemy. Leaving the DR he took the troop up a track for a short way to the left of the Steenvoorde road. The track led back on to the main road.

Corporal Parnaby, commanding one of the tanks, said, "As we drove on to the main road we ran into a column of German tanks – literally! Our lead tank commanded by Corporal Rowe came out of the green lane on to the metalled road right in amongst the moving enemy column. He, Corporal Rowe, realized the error of the position and gave the order to his driver 'tank about'. The driver pulled the tank around hard to get back on the green lane, but finished up with one track in a deep ditch and stuck there.

"The Germans, apparently did not realize what had happened and went on their way. Second Lieutenant Lindley ordered us to dismount, which we did after immobilizing the guns and the tanks and we started to make our way back to Cassel on foot."

Lindley had seen the enemy tanks on the road and knew he could not move, and as an anti-tank gun started to shoot straight down the road, he ordered the men to make their way on foot across the Steenvoorde road on to the Le Riveld road some distance away. It had got dark by then and Corporal Parnaby remembers walking right into an enemy bivouac but got away with it. A sentry challenged them, but did not rouse his comrades when they didn't answer. They crept silently away, found an empty hay loft and slept for a few hours.

Back at Cassel enemy patrols were becoming more frequent, as was the shelling. At RHQ a direct hit caused much damage and several officers were wounded or concussed. A major from the Gloucesters had come in for shelter and was cut in two. They moved out to the stables of the house where somehow or other a meal had been prepared. "The last meal we had prepared by the British Army," Carmichael noted. "It was good. The troop had caught six chickens and Gray made a superlative broth and then stewed chicken with tinned peas. It was a great meal, in which the whole troop joined, and gave us heart for any job the night might bring forth."

A Squadron fired on various German patrols; B Squadron maintained its positions, suffering bombing or shelling, but no offensive German action; and C Squadron, like the others, waited, although 5 Troop was sent out to deal with a reported enemy tank, which wasn't there. No further patrols were sent out.

★   ★   ★

At 2100hrs the Brigade started to withdraw from Cassel, but it was not until 2400hrs (midnight) that the ERY commenced its own withdrawal. All vehicles other than carriers were to be destroyed. The CO had realized that wheeled vehicles were now a hindrance and were useless to their escape. Some tanks remained, however. Hurried orders came through to the troops, men doubled up on carriers, and all stores, other than hard rations, were dumped. The Regiment was the last to leave Cassel and had the greatest difficulty in navigating past a number of burning buildings.

It was a desperately slow departure. The ERY first had to wait for the remainder of the Brigade to pull out – men marching, with vehicles bunched together trying to get round or through debris and rubble, to form into an order of march – shells falling, mortars blasting, small-arms fire constantly cutting through the night. The carrier platoons of the two infantry regiments came under command of the Regiment. The infantry had left flickering fires which still burned, with some skeleton posts. All arms except personal weapons had been abandoned; even so it was a slow descent off Mont Cassel and Mont de Recollets.

Once they began to move they went along the road reconnoitred by Wilmot-Smith from Cassel, second left to Riveld, then Winnezeele. Carmichael led the RHQ carrier troop in pitch darkness, having assured his senior officers he knew the way. But he went first left instead of second. After much doubt by him and no small amount of comment from Major John Hodgson (2i/c of the Regiment, who had only just returned from leave in the UK) they rejoined the right route at Le Temple, where, the day before, Major Mercer's anti-tank guns had covered the crossroads. Nobody moved fast, in fact the whole column went at walking pace.

As daylight broke and the mist cleared away, the forward part of the Yeomanry reached Winnezeele and were approaching Droogland when there started up a continuous anti-tank gun barrage, supported by tanks. Two of the carrier troops were sent forward to see if they could push through, but were destroyed. This unit was from the 2nd Gloucesters, but no report nor communication was received from them. Part of A Squadron was sent out on a reconnaissance, but no way through could be found. They were completely outnumbered and appeared to be totally surrounded. They were by then separated from the remainder of the column and suffering heavy casualties. They advanced across country in a north-westerly direction, until the carrier in which Second Lieutenant Bonner was travelling was hit at about 0600hrs. He, Captain Hall and the crew walked along ditches and came across one of the infantry's deserted carriers. They immediately took this over, joined up with Second Lieutenant John Cockin and went to a wood to the WSW of Watou. There they found several C Squadron vehicles. At 0630hrs Major Ratcliffe (OC C Squadron) told them to follow his tank towards Houtkerque to the north-west of Watou. They missed the tank after travelling for about fifteen minutes at a divergence of cart tracks and then ran into heavy enemy fire. Several of the men were wounded and Captain Hall was killed. Cockin tried to get round Watou to the east. His carrier was carrying considerably more than a normal crew.

Setting off on this course, they went past several farm buildings, which seemed deserted. Not so, for suddenly they were heavily fired on from the buildings, the carrier was knocked out and one man at least was killed. Bonner leapt into a ditch with some of the crew and they crawled along the bottom until they came to a stream. They waded through it getting soaked, then ran straight into some enemy troops who took them all prisoner, Bonner himself being slightly wounded.

Second Lieutenant Dixon in C Squadron was in a troop which had been ordered to make its own way back as best it could. They were under heavy fire, with smoke and chaos all around. This was the troop which Bonner joined with John Cockin in command. Whereas Bonner's carrier had been knocked out before the stream, Cockin and Dixon with their troops actually reached the outskirts of Watou from the SE in extended echelon formation from the left. The carriers all reached the road, climbed on to it, but the leading two were immediately hit by anti-tank gun fire and blew up. Dixon and Sergeant Clare's carriers plunged straight into a steep ditch headfirst and stuck fast. The force of the impact threw Dixon and his driver, Trooper Dodsworth, out of the carrier into the middle of the road. Bullets were whizzing over their heads from a machine gun firing straight down the road. They rolled into the ditch on the other side and hardly had they landed in the ditch than Germans appeared on the bank and took them prisoner. "What humiliation," wrote Dixon in his Diary.

B Squadron were also pushing on to find a way out, but the forces against them were too strong; nor was the ground suitable for the type of vehicles used by the Regiment. Under Major Wade a group of carriers decided to break through if they could, but the going was so bad and the carriers so much of a liability that every one of them was destroyed. Major Wade took all the fire himself so the others could escape on foot. After about two hours they walked straight into an ambush and were taken prisoner by a Sudeten Regiment. They were lined up by the Germans and Trooper Unwin thought that they were going to be shot. The Germans shot at their feet to give themselves some cold humour at the expense of the exhausted and defeated British soldiers. Then they fed them and gave them blankets, which was something of a paradox.

The composite troop under Second Lieutenant Lindley had tried to get back to Cassel on foot. They had slept for hours in the deserted hay-loft undisturbed and left at dawn. It was misty, but by mid morning they spotted a 5cwt Morris Utility travelling along a road as they were crossing a field. They made towards it hoping for a lift. It was in enemy hands and they set up a machine gun when they spotted the British soldiers crossing the field and opened fire on an easy target. Corporal Parnaby charged head first through a thorn hedge, two others followed in short order. Those left in the original field were either casualties or were captured. However, behind Parnaby and his two friends a group of Germans loomed up, heavily armed and menacing. The Yeomanry had revolvers only – capture was their only option.

Gradually during that long day the enemy pressure increased and the noose tightened around the remnants of the column of the East Riding Yeomanry. The CO tried to keep a coherent and disciplined formation, but eventually the order had to be given: "Every man for himself". It is clear from the Diary that communication was poor and smoke bombs non-existent, ammunition limited in the extreme, the enemy forces and armour superior in all respects bar one. That one was the courage, tenacity and sheer bloody-mindedness of the British troops and particularly of the Yeomanry. Even with the will to break through, the task was an unequal one. Even so, some of the ERY escaped from Cassel and reached the beaches in time to be taken off, one or two having made it to the beaches after 30 May by walking on roads and dodging any German troops.

Many good officers and men were killed. Major Ratcliffe was never seen nor heard of again after he went off into the woods near Watou. Captain Ted Sissons was killed and so were Captain Donald Hall and Second Lieutenant Hudson. The latter's death was recorded by Dick Harvey in his book *Yeomanry Soldier, Prussian Farmer*. No one has ever been able to find out how Second Lieutenant Brabook died, but it was assumed that he had been killed in one of the many individual skirmishes that took place on that day.

The CO and most of the other officers were taken prisoner. The Medical

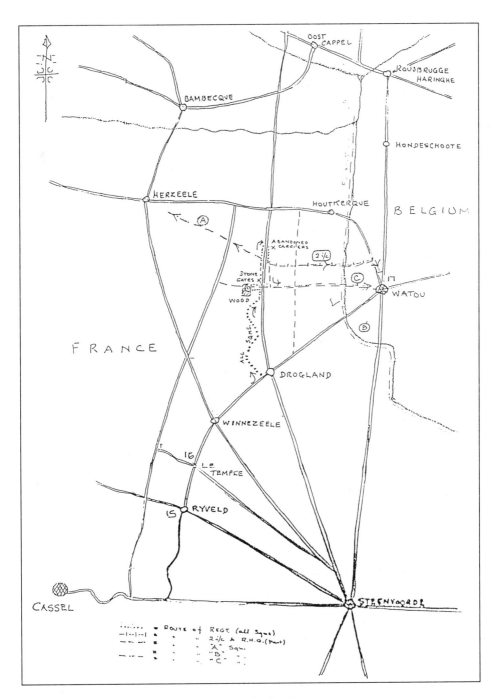

The Regiment's final moves

Officer had set up his Regimental Aid Post at the "Stone Gates", and there he tended the wounded until he was overrun by the enemy. Carmichael lost his carrier in a ditch and was caught trying to make his way out.

The Regiment ceased to be a fighting force by 30 May, having fought innumerable rearguard actions for most of the time they were in action.

It is obvious that, during the defence that the ERY put up, the holding and rearguard actions they mounted were instrumental in keeping large German forces occupied, thus helping the remainder of the BEF to escape from Dunkirk. Never should these men be forgotten. Never should these men have their actions either underestimated or ignored.

The War Diary of 145 Armoured Brigade was not accurate in describing the last days of the Regiment. After the War was over the CO had correspondence with the War Office pointing out how misleading the Diary was. It said in essence that the Regiment virtually immobilized its vehicles and ran for cover. After the war Lieutenant Colonel Thompson launched a vigorous challenge of the contents of the Brigade's Diary and the report was eventually corrected. The correspondence is summarized in Appendix 1.

Also, I set out a communication by the Commander of 145 Brigade, Brigadier Somerset, to Lieutenant Colonel D. Thompson and circulated to the Regiment's officers in the prison camp at Warburg (Oglag VIB) in 1942:

"To all Units 145 Brigade and attached troops:
After leaving Laufen a year ago I received the following letter from Major General Thorn, who at the time of the 'Blitz' was commanding 48th Division in which 145 Brigade was. The following extracts may be of interest.
'I am so glad to have this opportunity of acknowledging to you and your wonderful command . . .'
"I also had reliable information that a senior General in a public address stated that the country did not realise what it owed to 145 Brigade Group.
"Practically everyone in the Brigade who got home received, so far as I can gather, some honour or award and this, I think, can be taken as 'reflected glory' on our Brigade Group.
"Most of 44th Division which was south of Hazebrouck on 27 May 1940 got home via, as far as I can gather, Mont des Cats. Had we, therefore, not stuck to Hazebrouck and Cassel it is obviously improbable that any of that Division would have got away. This also

applies to any other formation East of a line drawn through Cassel from E to W (sic N to S).

'I would personally like to add that I am convinced that none of our Brigade Group should feel that the sacrifice of their liberty will have been in vain or that their conduct will not have been fully vindicated by history.

Signed

N. F. Somerset

Brigadier."

Chapter 6

PRISONERS OF WAR

The sounds of battle moved away, but the turmoil of men being herded into the square at Watou was continuous, men from all units, in all conditions and of all ranks. They had been overrun and forced to surrender to the unstoppable German war machine. The remnants of that once buoyant British Expeditionary Force were being rounded up in readiness to being marched off as prisoners of war. It is true to say that hardly one of them (unless they had been prisoners in the First World War) had ever contemplated being taken prisoner. They were tired, exhausted, dirty, hungry and thirsty. They were despondent, lost, low in morale and desperately lonely. They couldn't get home; how long it would be before they saw their families again didn't bear consideration.

Many of the members of the Yeomanry were brought into the Square at Watou during that long, hot day. Second Lieutenant Bonner was one of the first, he watched as Second Lieutenant Dixon was brought in with several troopers and many other soldiers. Several more East Riding Yeomanry officers straggled in, including the CO, most of RHQ and the surviving officers of the fighting squadrons. The Doctor arrived and set up a medical post and was soon extremely busy dealing with the many wounded and with not much medical equipment to help him.

All the while German guards lined the outskirts of the square, where machine guns were trained on the prisoners. Most of the guards were impassive, some showing contempt and some compassion. They too were tired but exultant that at last Cassel had been overrun and that they had knocked out those hardy defenders of Mont de Cassel and Mont de Recollets. The eight rearguard actions fought by the Regiment and 145 Brigade group had held up the German advance, enabling so many more to escape back to England. The members of the ERY did not realize what they had achieved, they thought in their misery that they had somehow failed. They had *not*. They also felt it had been one of the biggest series of military cock-ups ever known and that they had been abandoned as hostages to fortune.

One of Corporal Harold Parnaby's first thoughts on seeing so many taken prisoner was "How on earth are they going to supply us with enough spoons, forks and food?" The simple answer is that they [the Germans] didn't.

After waiting most of the day in the Square, with little or no food or water, in hot sunshine, the officers were taken by lorry to Steenvoorde. Some were given food by the guards, but most little or nothing.

Trooper Unwin and his comrades were then marched for five days to Cambrai. They had to cadge food from the locals on the way as the Germans supplied only thin soup and hard biscuits. The officers, after a night at Steenvoorde in a cafe, marched on foot also.

At Cambrai volunteers were sought who could handle horses, so Troopers Unwin and Matson volunteered and rode on horseback and looked after three other horses. It seemed to Unwin that they were taking all the horses from France back to Germany.

It was a physically and mentally trying time for these men, deprived of their liberty, at the mercy of a bullying enemy, short of food and water, made to march many miles a day and pushed and beaten to keep in the endless file of men being taken to Germany to prison camps. Sometimes they were given food by the locals; occasionally the views in the Ardennes were spectacularly beautiful, with a river to dive into to clean themselves up. These were highlights in a very dull time.

At Limberg Unwin and his friends were parted from their horses, herded into cattle trucks, eighty at a time, and after a terrible journey arrived at Lansdorf in Upper Silesia. It was the sort of hellish journey that only the Germans could conceive; hardly ever allowed out of the trucks when the train stopped (which it frequently did). To relieve themselves the men either had to hold their water until they could get out or piss in the next man's pocket. They were so closely packed together they could not lie down and to move was a contortion few tried to undertake.

The officers who had been segregated were no better off. After marching through parts of Belgium they were taken by truck to Liège, then on foot again through the Ardennes arriving at Bastogne on 7 June and left in a railway yard in boiling sun for hours. Eventually at about 0330hrs the following morning they were crushed into cattle trucks, between sixty and eighty per truck. They were taken from Bastogne to Trier in Germany;

from there to their first permanent camp at Oflag VIIC/H at Laufen am Saalach. This was a massive type of "Schloss" right on the edge of the River Saalach with marvellous views to the mountains of Austria. These views were not much good as there was so little food and no cigarettes, the Germans deliberately keeping them on near starvation rations. There were no Red Cross parcels at that time; their usual daily ration was a seventh of a loaf of German army bread that appeared to be made of sawdust, ersatz coffee, jam and a midday helping of what was called soup, but which was so thin that it hardly qualified to be called anything. If there was any meat in it, it was found to be guts or entrails. There was the usual ration of potatoes but at Laufen they were so rotten that the stench made them sick.

Unlike the other ranks, officers were forbidden under the Geneva Convention to work. This was one of the anomalies of German thought that they had the idea that they were treating their prisoners humanely. What were they to do all day? That was the big question especially at the beginning after the two roll calls daily taking about twenty minutes each. In time there were lectures on every conceivable subject. It was like a University with the professors coming from the ranks of the many experts and professional men in all sorts of activities. The officers attended these lectures, as well as putting on stage shows and concerts.

The men, on the other hand, went to other permanent camps. Unwin was sent to Lamsdorf in Upper Silesia on the Polish border. It appeared to him that they were starving all the fight out of the prisoners. Lamsdorf was a hell-hole. Stalag VIIIB was their home for the next five years. No Red Cross parcels arrived until three months into 1941. Unwin and Matson volunteered for working parties to get out of the camp with the opportunity of getting more food by any means at their disposal and also to explore escape possibilities. Early, Unwin and a number of his friends started "Goon-baiting". In other words, they did all they could to make life difficult for the guards. They flatly refused to learn or understand German. If an order was given to go forward, they went backward. How they weren't shot in those early days, Unwin never knew. He did say that the various units blamed each other for their predicament and there were several fights with regimental rivalry involved. Heaven help the Huns if they interfered, as ranks were closed against them if they tried to break up any of the disputes. Being out on a working party the food was slightly better than in the camp. Food was the main topic of conversation. In October it started to freeze and they were confined to their billets in a community centre until it thawed. Every three months they were returned to Lamsdorf to be deloused, as there were no proper washing facilities in the community centre.

It was a great day when Red Cross parcels were first issued. Unwin received one in early 1941 to be shared between four men. The guards in their usual bloodyminded way had opened all the tins and packets and emptied everything into one dish. But, as Unwin said, when you are starved for so long you lose your sense of taste for individual items of food. So custard powder went down with marmalade and pilchards, but at least the food parcels came through regularly and the men for several years were able to supplement the meagre rations handed out by their captors.

Trooper Elsey who had also been captured at Watau was sent from Stalag VIIIB to "Lababdand" on 29 June 1940 and was forced to march six kilometres to Rettbach working camp, building a new railway line. When that was finished he was sent to a sugar factory at "Ottmaghow" for the winter beet season, then he was sent to "Blackhammer" to a large building site, which was later heavily bombed by the Americans. Although he makes no mention of the food situation, they were in fact issued with Red Cross parcels and able to scrounge extras to keep them going.

Letters from home started to arrive in September 1940, both the troops and officers had been allowed to send an occasional letter-card in the early stages of their captivity to inform their families of their capture and where to send parcels.

As both Dixon and Bonner said, they were somewhat ashamed later when they realized how much they wrote about receiving food parcels. Cigarettes, like food, were short in those early days, so many ingenious ways were invented to enable them to have the odd smoke until parcels arrived in regular batches.

The officers were caged in their camps in long huts subdivided into messes of between ten and fifteen to a mess. They would change around when they fell out with a member of a mess and team up with new friends. Dixon made some lifelong friends from those he met as a POW.

In March 1941 about 500 junior officers, but headed by Major General Victor Fortune, the first TA Officer to become a General, who had commanded 51st Highland Division when they surrendered at St Valery, and Brigadier Somerset to whose brigade the ERY were attached in the last days, were sent on reprisal to Poland. Bonner was in hospital at the time and he, the CO and the other senior ERY Officers did not go with them but stayed at Laufen. It appeared that German officers in Canada after a drunken party had burnt down their accommodation and as a temporary measure had been put into an old fort while repairs were carried out. As far as Hitler was concerned this was a slur on the German Army and Dixon and the other ERY subalterns were among those selected and sent to another old fort near Posnan where their accommodation was underground. His particular room was quite small with twenty-four officers. There were wooden bunks in pairs on each side of the room with straw palliasses and they slept six on top and six below. Early in the evening the doors were locked and a large cauldron, similar to those in which their soup was delivered, placed in the middle of the room to serve as a latrine. The primitive washing facilities were cold water and the single exercise ground, which they were only allowed to use for a limited time, was in the moat which was swimming in excrement. After a month the Hun realized that a mistake had been made, the top of the fort was opened up and volunteers were asked for to go to a similar camp to the north at Thorn. Dixon volunteered on the basis that a change was as good as a rest and there could be a chance of escape. But after two months they were transferred to a camp at Biberach in Wurtemburg. The journey took about three days by train, this time they travelled in carriages with wooden seats. This was the nearest they ever came to the Swiss border and several escapes were made from the train. The accommodation in this camp was good in comparison with the others. However, they were then sent off to Warburg über Dossel not far from Kassel. This was Oflag VIB and included amongst its occupants Group Captain Douglas Bader. Here many daring escapes took place, and Dixon and the other Yeomanry officers who were there helped in the preparations.

A big escape was organized but the Senior British Officer got wind of an impending move; so the escape had to be hurried forward with the result that not so many were able to get away. All except three were caught, but these three elderly officers made it home.

Their final camp was at Eichstatt, Oflag VIIB. To Dixon and the other officers who had been at Oflag VIIC it seemed the most pleasant camp in which they had lived. Pleasant is too strong a word for what was still a prison camp, but they were in some beautiful countryside and the camp was huge and well laid-out. Dixon was in the central block called "Garden City". They were there from September 1942 for two and a half years. This was the time when the war turned in the Allies' favour. They listened to the news every night on their clandestine radio and were able to report to the rest of the camp how things were going in the war. There were plenty of Red Cross parcels; so they were able to supplement their rations and had plenty of cigarettes. The weather also played a part, heat during the day and cold nights. Beautiful summer days for sunbathing, but the winter had the bitter cold which seemed to get into every part of the body. Unable to work, time could hang heavily, but most of the officers were able to study either for a university or professional exam, or were engaged in various manual activities.

Still there were dedicated escapers, and planning and carrying out escapes and producing the means to escape was a regular pastime. All the men in the camp involved themselves in "Goon-baiting", a means of making life difficult for the Germans, and they were in the escaping organ-ization as well.

They lived in long, low wooden buildings divided into "messes" by using the bunk tiers as separators from other messes. Heating was primitive and not too effective in winter but the heat in summer was intense, as they were locked in the huts from last Appel or rollcall in the evening until first Appel in the morning.

Appel could take from twenty minutes to several hours, depending on the tricks of the British officers to confuse their captors (Goon baiting) or the stupidity and inability of the Germans to count correctly. The British helped this constantly by altering the numbers of men in a row or slipping one row of men and adding them on to the end. This was "played" until the Germans lost their tempers and threatened to shoot people.

The men in their Stalags got up to the same tricks; Trooper Unwin was well practised in Goon baiting during his time as a prisoner of war. The Stalags were run very much on Army lines. The warrant officers and sergeants kept up discipline as well as morale. Some were good and some not so good, but on the whole by keeping a grip on things they were able to fend off the excesses of German "Teutonic" behaviour and bullying. Escapes were organized and men got out, but not many made a home-run until the war was nearly ended. Trooper Unwin escaped several times, but each time he was caught and put in the "cooler" under solitary confine-ment for seven or fourteen days.

In one place in which they were housed on an out-of-camp working party they were all stuffed into a room at the top of a house. They were always locked in at night. The urinal was a large wooden tub which stood in the middle of the floor. Used by eighty blokes, it was always brim full in the morning and was the cause of many good jokes when carried out on the two carrying poles. Unwin's friend Matson was diagnosed with TB and was repatriated in 1943.

Then Unwin and a work-party were sent to a coal mine. They all refused to go down the mine, so ten men were picked at random lined up against a wall, and they were told that if the rest of them were not in the "shalley" by the count of ten they would be shot. "So," said Unwin, "we went down." This was when they went to "Abwehr" pit which was more dangerous than the first one they were sent to, as they worked from some 580 metres below ground up to a level of 380 metres. A good few of the British POWs working in this mine were killed or badly injured. Unwin himself was buried in a fall of coal when he was at the coal face, and the guards who had fled at the first sign of danger had to come back and dig him out. One of those who was killed was buried, and the Red Cross, who at the time were investigating the death of a Scot who had been shot and left lying for five days (see later), when told of the conditions in which our men had to work down the mine, made very strong representations to the Germans. In these circumstances Unwin made plans for his next escape. He and several men dug a tunnel from one of the empty huts. Getting rid of the earth was no problem, but getting air in was. They dug six feet down and then forward to the fence – it took a number of weeks to complete. When all was ready and they had disguised their uniforms as civilian clothes, they broke out. Six of them went initially. Unwin had teamed up with a soldier from the East Kents and they managed to reach a railway and hide in a coal truck going west. They buried themselves in the coal and travelled through the night, but they were spotted by a signalman who saw disturbed coal and alerted the authorities. The train was stopped at Oppehen and they were found and thrown into a civilian prison for two days and then into a POW camp at Oppehen Harbour where he managed to learn a great deal about loading barges with cement for Sweden going via Stettin. He was, however, sent back to his old camp where he did a month in the cooler.

Once back at the main camp he and the others soon realized how they could delay Appel by miscounts and altering the columns. The Germans got so angry one day that a shot rang out. The Feldwebel (corporal) had shot a Scots lad. He dropped badly wounded but no one was allowed to go near him for five days. The other prisoners knew he was still alive as they could hear him groaning. On the sixth day the British Medical Officer was allowed to move him into his clinic where he died two hours later. It was this death that the International Red Cross were also investigating at the time of the mine-investigation. The POWs were very angry and sullen at this needless act of barbarism.

Lance Corporal Dick Harvey spent his war working on farms in Germany sometimes with good employers and sometimes not. He describes his experiences in *Yeoman Soldier, Prussian Farmer*.

Lance Corporal Fred Kettner was also farming, but he managed to escape by selecting a docile cow from a herd grazing near his farm and driving it in an eastern direction. Whenever he was stopped he explained that he had "to take her to seek the pleasure of the bull on the next farm down the road". He wandered for 2½ weeks, sleeping in forests, gathering food from crops in the fields and milking the cow when he wanted a drink. But it was too good to last and he was caught on a bridge by guards who recognized his army boots and sent to Marienberg Prison. The cow had to be transported back and Fred was told to pay 1½d per week in compensation. He still owes the money.

Some of the men stayed in the camps and did work around the camp like cooking, repairing and tidying up. Some helped arrange concerts, plays and revues to relieve the harshness and boredom of prison life. Others just survived or tried to escape at every opportunity. They had excellent communications with the outside world with a clandestine wireless. They knew the tide of war had changed and the Allies were on the offensive. They heard of the D-Day landings in June 1944 and kept a close ear to the advances made by the Allies. It was not until the beginning of 1945, when the winter was at its worst and the sound of gunfire seemed to be coming nearer and nearer, that there was any major upheaval in their lives.

Chapter 7

EVACUATION FROM DUNKIRK AND HOME

Some members of the Regiment who had had their tanks, carriers and other vehicles knocked out were sent back with B Echelon to join those on the beaches at Dunkirk. Many wounded were also evacuated from the fighting and were sent back to England. There are many personal stories about escapes by the Yeomen from the enemy before evacuation from the beaches of Dunkirk.

The bulk of those who got away from Cassel itself were the B Echelon detachment commanded by Second Lieutenant Edmund Scott who was sent off by the Adjutant on orders from the CO. They had the support of Corporal Moor and his troop of carriers and they included many crews who had lost their tanks, two officers and the Quartermaster. A few others made their own way back.

Trooper Richardson had left Cassel with the Welsh Guards, having gone back there on foot after the loss of his tank. Once with the Guards, he lost touch with the Regiment and joined the general retreat to Dunkirk. At one time he took refuge in a cellar as they were being shelled and bombed. Two wounded men were also in the cellar and whilst trying to get them out a shell exploded close by and this blew him back inside. Eventually he was able to escort the two wounded men to a First Aid Post near the beach. "I was then told to join the queues on the beach. As I walked away, one of the marines on guard at the FAP told me 'to put my hands up'. Though not knowing the reason I did so and felt excruciating pain between my shoulders. I was told to return to the FAP and undressed to find that I had a lot of shrapnel wounds in my back. The wounds were given a temporary dressing and I was then escorted to a jetty and put on board a destroyer in the late evening of 3 June."

Trooper Albert Westlake, the DR, after delivering his dispatches to a carrier troop on the outskirts of Cassel who were expecting a German attack at any moment, had started back when the engine of his bike gave out. It would not restart whatever he did and just then a 15cwt truck stopped and a Signals Corporal in the back shouted, "Jump in mate, we've got with-drawal orders and we're going to get the hell out of here as quickly as possible with all the Echelon vehicles". Westgate jumped aboard and the truck flew off at break-neck speed, down the hill the Regiment had climbed a few days before. After a few miles the truck suddenly stopped as they arrived at a crossroads. They were sent down a side-road and then reached the main Poperinghe to Dunkirk road and so missed the German advance. There they ran into a procession of both men and vehicles and the road was blocked solid. Westlake spoke to SSM Philpots of the ERY who was riding with the driver in the front of the truck, "It's every man for himself, Bert," Philpots said. Westlake goes on: "It was now dusk; I set off with two others to pick our way along the road heartened by the thought that if we were shipped home, the ordeal might be over at least for the immediate future." There was a great deal of noise, smoke, fire, bombs and shelling, so that once it was completely dark it showed up vividly the burning buildings in towns and villages. The devastation at Bergues was nearly total, and every other building seemed to be in flames. They pushed on and reached the bridge over the Bergues canal where they were hurried over by the Royal Engineers and Military Police as it was about to be blown up. At last they were inside the Dunkirk perimeter and day was just breaking. His feet were giving him hell and he had discarded most of his equipment, but had kept the rifle and twenty or thirty rounds of ammunition he had "found". He was sick, tired, hungry and thirsty and didn't care a lot what happened next. "But I knew we had to keep going," he wrote. As they approached Dunkirk Westlake remembered seeing piles of bodies covered by ground-sheets or blankets. He and his companions picked their way into the town through streets all cratered and blocked at times by rubble from the shelled and bombed buildings, as they sought a way to the dock area. Somehow, prob-ably guided by instinct or even the smoke of burning oil tanks, they emerged on to the water front at about 0700hrs.

There they saw a queue of soldiers standing right along the mole which stretched out to sea, at times the queue was five or six men wide. They decided to take their chance and tacked on the end. There was little bombing, but shelling was constant. Once, however, they were strafed by a low-flying aircraft. They shuffled forward slowly, while ships moored at the mole picked up all the men they could carry, then moved out to sea, to let the next ship in. Westgate didn't know how long he waited in that queue but it seemed like a lifetime. Eventually, after carefully treading their way over a makeshift bridge which spanned a shell hole in the mole, their turn came and they clambered aboard a ship helped by a naval rating. His feelings were numbed, but he was glad to be getting away from Dunkirk at last.

Trooper Ernest Asbrey remembered digging in on the beach, sheltering from dive bombers and enemy aircraft. The Padre came along and said to him, "As long as I see you puffing that pipe of yours, Asbrey, things will be all right". Asbrey got back safely.

Corporal Brown reckoned he was one of the last to leave Dunkirk, having walked all night and the next day to the west, following the sunset. It was thirty miles to Dunkirk and he was totally alone, only missing the Germans by keeping to minor roads. He arrived at the beach and then was taken aboard a destroyer, where he was given tea and bread and butter and slept solidly until he reached England.

Trooper Barlow, a DR, remembered most of the unforgettable horrors of the beaches north of Dunkirk, of the dive-bombing by Stukas which was endless and the dreadful pall of smoke over the town.

Second Lieutenant Ellison, as Brigade Liaison Officer and thus detached from the Regiment, was at Lord Gort's GHQ when the decision was taken to evacuate as many as possible from Dunkirk. There was no flap and orders were given and carried out with great calmness. It was Brigadier Oliver Lees who later rose to high command in the Desert and Italy who gave him his orders. Having a motor cycle was the only way of getting near the beaches and even so he had to leave his faithful Norton about a mile away. He could not remember how long he waited on the beaches, it was either one or two nights. It was late May but not very warm. They were strafed incessantly by Stukas; but he did not see one counter-attack by the RAF, though when one German plane was shot down it did a lot for morale. Most people were so tired, however, that they were not actually afraid but merely numb from lack of sleep. Eventually he was able to wade out to a small boat and was hauled aboard HMS *Worcester*. His comment on the beaches was, "There was little of the worst of our soldiers and an awful lot of the magnificent".

These are some of the memories of a few of those who got away, told very much in their own words. When they arrived in England they were, rightly, given a hero's welcome. They were given food and cigarettes, cleaned, cheered and sent to collection centres. Then they were sent home on leave.

Chapter 8

RELEASE AND HOME 1945

After nearly five years of life as POWs, of attempted escapes, of making their own entertainments out of very little, and of living in a confined space amongst many others, the battle came nearer.

After Christmas 1944 some of the POWs, including Unwin, were told to get ready to march. It was bitterly cold weather and snow was deep; so they were grudgingly given permission to make sledges with bed boards. They started their journey on New Year's Day 1945. After a week of constant snow and continuous marching Unwin hardly knew where they were; but they met up with some more POWs and were told to conserve their food, as it was impossible to give them Red Cross parcels. A further ten days' marching and still snowing – then some Russian POWs joined them, but were kept separately. This was the time of the Ardennes counter-offensive when the whole of Europe was suffering under freezing conditions. The men had to walk, but if they fell they were left and many died on those marches. A Canadian warned Trooper Unwin and his comrades not to wash nor take off their clothes as otherwise they would get frostbite. So he wore all the clothes he possessed, two vests, two pairs of longjohns, two shirts, cardigans, battle dress and greatcoat, balaclava and gloves. He wore one pair of socks and had ten more pairs threaded on a belt under his great-coat to dry. At the end of each day wet socks were exchanged for dry ones to prevent frostbite. He changed his clothes round each week. Sometimes they were able to sleep in a barn at night. At others they slept in the open huddled together for warmth. They had people foraging ahead to find any food they could. One luxury was to have steamed potatoes to start the day with. Unwin managed to pinch a cow lick which he sucked twice a day, hoping to tighten up his loosening teeth. They had to carry their sick; other-wise they would have been left to die.

The harsh weather was with them nearly until March. They had, by this

65

time, arrived at the River Elbe and passed Koenigstein, where they begged food from the Oflag there. A Red Cross parcel between five was given to them, but the Germans insisted they share equally with the Russians, so it became one parcel between ten.

One of the men was caught stealing from his mates. Instead of handing him over to the guards, the British tried him and sentenced him to run a gauntlet of two hundred men. He was a sorry sight at the end of it, still alive but he was unlikely ever to steal again.

The column arrived at the small town of Koenigswald on the Elbe. The guards who were still with them just disappeared. The Russian forces arrived the following morning. They were nearly as bad as the Germans, leaving the POWs to their own devices but not allowing them to move. After fourteen days they did, however, move towards Chemnitz in small groups. After three days with a horse and cart they met some Canadians. They were then taken by truck to Prague and handed over to the Americans. There they were treated well, unlike the officers from the ERY who had a rather worse experience.

Lieutenant Waterhouse explained that in April his camp were ordered out; they started to leave when two American fighters flew down the column and machine-gunned them. Waterhouse found a white flag, which he waved frantically, standing in the middle of the road, oblivious of the bullets all round him. The two fighters flew off leaving forty wounded. When the officers did meet up with the American troops they were kept in filthy conditions, badly fed, the only difference being that they were guarded by Americans instead of Germans. It has to be said, however, that most POWS who came into American hands were well looked after and well fed.

They were at last handed over to the British, sent to Belgium, kitted out in British uniforms, after delousing and baths and time for rest. They were all sent home in Lancaster bombers, in the bomb bays. The aircraft were not altered to take passengers; so the journey was none too comfortable.

They arrived in England and were all sent on leave. Both Dixon and Waterhouse surprised their families by arriving before the telegrams announcing their return.

Unwin's home-coming was different. He landed at Hove in Sussex. "There must have been a thousand of us herded into a huge dining room. Here a senior RAF warrant officer started screaming and abusing us, calling us 'Yellow Scum' and other foul and insulting words and names." The CO intervened and ordered the WO to leave the men alone and get out. Unwin's final comment in his account was "Why were we, one of the regiments who helped all those thousands to get back from Dunkirk, termed 'Yellow Scum' and those who got back in 1940 'Heroes'?" Why indeed?

We of the Yeomanry who fought in 1944/5 owe those men of 1940 a great debt of gratitude, as does the whole country. It was their spirit which helped to make the East Riding Yeomanry the first-class Regiment it was.

PART III

REGROUPING AND PREPARING FOR INVASION

Chapter 9

HOME FORCES

Nearly a quarter of a million British troops were evacuated home from Dunkirk and over one hundred thousand French, who were mostly restored to their home-land to continue the fight. With only a few exceptions the survivors arrived back in Britain without even small arms and no artillery, armour or transport. Existing home defence formations were themselves not fully equipped and there was a shortage of everything from weapons and ammunition to transport and stores of all kinds. While the army was hastily being reorganized and re-equipped, the first priority was coastal defence with a quick-reacting mobile reserve behind it, equipped with makeshift armoured vehicles. In the air, a nucleus of fifty fighter squadrons had been held back by the RAF in spite of strenuous entreaties by the French to move them to France. This was the bare minimum required for home defence and even part of this was committed to cover Dunkirk during the last days of the beachhead. Direct defence against invasion rested with the Royal Navy which had already suffered grievous losses in the evacuation.

Only seven officers and 230 other ranks of 1 ERY returned from the BEF. (This was the strength on 1 July 1940 as reported in the Regimental Diary. The Diary up to the end of May was lost when the ERY was overrun at Cassel and there is no record of a Diary for June 1940.) On 2 July nineteen officers and 231 other ranks were posted to the Regiment from 2 ERY, then stationed at Tidworth. Lieutenant Colonel R. B. B. Cooke from 17th/21st Lancers was given command of the reformed regiment and several senior officers were posted in to fill the vacancies left by those killed or captured in France. The Regiment was stationed at Bovington Camp, Dorset. In various accounts from officers and men who had been with the 2 ERY, the remnants of the 1st Regiment arrived from Dunkirk at Tidworth. As will be seen above, the War Diary shows a different story and 2 ERY postings were direct to Bovington rather than from one unit to another at Tidworth.

Second Lieutenant Tony Mitchell, who had been commissioned in April 1940 and had been posted to 2 ERY at Tidworth, stated clearly that during the weeks preceding Dunkirk they had lived a most gentlemanly life in a pleasant mess. Their main occupation was inspecting the troops' quarters, playing tennis or taking afternoon tea with trainee nurses. In the evening there were dinners and dances.

It was a shock of the greatest magnitude when they started to meet the survivors from Dunkirk. These men were tired, disillusioned and dispirited. The CO of 2 ERY, Lieutenant Colonel Nigel Birch, not having taken a Staff Course and considered too old to command a fighting regiment, was relieved of command.

One of the new Squadron Leaders was Major David Barbour, also of 17th/21st Lancers. When he arrived at the regiment at the end of June he was told by Cookie (the Colonel's nickname) to take over C Squadron. Other senior officers were also regulars: Major John Leigh of A Squadron (4th/7th Dragoon Guards) and Major Lord Apsley B Squadron (11th Hussars); but the junior officers were mainly East Riding Yeomen, who naturally clubbed together and talked about life north of the Humber. This was foreign soil to the senior officers who had never been to that part of the country. The new Adjutant was Captain Tony Fitzwilliam Hyde of 4th/7thDG. The new combined Regiment was entitled plain East Riding Yeomanry without 1st or 2nd designation.

Second Lieutenant Victor Ellison on his return was sent to Tidworth where he was totally unable to locate either the Regiment or the Brigade HQ, so he was left with a First World War colonel who had no interest in him. It was only after three weeks of constant badgering and making a lot of noise that, finally, he was allowed to contact the 1st Armoured Recce Brigade and return to the Yeomanry. Once the ERY had arrived at Bovington, it became part of the anti-invasion force; their sector was between Weymouth to the west and Lulworth to the east, a front of some 30 miles with 400 men to guard it. There were no army maps available so the officers had to buy what they could from the local shops. The ERY was issued with the old long bayonet and Lee Enfield rifle, and Major David Barbour was told to train his Squadron accordingly. This meant, he wrote, that after dinner each evening he retired to his room with the bayonet-fighting manual and learnt his lesson for the next day. Before breakfast next morning the Squadron went for a run or had PT. During that time he taught his NCOs to fight with the bayonet. After breakfast these same NCOs had to teach their troops what they had just learnt from their Squadron Leader before breakfast.

At that time there were no armoured vehicles, or fighting vehicles of any kind for that matter.

In July Second Lieutenant Ellison was awarded the MC for his work in France as Brigade Liaison Officer. When the award was being discussed he was asked whether he would like an MC or OBE. He chose the MC as he thought it more appropriate to the duties he had carried out. The OBE was nicknamed "Other Buggers' Efforts". At least Ellison reckoned that he had used his own effort throughout. At last somebody in the Yeomanry had been recognized for what was done in France. No further awards were made for the 1940 campaign until after the war ended.

Once the ERY was up to strength, those of the 2nd Regiment not required formed the nucleus of a new infantry battalion, 11 Green Howards, which subsequently became an Airborne Unit and landed by parachute in the invasion of Normandy. Gradually at last the Regiment became a little more mobile with a bus to each squadron and trucks arriving so they could patrol their long front more effectively.

There were many changes as both officers and men were drafted into and away from the Regiment, because with the return of so many men from France experienced soldiers were needed throughout the new units then being formed.

Ted Wright, who was at Bovington at the time doing a D&M Course as a Sandhurst Cadet, remembers the occasion well. The officers, mortally terrified of "Cookie", had even to polish the brass eyelets and buckles of their gaiters to be sure of passing his eagle eye. His contact was with Tom Robinson (later OC, B Squadron and MC) who had joined them from the Second Line. The cap badge of 17th/21st Lancers was a skull-and-cross-bones and Cookie reportedly looked much like it.

About the third Sunday of their stay at Bovington the CO decided that it would do everyone good if they had a ceremonial church parade. All the officers marched at the front of the Regiment and, as the senior officers all came from different regiments, the various colours of their side-caps caused one passing soldier to remark to his companion in a loud voice, "Bloody fruit-salad I call it"! Captain Hyde, the Adjutant, heard this and told the CO, and from then on they had to drop their various regimental badges and side-caps and wear the ERY fox. This, Major Barbour writes, was timely and accepted. In later years David and his wife attended a few reunions and she always wore a handsome fox badge with diamonds given her as a wedding present by her husband, a regular 17th/21st Lancer, which showed a nice sense of loyalty to his new unit although it might be said that a Forrard badge made a nicer brooch than the 17th/21st Lancers' "Death's Head".

Whilst the reorganization was progressing towards the end of July, news began to filter through of those who had been taken prisoner, including the CO, Lieutenant Colonel Douglas Thompson, the 2i/c, Major Hodgson, other senior and junior officers, and many of the troops including the RSM.

On 6 August they moved from Bovington to Braxted Park near Witham in Essex, as part of the 1st Armoured Recce Brigade. Although no mention is made in the War Diary, the first "armoured vehicles began to arrive". These were "Beaverettes", open-topped vehicles on Standard 14 car-chassis with front, sides and rear armoured with boiler-plate. On test this proved not to be proof even against small arms fire so the makers lined the steel with three-inch-thick layers of oak-timber. There was an aperture in the front for a Bren gun and a slit with a bullet-proof glass cover for the driver to see through. In addition to the Brens each troop had one Boyes Anti-tank Rifle and the vehicles were very top-heavy and could, and did, roll over on a tight corner. The general consensus was that the Beaverettes were pretty useless as fighting vehicles, but better than nothing; and a role was found for them on reconnaissance as well as for quick reaction against invasion landings or for airfield defence. They were fairly fast and the Yeomanry at least learned to read a map after all the signposts had been taken away.

Braxted Park was a large bracken-covered park and the Regiment was housed in tents, but, according to Lieutenant Mitchell, it was all pretty primitive. They spent much of their time out on exercises, on reconnaissance or on airfield guard duty.

They took part in one full XI Corps exercise and on 28 August received forty-two wireless sets to complete establishment.

After one exercise on returning to camp a few bombs were dropped in the regimental area during a raid. None exploded and there were no casualties. During September the Battle of Britain was at its height; there was some enemy air activity in the area, but there were no direct hits. The facilities in the camp were improved, but the threat of invasion was so intense that the ERY was kept on 10-minute notice to move. All vehicles were kept loaded, all were armed and all were ready to go with guards doubled. This state of readiness was maintained for two weeks when the notice to move was extended to 2 hours.

Second Lieutenant Ellison was posted to Brigade HQ and appointed Staff Captain. Even at this state of readiness normal things happened as the Yeomanry took part in a Corps Traffic Check of suspected vehicles but not one suspect was apprehended. It also took part in a Brigade exercise for which the whole Regiment was personally congratulated by the Brigadier.

The CO, Lieutenant Colonel Cooke, left the Regiment in September to attend the Senior Staff Course at Camberley, and the next day Lieutenant Colonel A. F. Fisher ("Fish") took over command. He had previously been at the War Office as Military Assistant (MA) to the Director of Military Training, Major General P. C. S. Hobart ("Hobo") of whom more is recorded later. Fish told the story of how a few weeks after Hobo became DMT all three of the Directors at the War Office (Ops, Plans and Training) who were meant to work in close co-operation with each other had ceased to be on speaking terms. Thereafter all communication was through their Military Assistants. Hobo left the War Office in 1939 to raise the 7th Armoured Division ("The Desert Rats") in Egypt. Just before the Italians entered the war on the German side in 1940, the British forces in the Western Desert held a comprehensive exercise with 7th Armoured Division acting as the "enemy". Hobo exercised a classic "right hook" as Rommel did later and brought the exercise to a premature close by capturing the "defenders'" HQ. He was found to have exceeded the permitted track-mileage on his tanks during this manoeuvre and was sent home with a bowler hat. Apparently he later became a Corporal in the Home Guard, but was rescued by Winston Churchill and given the task of forming the new 79th Armoured Division. The number was said to have been derived from 7 of the Desert Rats, 9 from 9th Armoured Division, from which 27 Armoured Brigade came, including the ERY. For the invasion of Normandy, 79th Armoured Division included all the special tanks used for attacking heavily fortified positions and known as "Funnies".

A few changes were made as a result of this; Major Barbour was posted to command HQ Squadron and Major Sam Strang, a 12th Lancer like the CO, took over his C Squadron. The Regiment was constantly out on schemes to learn, to train and become efficient, effective and moulded into a unit to carry out its duties in rapid-reaction armoured warfare. There was a constant ebb and flow of personnel of both officers and men to and from the Yeomanry, but there was a nucleus of all ranks who were the backbone on which the ERY had been rebuilt.

1. The original stone outside the barracks in Hull.

2. Captain Victor Ellison MC in 1941.

3. Lieutenant Ted Wright in 1942.

4. 2nd Lieutenant Paul Mace in October, 1944.

5. An original Yeoman.

6. ERY marching up the Toll Gate in Beverley in about 1910.

7. Camp, pre-1914.

8. 26th Armoured Car Company, RTC, 1933, with Rolls Royce armoured cars.

9. A full complement of Despatch Riders, Tidworth, 1939.

10. Amalgamation of the remnants of 1st and 2nd ERY, 1940.

11. Destroyed bridge over Belgian canal, 1940.

12. Bridge over the Albert Canal destroyed by the Allies, 1940.

13. POW ERY Officers in 1940.

14. POW ERY Officers at Oflag V11B, Eichstatt, 1944.

15. Lieutenant Ted Wright explains the details of a new American tank to the Prime Minister, Mr Winston Churchill.

16. D-Day, 6 June, 1944. Somewhere near Ouistreham.

17. D-Day. Knocked-out tanks near Lion-sur-Mer.

18. Crossing the Seine at Elbeuf.

19. 'A' Squadron driving through Rouen.

20. 'B' Squadron approaching 's-Hertogenbosch, October 1944.

21. Clearing the entry to 's-Hertogenbosch.

22. Rescuing a family during the bitter fighting in the centre of 's-Hertogenbosch.

23. 'B' Squadron crossing the Nederwert Canal Bridge: 2nd Lieutenant Paul Mace is in the tank on the right.

24. Members of the Recce Troop, Holland, November 1944.

25. Rest at Oudenbosch November 1944.

26. Supporting the Infantry in canal-hopping operations in November 1944.

27. The liberated torpedo boats *Hull* and *Humber* used by the Regiment.

28. The only known photograph of Major Salmon, centre, in shirt sleeves.

29. A good British tank at last: the Comet.

30. Hitler at the German U Boat Memorial at Laboe.

31. Sergeant Morrell in the same place, later.

32. ERY Officers, May, 1945.

33. Officers of the re-formed Regiment, 1947.

34. Paul Mace and Ted Wright, 6 June 2000.

Between September and November the Regiment moved to Brackley in Northamptonshire. HQ, A and C Squadrons were stationed in the town and B Squadron at nearby Evenly Hall, a beautiful country house with lovely grounds, a marked contrast to the mud and discomfort of tent life at Braxted Park. Shortly after arriving at Brackley, Lieutenant Mitchell was posted to the Wireless Wing at Bovington where he remained until 1943, when he was posted back to the Regiment and appointed Signals Officer.

Major Barbour took over B Squadron in late 1940 from Lord Apsley who was posted to the 11th Hussars in the Middle East. Major Barbour said of his predecessor, "Of course the most outstanding officer in the Regiment was Lord Apsley, who was delightful, had a bubbling sense of humour and was inexhaustible. He was, in addition, a very active MP and spent more time in the House than in B Squadron. He was always getting into hot water for doing something astonishing like ordering the whole of B Squadron to RV in Parliament Square in their Beaverettes. This infuriated the powers-that-be that an armed and armoured force should exercise in Parliament Square without having first obtained permission from the Lord Mayor, the Brigade of Guards, Scotland Yard and any other Panjandrum one could think of".

Major Barbour was married in December 1940 and was presented with the customary silver cigarette box with the ERY crest on it by his fellow officers. It has remained with his family as a treasured possession ever since. He went on to become a Brigadier in Italy but said, "I like to think that the ERY taught me more than I ever taught the ERY. But it was the best of all company, both officers and men."

In November 1940 one Edward Vere Wright, the youngest brother of Major Maylin Wright who had been with 1 ERY and was captured at Watou in May, was commissioned into the ERY, his first choice of regiment at Sandhurst, which caused some gentle amusement among the regulars there. Appropriately he was posted to A Squadron, his brother's old Squadron, given No 1 Troop, and was, in his own words, "a callow and woefully conceited Second Lieutenant".

The Regiment was now well established with the 1st Armoured Recce Brigade soon to become 27 Armoured Brigade. The other regiments in the Brigade were 4th/7th Dragoon Guards and 13th/18th Hussars. They did many exercises together and with a full compliment of Beaverettes much training was carried out. As much fun as possible was derived from these exercises – radio especially, not least one evening exercise in early summer 1941 when one Sergeant from A Squadron came in with the poetic remark, "The fucking 'uunysuckles were fucking luvly"! There was a great deal of regimental entertainment; they had a good band and some gifted people to enhance the shows.

The summer and autumn of 1940 saw what will ever be known as the Battle of Britain when Fighter Command of the RAF met and finally defeated the German Luftwaffe. The German air force had been given the task of gaining air superiority over the Channel and Southern England without which the enemy were not prepared to launch their land-invasion, Operation Sea-Lion. Plans were made and much sea-transport assembled in the Channel Ports for this; but the hopes for air superiority never materialized so that by the winter of 1940–41 the enemy's plans were changed. This became fully known only later and mean-while the chief priority for Home Forces remained a counter-invasion role well into 1941. After the fall of France and while the fate of the air battle was still in the balance, the centre of gravity for land operations shifted eastwards with Italy declaring war on the German side on 10 June 1940. As early as July 1940 measures were taken to reinforce our position in the Eastern Mediterranean with warships and ill-spared tanks since an Italian invasion of Egypt was expected. Meanwhile the Italians extended their efforts in the Balkans by attacking Greece in October 1940.

Chapter 10

ARMOURED REGIMENT

In December 1940 the Desert Army advanced into action against the Italians and in six weeks had annihilated the forces which had invaded Egypt. Having captured the Italian garrisons in Cyrenaica at Sidi Barrani, Bardia, Tobruk and Benghazi they were pushing on towards Tripolitania. The Mark II Infantry Tank with its heavy armour proved a decisive weapon and first got its nickname of "Matilda" from the Australians in these battles. Over 110,000 prisoners were captured, but as this first victory was being celebrated General Wavell, C in C Middle East, was called to shore up the Greek defence against a German invasion through the Balkans. Greece was soon overrun and the Navy carried out the evacuation of allied troops without most of their heavy equipment, some being landed to reinforce Crete, the remainder to Egypt. Crete was soon invaded in turn and this was the only occasion when the German Parachute Division was used in is proper role, but with severe losses. Hopelessly outnumbered and outgunned, the garrison fought with great gallantry and the survivors then marched over the mountains to the south coast to be picked up by the Navy and shipped to Egypt. Naval losses during these operations were very severe. The Germans then took command in the Western Desert from the failing Italians, landed the first elements of the Afrika Korps and defeated the over-extended British Army which had reached El Agheila on the Tripolitanian border. The German onslaught carried them right through to the Egyptian frontier; but Tobruk, though surrounded, still held out.

In the early summer of 1941 the Beaverettes of the ERY began to be replaced by Cruiser tanks and the Armoured Recce Brigade became 27 Armoured Brigade in 9th Armoured Division whose sign was a black-and-white panda's face, very distinctive and conveniently easy for the signwriters to paint. A Squadron received Covenanters (Cruiser MKV) and B and C Crusaders (Cruiser MKVI). Both these had the renowned Christie suspension and were notably fast, the Covenanter with a "flat-12"

75

Meadows engine and the Crusader with a V-12 Liberty engine whose design went back to the First World War when it was made in quantity in the USA. The Yeomen took to them like ducks to water, the speed with which the Regiment became a fully equipped armoured regiment in two or three months being outstanding. Both models were reasonably reliable given care, but of course were under-armoured and undergunned. A weakness was the ease with which they could break a track on soft going. Nor was the standard tool-kit issued with the tanks remotely up to the job.

Second Lieutenant Wright remembers going over to Oxford with Lieutenant Robinson one Saturday evening to dine with the fellows at his old college. The two of them got talking after dinner to Professor Lindemann (Lord Cherwell), Winston Churchill's Scientific Advisor, and told him just what they thought of the tools, especially the special punches used with the aid of a sledge-hammer to drive out the track-pins, and in constant use to effect repairs. As was his custom the "Prof", as he was always known, listened to the two young subalterns very sympathetically; and literally within weeks good-quality tools were issued. It clearly paid to have a chance of complaining to someone with influence at the top.

Corporal Colin Brown felt that the time at Brackley was more like peace-time soldiering, the food above all was excellent; the troops played football (both sorts) and cricket, the regimental teams excelling themselves. Training was in the usual disciplines of D&M (Driving & Maintenance), Wireless and Gunnery. On a course at Bovington he even learned on the old Matilda Infantry Tank and on his return was made up to Sergeant.

Sport was always encouraged and the Rugby team was especially strong, with several players who had been with the Hull and East Riding Club for the RU game, vigorously reinforced by League players, some of whom had played for Hull or Hull Kingston Rovers, notables among them being Corporal "Bunk" Bedford, Trooper Alf Broadley, Sergeants Freddie McBain, Alec Morland and the formidable "Max" Tindall who was not only large but reputed to be able to run the 100 yards in even time.

The CO took a keen interest in the cricket team and was playing in one match against a strong Northampton side containing a senior ex-Test Match bowler, V. W. C. Jupp. Ted Wright opened the batting and had the temerity to hit the first ball he received from Jupp for six. The expert was much too clever for that sort of treatment and clean-bowled him next ball. Fish was furious and gave Ted a proper rocket.

Other athletic activities took place as well as such team games. Captain Ellison, who had been a County player, duly won the Divisional Squash competition, and to the dismay of the infantry of the Motor Battalion, the Brigade cross-country run too. Lieutenant Robinson, who had been a keen cross-country runner at school, won the Divisional Assault Course and received a Commando stabbing knife as his prize from the GOC himself which was mockingly known afterwards as the "Brocas Burrows Fruit Knife" by his fellow officers.

By the late summer of 1941 9th Armoured Division had worked up to operate as a division and the climax came in September when a full-scale Home Forces exercise took place, Exercise "Bumper". By September the harvest was in and the participants were free to travel across country with only such areas as market gardens out of bounds. Special repair parties were organized to follow up the action to mend fences and hedges and generally tidy up. Virtually the whole of the front-line army in England took part and 9th Armoured Division's role was to spearhead a mock enemy attack, while 8th Armoured Division (with Valentines) and 11th Armoured Division (with Cruisers) formed the mobile defence. An armoured division at that time consisted of two armoured brigades and a motorized infantry brigade of three battalions. In addition there were four artillery regiments and divisional troops. All these amounted to hundreds of tracked and wheeled vehicles so that manoeuvring forces on this scale took up much of the southern midlands.

The ERY started in their enemy role by entraining at Brackley and travelling to Newmarket where they blotted their copy-book by motoring on their tracks straight across the Limekilns gallops to their billets for the night in the commodious racing stables. The track-marks of the tanks could still be seen on aerial photographs several years later. The next morning the mock invasion began and it was not long before the Regiment lost its inhibitions about leaving the roads and was charging across country firing blanks from their 2pdr guns. The attackers made notable advances in the first two days, Second Lieutenant Wright's No1 Troop of A Squadron even reached the village of Islip just outside Oxford when acting as point troop for the Yeomanry. Here they were assailed with great ferocity by the Home Guard, one brick thrown at the tank missing his elbow by inches. He later met a 4th/7th DG officer, Philip Verdin, who lost an eye to a Home Guard smoke grenade on the same exercise. The ERY were then pulled back into Buckinghamshire where at one time they had the complete soft "tail" of the transport of 8th Armoured Division under their guns, but were prevented by the umpires from firing and possibly upsetting the later course of the exercise which the home side of course had to win. That night, again under pressure from the umpires, 9th Armoured Division was made to retreat into the rural areas near where Milton Keynes now is. This was a night march and everyone had been going for two or three nights without any sleep. The Troop Leader of No1 Troop in A Squadron and his driver Trooper Robinson reckoned that their tank which was leading the Regiment was the only one out of the thirty odd survivors which had two of the crew awake all through the march. In all the others either the driver or the tank commander used to drop off to sleep. But the march went on and while it was still dark the column arrived at the wood where the ERY had to laager for the rest of the night. To get there they had to go through a gate only a couple of inches wider than the tanks on either side and in complete darkness too. All thirty tanks made it without a scratch on the gateposts. Unfortunately when daylight came there was an alarm and, as they rushed to deploy, the second tank through carried one of the gateposts clean away.

The "enemy" had been cut off from their transport by that stage and tanks were running low on fuel. Some still had the 30-gallon reserve "saddle tanks" strapped on to the rear engine compartment, and full up too. During the wakeful hours of his third night with no sleep Second Lieutenant Wright tells how he worked out that if the fifteen best "runners" left replenished their fuel from the available "saddle-tanks" they would have just enough to make a despairing suicide raid on Whitehall. When dawn broke he tried out the idea on Fish who admitted that the estimates were reliable, but he was far too wary an ex-Senior Staff Officer to risk his Army future on any such hare-brained idea, however attractive it might seem. No more was heard of it and the "enemy" remnant were duly umpired to an inglorious defeat.

The late summer/autumn manoeuvre season was not yet over, because after a week for rest and much-needed maintenance, the 9th Armoured Division once again took to the railway and travelled north to Northumberland for Exercise "Percy" which was on nearly as ambitious a scale as "Bumper" had been. Second Lieutenant Wright was unable to observe this battle as he was left behind at Brackley in charge of the rear party. The disturbance of manoeuvres on this sort of scale and the inevitable, large increase in radio traffic was used to cover major redisposition of formations up and down the country, so that a division might find itself permanently relocated. Fortunately this did not happen to the Yeomanry who enjoyed their old billets at Brackley for some time longer.

Soon after these exercises, the commander of 27 Armoured Brigade, Brigadier Charles Norman, was promoted to become GOC 8th Armoured Division and the ERY's CO was moved up to take his place at Brigade. His successor in command of ERY was the very popular Dick Agnew, a 15th/19th Hussar whose home was by chance near Brackley, which enhanced the social amenities available. Another departure among the senior ranks was Major Roddy Verelst, a long-serving 11th Hussar officer who had been attached to RHQ effectively as 2i/c for nearly a year. He departed with his old friend, now a Major General, Charles Norman, whose 8th Armoured Division soon embarked on the long voyage round the Cape for Egypt. In the 8th Army they fought doggedly at Alamein in spite of the deficiencies in gun-power of their Valentines and when that battle was won led the pursuit through Cyrenaica where reliability rather than gunpower was at a premium. Poor Roddy Verelst, however, was indiscreet enough to write a highly critical letter about what he saw as the deficiencies of the army's set-up in Cairo and give it to a fellow-officer who was flying home to post when he got back. When he got there he put it in the "out" tray in the War Office where it was opened by the censors. In the row that followed Roddy was "given the bowler hat" and sent home in disgrace for breach of discipline. He was a great character, however, and kept the officers' mess entertained by accompanying rather croaky renderings of Kipling's Barrack Room Ballads on his ukulele. One of his more memorable remarks, when told that one of the subalterns had become rather moody, was to say that he must be suffering from "ingrowing greens".

Before all this took place a few more sketches of "goings on" at Brackley may illuminate the scene and illustrate what genuine fun survives in the memories of those who were there. One concerns the D&M "School" which was run by Captain James Wright, a cousin of Major Maylin Wright of A Squadron renown in 1940 and his youngest brother Ted. Captain Wright, who had a Cambridge degree in mechanical engineering, duly went down to Bovington to take the long instructor's course in D&M and passed with a "D" for Distinction. The climax of such courses was the TP or Teaching Practice by which all candidates were finally judged. The subject was chosen by the candidate himself and involved much coloured chalk drawing of sectioned elements of engine-design to illustrate the spoken piece. Captain Wright chose a compelling "spoof" invention of his own entitled the "bubble engine" which was fuelled with soapy water, the induction stroke drawing a bubble into the cylinder-head to be pierced on compression by a descending pin in lieu of the more conventional spark. The expanding gases thus released drove down the piston and the cycle continued. This was all delivered in impeccable instructor's jargon and illustrated with classic chalk drawings of the mechanism. Under pressure, he sometimes repeated the discourse to an audience at Brackley and anyone who was fortunate to hear this masterpiece was reduced to gales of laughter. No wonder he achieved a "D"! Later, when drafting to the Middle East set in, Captain Wright went out to Egypt to take charge of the D&M School in Cairo and used to keep a weather eye open for "Fox Badges", finding jobs for ERY chaps at his school as often as possible.

One arrival at the Regiment during the Brackley period was Captain Noel Sissons, a cousin of the Captain Ted Sissons who was killed with the ERY in the Dunkirk campaign. Noel had been in 2ERY but had gone to Camberley to take the wartime Staff Course, successful candidates being designated "psc" (for "passed Staff College") as opposed to "sc" for achieving the full regular Staff qualification. All the suitable appointments being already filled, he was made President of the Mess Committee and for a few months ran the Officers' Mess with considerable style. He was a some-what bland individual and was given the name "Uncle Quag" (after Quaglino's Restaurant in London). After a while Noel Sissons, who could always land on his feet, got the job of running a Combined Operations D&M School with headquarters at the luxurious Sandbanks Hotel at Sandbanks in Dorset. Among his staff were reported to be some of the comeliest female officers in the British Army.

But Brackley was a welcoming place and several of the Yeoman married local girls and settled there after the war. The name of Cone (one of two brothers in A Squadron with a Fish-Dock background in Hull) was for many years associated with the Brackley fish-and-chip shop.

The summer of 1941 was a hot one and Northamptonshire was beset by a drought, so that water for showers had to be rationed. The CO had the bright idea that the dried-up, open-air swimming pool belonging to the town might be brought back into use. A party was duly organized to dig on the hill above the swimming bath to locate a supply of spring water, the lie of the land suggesting that this was a promising place. After they had started, Second Lieutenant Wright, being a bit of an amateur dowser, heard about it and went along to see what they were up to. Cutting a suitable forked twig, he started testing for indications of underground water. Quite soon his twig signalled the presence of water some distance from where the party was at work, so he shifted their efforts to the more likely spot and it was not long before the diggers uncovered a wet pipe from which a little water was seeping, right by the swimming-pool. This was soon identified as the original piped source of supply when the pool had first been opened. Alas, however, as a hoary old local was quick to point out, the supply had been blocked by what he called "running sand" and the council had had to abandon the project some years before. It might have paid to make a few enquiries among the locals in the first place. The Yeomanry swimming-pool became a "might have been" too.

One of the penances for a subaltern during the later stages at Brackley was to be sent off to take charge of a scratch troop of old light tanks doing guard duty at a satellite airfield of the RAF base at Wittering near Stamford. These even included two machines of Marks which preceded the MkVIB of 1 ERY fame. It was difficult enough to keep these antiques running at all, let alone lift the low morale of the crews. One unfortunate subaltern describes how, during his tenure of the post, the RAF Squadron at the airfield had just been issued with Spitfire VI fighters. These were the first Spitfires to have pressurized cabins for high-altitude flying. The squadron was commanded by "Johnny" Johnson, a famous Yorkshire fighter-pilot who later rose to the rank of Air Vice Marshal, and they kept suffering a series of fatal accidents. This turned out to be mainly due to the Squadron being used for low-level defence of East Coast convoys which caused the cabin temperatures to rise so much that the pilots blacked out. The Army did not have a monopoly on foul-ups.

Around this time Captain Fitzwilliam Hyde, who had been Adjutant for more than a year, moved to Brigade HQ to command Brigade HQ Squadron and handed over to Captain Michael Argyle, one of the band of mainly 11th Hussar officers who used to spend long periods with the ERY while awaiting posting to the Middle East. Other regiments were represented too, for instance Lieutenant Norman Hall of the 8th Hussars who is remembered for a remarkable green- and gold-braided side-cap of a box-shape, the pattern being worn by officers of the regiment to this day as could be seen when the 8th Hussars took their Challenger II tanks to the Gulf War in 1992. The "fruit-salad" effect first forbidden by Lieutenant Colonal Cooke in 1940 at Bovington was for a time revived. By a strange co-incidence the author of a book on regimental silver made contact with the Old Comrades Association in 1998 having been offered by a dealer a silver cigarette box with an engraving of the Forrard badge on the lid and an inscription to say that it had been presented to one Lieutenant A. H. Cockbain by the officers of the ERY on the occasion of his marriage in 1941. Tony Cockbain had been one of this group, had gone out to fight with the 11th Hussars in the Middle East and had died in Palestine in 1942 after a severe bout of jaundice. The box must have found its way back into the trade in Cornwall when his family possessions were dispersed. A similar badge has been incorporated in a little beaker made by an amateur silver-smithing friend which Ted Wright uses at reunions at his house.

One or two episodes will serve to round out the varied and usually enter-taining life led by all ranks at Brackley. There was the occasion when the Officers' Mess Sergeant Valler was in the Magistrates' Court at Brackley for obtaining over-the-ration meat for the mess who were in fact nobly fed. Captain David Barton, a Hull solicitor in civil life, defended him and got him off with a caution; but the real trouble was that the then Mayor – and Chairman of the Bench – was the butcher who had sold him the meat. The poor man had to resign from both positions in deep disgrace which was apparently nothing in comparison with the telling-off he received from his fellow-magistrates for letting the institution down. Another one concerns the first trip to the ranges at Linney Head in Pembrokeshire. All went well to begin with and all enjoyed firing off live ammunition with abandon. But the gearboxes on the Covenanters began seizing up. Lieutenant Wright well remembers Trooper Richardson, who was one of his drivers, coming in to the finish of the run waving the gear-lever out of the driver's hatch, having broken it off in his efforts to change gear. The Technical Adjutant, Captain Peter Northcotes, was well qualified as an engineer and decided to set about the cure without incurring the disruption of sending the tanks off to base workshops. Entirely on his own initiative he had his own fitters in the Regimental Workshops remove and strip down the faulty gear boxes, grind down the splines with hand-tools to free the sliding pinions and return the offending casualties to service in a matter of a couple of days instead of the weeks it would otherwise have taken. This was entirely against the rules and he might have been in very hot water if he had been found out; but the shooting programme was completed without interruption. One Mechanical Sergeant, L. A. Davis, remembered that, on one excursion to the firing ranges at Linney Head, the tanks were prepared and loaded with shells and fuel to fire in their main armaments. They were to be loaded on the wagons known as "war-flats"; but there had been a sharp frost during the night and the first two tanks slipped off sideways and lay on their sides across the main railway lines. The London train was diverted and the fitters laid sleepers in between the tracks and winched them back, inch by inch. It was a very slow process.

A final episode was really quite a feather in the cap for the ERY who were ordered to send one each of the three sorts of tanks then on their strength: a Covenanter, a Crusader and the first American Light Tank – the Stuart or Honey as it later became known – to be issued to a fighting unit in Britain.

Lieutenant Wright and one of his sergeants in 1 Troop of A Squadron, Eric Bean, who had been on a short learning course on it at Bovington provided the crew. The party set off for their first journey on road transports to a "secret" location near Luton and on arrival found that a specimen of every tank in the army was being assembled for some grand demonstration. The first day was spent in a rehearsal and our two representatives suggested that their Stuart, which could turn on a sixpence but at best could only do 37 mph flat out, might have a race with the little Tetrarch Light Tank (which eventually landed in gliders in Normandy on D-Day) round the circuit provided in a large park – Tetrarchs were very fast, with a top speed of over 45mph; but had a very wide turning circle and Sergeant Bean reckoned that by cutting the corners as close as possible to the markers on the course the Stuart had some chance. All went well until after the half-way mark when the Tetrarch started to gain and Sergeant Bean, who was driving the Stuart, went full speed hard up to the last corner. Alas, the Stuart jumped off its tracks and nearly rolled over. Of course we had no spares, so the organizers had to send a truck down to Farnborough to pick up what was needed to repair the damage overnight and the crew had to work long hours to get the tank fit to take part, albeit rather groggily, in the more sober parade the next day. During the evening Lieutenant Wright tried to winkle out of the organizers what the show was in aid of and who was coming. HM The King was seriously suggested as one possibility; but they would not break security. They did, however, give a broad hint by mentioning that a very special bottle of brandy had been secured for the lunch. This could only mean Winston Churchill. And so it was the next day with generals and cabinet ministers and all the top brass assembled and the Prime Minister went round the lines of tanks drawn up for inspection. Lieutenant Wright got his picture taken talking to the great man on the Stuart's turret, he complete with cigar and the famous square-sided bowler hat. Ted never knew that he had been photographed until his mother saw the picture in the *Yorkshire Post* and sent for some prints, one of which is reproduced here. The really big attraction of the show, however, was the unveiling of the new A22 Infantry Tank Mark IV made at Luton by Vauxhall Motors. Winston of course had to have a ride in it himself, so he donned a white coat and exchanged his bowler for a Tank Corps beret borrowed from the head organizer Major Liardet (the next up among them was Captain Creagh Gibson of 5RIDG (the Skins) who later came to the ERY in Laboe in 1946). The crews of the parading tanks were fallen out on the edge of the park and could not see what was going on in the middle of the arena, but found out later that there had been a brief pause followed by a cheer which all could hear. This was the PM relieving himself in full view before setting off on his ride. It was just like the British generals to cheer the Boss at such a moment. Not surprisingly the A22 became known as the Churchill from that time on, properly baptised too.

Around this time, there were two significant changes in the senior ranks. At long last Captain Ellison got his way back and was promoted to Major on taking over C Squadron from Major Sam Strang who was transferred to another appointment. As will be clearly seen in his book *Europe Revisited*, C Squadron became the love of his life even after he became 2i/c. The second change was in A Squadron where Major Johnnie Leigh ("Jigger" to the troops) became 2i/c of the Regiment when that post was formalized, having previously been filled unofficially by Major Verelst. The vacancy in A Squadron was filled by the much admired Major Brian Burstall ("Busty") who had returned after a long convalescence from a serious operation. Brian was another Hull solicitor, and slightly elderly for the job; but he had an adventurous nature and although accident-prone – he was credibly reported to have broken nearly every bone in his body at one time or another – drew great affection from all ranks. He was a notable bird-watcher as well. B Squadron having been taken over earlier by Major Edmund Scott, who is mentioned in the 1940 Cassel stand, all three fighting squadrons were commanded by Yeomanry officers. Another change at this time was the promotion of Sergeant Major Medhurst to Lieutenant QM in place of Captain Martin Mulchinock who had successfully escaped from Dunkirk. Bert Medhurst was a First World War Tank Corps veteran whose face can be identified in a group photograph of 26th Armoured Car Company. Usually known as "Pop", due to his age, he was very popular with all ranks and this proved to be one of the most satisfactory of appointments as he served through until after the end of hostilities in Europe.

To his great regret, Lieutenant Wright was sent off to RMC Sandhurst as an instructor in the Armoured Wing. There he took over a troop of Cadets in mid-course from another ERY officer called Jacques, but never found out where he had previously fitted into the Regiment. He found it something of an embarrassment to try to teach some of the Cadets who already had had battle experience in the Western Desert. After a frustrating winter spent much in the company of two other young instructors who had been invalided back from Egypt and drinking rather more than was good for them as a way of relieving their feelings, he at last got his way and was posted back to the ERY. One good thing which came out of it, however, was that he persuaded one Chris Moreton to opt for the ERY who was a great success but was killed in July 1944 when leading a troop in B Squadron. Lieutenant Wright was replaced at Sandhurst by Captain Pat Cummings, a rather older ERY officer much better suited for the job, who attracted several other good recruits to the Regiment.

Soon after returning to the Yeomanry, Major Ellison attended a course at the Senior Officers' School, designed to equip the candidates for future command. There he met a Major Tom Williamson of 5RIDG (the Royal Inniskilling Dragoon Guards or "Skins") who later became CO of the ERY. They had been at school together at Malvern and Major Ellison used to say to Williamson that, having successfully passed, he was then fitted to command a regiment, which did, as was intended, ruffle feathers some-what.

At last, after a good year of varied and comfortable existence at Brackley, the time came to move and the ERY went for some months to Easton-on-the-Hill near Stamford in Lincolnshire. The spell there left little impression on the record of events; but seemed to have been generally uninteresting.

⋆　　⋆　　⋆

The next phase in activities began with a move to the Breckland in Suffolk to the west of Thetford. "The Breck," as it was known, is a wide area of heathland divided by linear belts of pine trees to act as windbreaks. The ERY were in a tented camp near Elvedon called Canada Farm and part of the Guinness family estates. Elvedon was famous for its game-shooting and one of the Squadron Leaders used to carry a shot-gun in his turret on local exercises to take pot-shots at the birds put up by the tanks as they dashed about the countryside. Now all the heather area has gone under the plough for barley-growing, but in those days was a haven for the rare stone curlews which were often put up by the exercising tanks. One evening a message was passed to Major Burstall from the Sergeants' Mess asking him if he would kindly come over to tell them what the strange noise was in the pine trees above their tent – it was a nightjar "churring". It was a haven for all sorts of wild life and a paradise for anyone with an interest in natural history; but less attractive for many of the Regiment who were more used to town life.

While, throughout the long summer, the ERY either enjoyed or in some cases endured camp life at Canada Farm, exercising over the open heath-land or the wide Stamford Battle Area nearby, training in the usual tradesmen's skills to qualify as Driver Mechanics, Driver Operators or Gunners continued unabated as the drafting process intensified. The decisions as to who should be selected began to hurt as longstanding Yeomen who had sometimes been with the Regiment since pre-war days had to join drafts to make up the quotas of trade-tested men.

One day soon after rejoining from Sandhurst Lieutenant Wright was standing by the side of the main road through the Canada Farm camp chatting to Lieutenant Bert Medhurst, the QM, and trying to catch up with events during his absence when a Daimler Scout car drew up containing a tall grey-haired officer in a blue boiler-suit and wearing a general's gold-braided cap. They saluted smartly and Medhurst started talking to him, obviously knowing him already, while Lieutenant Wright was left at a complete loss. It turned out to be the new Divisional Commander, Major General Brian Horrocks. The General's first concern was with the welfare of the chaps with the question "Are you all right for water?" When Lieutenant Medhurst said that they were having difficulty in keeping up with the demand, Horrocks promised them an extra water-truck which duly arrived the next day. Lieutenant Wright goes on to say, "Horrocks (usually known as "Jorrocks") was the most genial and approachable general under whom the ERY ever served and he spread an air of confidence and good spirits wherever he went." Soon after this meeting some of the officers had slipped off for an afternoon's golf at the nearby Mildenhall club and after their round were tucking into tea and toast at the club-house when in walked Jorrocks and three of his staff on the same errand. The two parties joined up and the General gave the impression that he thoroughly approved of that sort of activity and "thought it quite right that we should have this bit of relaxation, leaving us quite unabashed".

One observer of the passing scene used to collect examples of what he called "Heard in the tank-park" and a couple from Canada Farm days have stuck in his memory. A tank-driver, Trooper Fred Turner of A Squadron, who had been the driver of the Squadron bus in the Bovington-Braxtead-Brackley days of 1940, was seen by a passer-by sitting on the turret of his Covenanter during one of the regular repainting programmes. He was covered up to his elbows in brown or green camouflage paint and the passer-by called to him, "How are you doing Fred?" to which without pause he replied "Fine; 'Itler started in a small way too!" Another gem, also from A Squadron, came from an occasion when another of the tank-drivers, Trooper Bartholemew, a very respectable mortician in civil life, had dropped something heavy on his toe and let out a stream of not very clean oaths. A notoriously foul-mouthed fellow-trooper overheard him and in solemn tones remarked, "Trooper Bartholemew, your language is fucking 'orrible!" There was always time for fun, given a receptive enough ear.

Morale was high and everyone was encouraged to adopt names for their tanks. Not to be outdone, No1 Troop, A Squadron chose the names of birds for theirs and the Troop Leader had trouble finding ones beginning with "A", eventually settling for Auk, Avocet and Albatross, the next possibility which fortunately was not needed being the Alpine Accentor. These tickled the fancy of their bird-loving Squadron Leader; so the Troop Leader being fairly good with a paint-brush painted three little steel panels to mount on the tanks with depictions of the chosen birds. When Major Burstall left A Squadron in 1943, the Troop Leader, having by then already left for HQ Squadron to start up the Recce Troop, he made off with the three plates – and kept them as a souvenir till his dying day in the 1980s.

General Horrocks once gave a memorable lecture to the assembled division in a nearby cinema in which he described the situation in the Middle East. One in the audience remembers how he gave high praise to General Auchinleck, the C-in-C, who had taken personal command of the defeated 8th Army and was not enjoying much of a press at the time. He had, however, organized the impregnable defensive position on the El Alamein line only 50 miles short of Alexandria on the Nile Delta. It was not long before Horrocks himself went out to Egypt to command XIII Corps at the Battle of Alamein and begin a spectacular career under Field Marshal Montgomery as one of his most successful Corps Commanders right up to the end of the NW Europe campaign.

The armoured forces in Britain were still being increased in 1942 and the Guards Armoured Division was formed, complete with two armoured and one infantry brigades. A special series of two-week courses was set up at Bulford on Salisbury Plain to teach armoured tactics to the somewhat inflexible guards officers. Lieutenant Wright was sent on one of these as part of the process of mixing experienced exponents of armoured practice with the novices. He relates how it was a very gentlemanly affair run by a Lieutenant Colonel Harry Floyd from the 15th/20th Hussars and several able instructors, one of whom got into the Cabinet after the war. Much of the time was taken up with the traditional TEWT (Tactical Exercise Without Troops) during which the mess-truck would arrive with the makings of a lavish picnic lunch ending with a glass of port. The result was that the afternoon's proceedings were a somewhat sleepy affair. A sequel to this was, perhaps not unexpectedly, the introduction of a system of Parade

Maintenance which may have suited the guards but not the ERY, who, having always coped quite satisfactorily with the mechanical side of things, regarded it as something of an impertinence suitable only for guardsmen.

In some peoples' memories Canada Farm was notorious for some very wild parties in the Officers' Mess which was housed in a large marquee. Often these happened quite spontaneously; but one of the more spectacular was a guest-night when the principal guest was a Lieutenant Colonel from Brigade HQ where he was in charge of training exercises. He was old, very senior and had been in the Indian Army cavalry, sporting a magnificent leather-belt affair which went over one shoulder and had silver fittings including a neat little box presumably for 'dispatches'. His name was Lieutenant Colonel Sartorius, known variously as "Sart" or "Old Happy and Glorious". As the frolics warmed up, a party led by Major Burstall had shinned up the outside of the marquee with a supply of thunderflashes which they started dropping through the ventilation-openings onto the company below. The Army thunderflash had a four-second delay before exploding, to allow a safe interval for the thrower; and those below started picking the fireworks up and throwing them back at their attackers. Soon the upper party beat this trick by counting to "three" before dropping the fireworks; but unfortunately "Sart" was too far gone to notice and picked up a thunderflash which promptly exploded in his hand. The cardboard base-plug went into his palm; but he refused to let the MO, John Carson, give him first aid, claiming that he was too drunk to know what he was doing. "Our observer" had been out all day with a bicycle on a train expedition to Norwich and was pedalling back up the hill to camp from Thetford Station. As he approached he could hear the uproar from nearly a mile away and realized that something entertaining was afoot. When he arrived he went in to find "Sart" sitting on the ground against the tent-flies, holding his wounded hand and moaning while the jollification went on around him. He concluded that for once it was better to stay sober and not try to catch up with the rest of the party, confessing that this was a rare event in his experience. "Sart" was an unusually game character for an elderly and very senior officer. His main role at Brigade HQ was organization of exercises and he could normally be seen out among the tanks as an incongruous figure riding a motorbike.

As the summer of 1942 was drawing in, the time at Canada Farm, which some relished but many disliked, had come to an end. The move was not too far to a hutted camp at Chippenham near Newmarket. This was close to an RAF Fighter Station at Snailwell and the traffic there became unusually heavy for one short period which turned out to coincide with the costly Canadian raid on Dieppe in mid-August. This was essentially a reconnaissance in force to probe the defences of the Atlantic Wall and many valuable lessons were learned, even though at the expense of very heavy casualties. The alleged shackling of German prisoners by the attacking Canadians led to harsh reprisals against Allied POWs, among whom some of the ERY officers suffered.

At Chippenham the establishment was increased to include a Recce Troop in HQ Squadron and Lieutenant Wright was moved from A Squadron to organize it. The equipment at first was ten old Daimler Scout Cars, or Dingoes as they became known, another nickname acquired from the Australians in the Western Desert. The early models had a remarkable reversing mechanism to enable them to retire quickly if they ran into unexpected danger. By the shift of a lever the driver could change the steering so that what had been the trailing wheels became the leading ones and all the gears in the self-changing box remained available instead of just reverse. The driver's seat was mounted at 45° so that he did not have to turn his neck too far to see where he was going when driving backwards. Trooper Richardson, driving his Covenanter in No 1 Troop of A Squadron, once had an entertaining encounter with one on an exercise. He was going along a winding road when a Dingo came round a corner and, immediately slapping into reverse, shot back the way it had come. Trooper Richardson gave chase and wound up the Covenanter to its top speed of over 40 mph which was near to the maximum a reversing Dingo could do. They went on like this for several miles which must have been a hair-raising experience for the scout car which was given no chance of escaping or turning round.

Not long after that the by then worn-out Dingoes were exchanged for Bren Carriers which with their tracks were thought better able to keep up with the tanks across country. These eventually gave way to a mixture of another model of wheeled scout car and a dozen or so Stuart light tanks which remained standard until the end of the war in Europe.

Chapter 11

79TH ARMOURED DIVISION AND
27TH ARMOURED BRIGADE

Instead of a narrative account, the events of 1941–42 are shown in the form of a diary. This was the lowest point of the war for the Allies and disaster followed disaster; but by August 1942 the tide had turned.

April–May	*Iraq occupied by Middle East forces.*
May	*Sinking of the* Bismarck
June	*Middle East forces invade Vichy French Syria.*
21/2 June	*Germans launch Operation Barbarossa against Russia.*
June–Sept	*Seesaw actions by 8th Army and Afrika Korps in Western Desert.*
Sept–Oct	*Occupation of Persia (Iran) to open supply line from Persian Gulf to Russia.*
Nov	*Germans drive into Russia peters out with the onset of winter at one point only 20 miles from Moscow. Russians launch counter-offensive and regain much lost ground.*
7 Dec	*Japanese launch surprise attack by carrier borne aircraft on Pearl Harbor. USA enters the war and declares war on Germany too.*
1942 – Feb onwards	*Japs invade Malaya and capture Singapore by 15 February, and the Philippines where the Americans hold out until April. East Indies and Burma overrun, advance eventually contained by May at carrier battle of Coral Sea*
End May onwards	*After fierce battles, 8th Army in Desert and retreat to El Alamein line fifty miles from Delta.*

At the end of 1942 the establishment of an armoured division was reduced to only one armoured and one infantry brigade. The 27 Armoured Brigade therefore left 9th Armoured Division and moved to the newly forming 79th Armoured Division under the formidable command of Major General Sir P. C. S. Hobart ("Hobo"). They exchanged their cruiser tanks for Valentines and in December moved to Bingley and Shipley in West Yorkshire. The wheeled vehicles travelled by road and, after a long and frustrating drive, the Recce Troop halted in Bingley alongside a gloomy wool-mill in the dusk with a steady drizzle falling. Lieutenant Wright leaned down to his driver, Corporal Frank Hodgson, and with thoughts of the Suffolk countryside in his mind said, "Isn't it awful?"; Frank replied: "Awful! I think it's lovely". The Hull chaps were back in a town at last. Once the Regiment were sorted out with A Squadron at Shipley and the rest around Bingley, everyone settled down for an interesting winter in the West Riding usually with "feet under the table" with many friends made locally.

The demand for trade-tested troops in the Middle East and elsewhere rose to its peak at this period and training became the first priority. The detailed programmes set up came under the direct and terrifying eye of Hobo himself who insisted on highly detailed systems designed to cover everyone in the Regiment. Woe betide any officer who did not know exactly what any of his men were doing at any time of the day. The Recce troop with their elderly vehicles parked in a damp area by the River Aire at Bingley were at a very low ebb at this period, but perked up somewhat when they received their Bren Carriers, although these were no better than the Valentines over the boggy North Yorkshire moors where many got stuck whenever they went out on exercises.

The locals were notably friendly and many good times were had, not least at the Ferens Arms in Bingley patronized especially by Captain John Carson, the MO, and Bert Medhurst, the Quartermaster. These two palled up with a group of like-minded people who used to retire to "The Snug" after licensing hours. One party there went on all night and the Doctor told afterwards how, after some preliminary drinking in the snug, a local and prosperous entrepreneur told the company that he had to be on firewatching duty at a bakery he owned at the Brontë village of Haworth not far away. So they called up one of the town's taxis, a Rolls Royce driven by a character called Nelson, loaded it up with everyone's favourite tipple (Champagne for the ladies and a case of "baby" Guinness for a chap who never drank anything else) and set out for the bakery. When they got there John Carson in his very Scottish accents told how there were hams hanging from the ceiling and a whole crate of eggs for traditional Yorkshire ham-and-eggs and he was not asked "Will ye have a whisky?" but "What sort of whisky wud ye like?", four of the choicer blends being on offer. So much for the firewatching stint, but the MO and QM rated it one of the best parties that they could remember. The prosperous entrepreneur (whose name is forgotten) was not above doing the Yeomanry a good turn either; for when one of Second Lieutenant the Hon James Lowther's tanks in C Squadron demolished a stretch of wall in the town (known as Jimmy's Hole) he had his builders repair it with no charge before any more could be said. It was here that Major Ellison had his affair with the 15cwt truck, whose driver failed to put any oil in the differential, thereby reducing the pinions to pieces, according to one witness, "no bigger than a sixpence". There was the usual Court of Enquiry whose proceedings went up to the GOC, who wrote across them "Squadron Leader to pay". They then found their way back to Major Ellison who did nothing about it for over a year and finally destroyed them when the ERY went over on the invasion of France in 1944.

Through all this time the training and the inevitable drafting overseas went on apace and the demands for quotas of tradesmen began to call for severe sacrifices of long-serving Yeomen. The experience of Trooper Richardson in A Squadron is typical, he having been with the ERY since the outbreak of war and become one of the best and most experienced drivers in the Regiment. He went on a draft to Egypt and after the war used to tell how he rose to be a sergeant in a reinforcement unit. On one mission to deliver by road-transporter a consignment of Grant tanks to a yeomanry regiment just out of battle, the CO said to him, "You know how to drive these things; so you can be my driver". Trooper Richardson had no option but to obey orders. On the first day back in action, he took an AP round (presumably an 88mm) clean through the front of the tank and then going through his leg. He was evacuated to hospital where the surgeons decided to shorten the other leg to match the wounded one. He eventually recovered from his ordeal after two years in hospital and was lucky to have survived. Old friends remember seeing him at reunions until 1998 when his health was already failing before he died in 1999, sadly missed by all. But somehow a firm nucleus of East Riding Yeoman remained with the Regiment.

Once a year it was standard practice for all the clerks, cooks and other administrative troops to parade for Mills Bomb throwing. This took place at a range on a piece of moorside near Bingley, where as usual the ground was somewhat soft. One corporal, who will be nameless, had chucked his grenade satisfactorily and retired about fifty yards behind the throwing point. The programme went on when without warning he fell to the ground with a cry, having been hit in the jaw by what turned out to be the base-plug of a grenade. He was taken off to hospital to have his broken jaw wired up and was visited by his Squadron Leader when he was well enough. As reported later by the officer in question, Major David Barton, perhaps embellishing the story somewhat, he seemed to be in some distress, but found it difficult to speak properly with all the rigging round his jaw. Eventually it turned out that his denture had been smashed to bits in the accident. Major Barton tried to reassure him and said that he need not worry as the army would give him a new one. This did not comfort him at all and at last the full story came out: "D'you see, Sir, it was like this; they weren't my dentures. They were a pair I was wearing in for one of the cooks". Can camaraderie go further? Reconstructing the event, it seems that the grenade must have landed in a patch of soft ground and acted like a miniature mortar, firing the base plug a hundred yards back to where it dropped among the spectators. Dangerous things, Mills Bombs!

In the spring of 1943, according to the official story, the much respected Colonel Agnew "sought a posting to a more active theatre of war" and Lieutenant Colonel Tom Williamson (the very same who was on the course with Major Ellison) was appointed to command the Regiment. He was tall and good looking, with a high opinion of his old Regiment and sported their green trousers when in service dress, even though he wore the badges of the East Riding Yeomanry. He was not universally popular.

About this time men started to be posted to the Yeomanry and to stay, as drafts to other theatres slowed and the Regiment gradually came up to strength. Lectures on every conceivable subject were given on tank warfare, from divisional to troop tactics. There was even a lecture on the Middle East given by Major General Martel who had commanded the abortive Arras counter-attack in 1940, although no one thought the Regiment would ever be fighting in desert conditions.

In April 1943 Major General Hobart gave an address at Bingley on the future operational role of the Brigade. It was to spearhead the invasion and to storm into Europe. Those who had come back from the mauling in France in 1940 were content that they were going to deliver a bloody nose to the Germans in return, whilst those who had spent years in training were glad at last to see a solid objective to train for. Secrecy was very much enforced.

The ERY moved that month to Rendlesham Hall in Suffolk, a large Victorian mansion which had been an inebriates' home, where the ex-butler had become janitor and made a steady income selling hard liquor to those who were paying good money to be cured from it.

Early in May enemy aircraft began hit-and-run attacks in the Ipswich area. Bombs were dropped in the vicinity of the camp from time to time, but no damage was done. Coming back late one night one of the NCOs and a trooper were stopped by a vehicle which had been hit by bombs. There were several bodies lying in the road. They stopped and went to help. There were many dead and some had had limbs blown off. The trooper calmly collected and stacked the limbs in neat piles which nearly made the Sergeant faint. "How on earth can you do that without throwing up?" he asked. "Oh, easy really, I was a butcher in civvy street and was always told to keep things neat and tidy"!

During the summer of 1943 a curious episode took place involving the Recce Troop and their Bren Carriers. Lieutenant Wright was asked to receive a young soldier from the infantry who had been in constant trouble. His only saving grace seemed to have been some aptitude in driving a carrier; so he was to be sent to the ERY for a last chance. When he arrived, he had a record-sheet consisting of four pages of the standard Army form listing a wide variety of misdemeanours, the most spectacular of which had been to drive away a motor road-roller on an airfield which they were guarding. Lieutenant Wright took his two sergeants, Stan Wilson and Max Tindall, into his confidence and asked them to do their best with the villain, Trooper (ex-Private) Bryant. The rest of his troop were not in the picture about his past; but he never seemed quite to fit in with the others. All went well, however, and he was made the official driver of one of the carriers. After a while he formed up to his Squadron Leader and asked for compassionate leave in order to attend his grandmother's funeral or some other similar pretext. Off he went and, of course, failed to return when his leave was up. A few weeks later he was picked up by the RMPs at a dog track in the East End of London and returned under arrest; so he had to spend every night with the guard while awaiting trial.

That was not the end of the saga, for one night when the Sergeant of the Guard was a rather mild individual called Shelton, a notable wireless instructor, Bryant planned his get-away. He asked to go to the latrines; so Shelton sent him off with one of the guard to stop him escaping. This happened twice more until the Guard Sergeant had had enough and sent him off on his own, but after taking the precaution of having him leave his boots and trousers behind. Off goes Bryant and disappears. It turned out that he had called in on the bunk of Corporal "Bomber" Mankel, the Provost Corporal (under Sergeant Parnaby DCM), and stolen his best boots and battledress trousers before making for London again. The RMPs arrested him once more and returned him to the ERY where he was duly court-martialled and sentenced to a spell in the "Glass House". But the proceedings of the court had to go to the GOC ("Hobo") for confirmation and he commuted the sentence and had Bryant put on a draft for Italy "where he might use his ingenuity more usefully against the enemy".

The pace continued as exercises were made tougher. Then in July 1943 the final phase of training started. They were let into the secret that they were to be one of the first regiments in the Army to train on DD tanks. These were tanks modified by adding a large canvas screen raised and lowered by a ring of rubber columns inflated with compressed air so that the tanks floated in the water suspended below a kind of reinforced water-proof bag. The Brigadier said at a conference that the Yeomanry were about to face the biggest test of physical and mental courage in their lives, and went on to explain their role with the DD tanks. DD stood for Duplex Drive with propellers in the rear as well as the normal tracks: hence "Duplex". The first tanks to be converted were Valentines on which initial training took place; but later Shermans were to be used for the invasion. At a Squadron Leader's conference after the talk Major Ellison and the other Squadron Leaders questioned the Brigadier, in a leg-pulling way, about his talk of the dangers with DDs, repeating the light-hearted comments made by some of his listeners, that if the role was that bad, "why couldn't they join the Paras and get more pay". The Brigadier then went off the deep end, saying, "They (the Squadron Leaders) were a lot of bloody ignorant civilians incapable of commanding their men".

95

The DDs were then being tried out extensively on a large sheet of water called Fritton Lake, originally a duck decoy. The area was surrounded by woods and enclosed in barbed wire and no unauthorized person was allowed in or out. One cantankerous retired admiral apparently refused to leave his home overlooking the lake, so he had to remain behind the wire for many months. The Navy described the DD Sherman as a "canvas boat with a 30-ton keel". It described well the contraption in its Sherman form as this had a canvas screen 20 foot high attached to the tank, big enough, in accordance with Archimedes' principle, to displace enough water to float. Unfortunately there were inevitably some casualties if the columns holding the screen collapsed or a hole was torn in the canvas, when it became only a "30-ton keel" and sank. The tank commander had to have a periscope to see over the edge of the screen.

In case of accidents all the crews had to undergo training and pass a test in the use of the Davis Submarine Escape apparatus, known as "the Joe Davis" after the then World Snooker and Billiards Champion. The apparatus consisted of an oxygen cylinder with an on/off tap, a mouth-piece with a tube connecting the cylinder to an airtight bag on the chest and a nose-clip so that all breathing was through the mouth-piece. Outside Navy instructors from Portsmouth came to teach the use of the apparatus and to pass out successful candidates. They had been trained in the heated waters of HMS *Dolphin*, the RN Submarine School, but the ERY learned their basic training in an outdoor swimming-pool at Yarmouth at 6 am.

First, troops had to learn how to breathe through the mouth and follow out the simple drill to switch on the air and control its inflow. They also had to learn how to rise to the surface from the bottom of the pool breathing through the apparatus as they rose and, most importantly, switch off the air-supply as soon as they surfaced. Gradually they gained confidence in the device and could breathe quite normally. Most people succeeded in passing, but there were occasional problems such as the case of one cheery cove who on surfacing took his mouth-piece out and shouted, "It's a piece of cake", whereupon his chest-bag exploded and he sank to the bottom of the pool and had to be rescued. He had forgotten to turn off the air-supply and his air-bag had blown up. A very few learners panicked and never mastered the drill. Trooper Burrows of C Squadron passed the test; but he said he was terrified the whole time because he had never been able to swim.

After the initiation in the swimming-pool the real test came. Each crew had to sit in the hull of a Valentine tank in their fighting positions. An area of Fritton Lake was dredged off and blocked from the main lake, so a pit could be made for the tank-hull with a large water-tower overhead. With all in position and their "Joe Davis" apparatus ready but not in place, the instructor pulled the plug and the pit filled with water from the tower, coming in through two great vents, all in a matter of seconds. This simulated the effect of a DD tank sinking. It was quite a job to fit the apparatus in the swirl of cold, murky water; and it was the commander's final job, breathing through his escape apparatus, to check that all his crew were safely out before surfacing himself.

The Brigadier, who watched these exercises, was asked if he would set a good example and do the test himself. Major Ellison and the other senior Yeomanry officers shamed him into it as they had all passed through with flying colours. Unwisely the Brigadier had not done the preliminary training in the swimming-pool; so when he came to the surface he passed out. At the next Squadron Leaders' conference they reminded him that the "ignorant civilians" had all passed successfully.

So the Regiment were then able to train on the main lake at Fritton, but with a threat hanging over them from General "Hobo" that if any DD was lost or damaged the commander would be court-martialled.

The first phase consisted of descending a ramp on the bank fashioned like that of a landing craft. They had to enter the water by this ramp which was very steep. On one such exercise Sergeant L. Davis, a Mechanical Sergeant, was attached to B Squadron for one of the exercises. He remembers that he was standing beside the ramp when the tanks came crashing through the wood and down into the water with their screens in place. One tank clipped the rear of the tank in front and tore its canvas screen. When it hit the water the cut opened up and by the time it was almost in the middle of the lake it went down. The crew baled out, but one member could not swim. Luckily a launch was standing by in case of such an incident and picked him up, none the worse for his ducking.

George Jenkin had recently joined the Regiment as a Second Lieutenant and was in charge of 3 Troop in B Squadron. He recalls a night training exercise: "I particularly remember going off the mock ramp into the water on a pitch black night. I led and entered successfully and moved away from the ramp, followed by Sergeant Smith, my troop Sergeant. He must have come down too fast, as he shipped water. The next thing I heard over the W/T was that his 'craft' was sinking and everyone was baling out. As a result of this Smith was court-martialled and busted, and I, as the 'responsible officer' (although nowhere near at the time) had to face a Court of Enquiry and was denied my promotion to full Lieutenant for six months." "I thought," George continued, "that I was hard done by, but learnt the hard way the meaning of the words 'responsible officer'." The Brigadier himself had imposed this punishment.

Some of the verbatim comments from the Yeomen on this training are illuminating:

Trooper A. J. King: "It was a pleasure to launch on 14th July 1943 on the lake and I can vividly remember the tanks crashing blind through the trees and plunging off the ramp in the darkness, and two sank!"

Sergeant W. Morrell: "Enjoyable cruising around a lake. Happy we did not have to be in them on D Day!"

Sergeant J. Moverly: "Enjoyed cruising down the river on a Sunday afternoon. Happy we did not have to take them in on D Day!"

Trooper Tims: "We had really good grub at Rendlesham, which made up for the training."

The War Diary notes that: "Training Phases 2 and 3 took place at 'Fritton Bridge Camp' as it was then coded".

Whilst at Rendlesham some of the officers had one night out which turned out to be quite exciting. It was early in November 1943, when a dozen or so officers joined forces to dine one of the C Squadron subalterns on his 21st birthday, the Hon James Lowther (now Lord Lonsdale) who was to celebrate his coming of age. They had booked a room at the Crown Hotel in Woodbridge, so, after several drinks in the mess, they set out for the dinner in two pick-ups and already in a fairly happy state of mind. The German air force had just paid one of their brief visits and dropped some incendiaries on a village in their path. The village was all agog with wardens and fire-fighters dashing around in the dark, and there was much shouting and scurrying about. The second pick-up with its load of happy officers stopped to help. They soon concentrated their attentions on a house with a burning incendiary bomb in the thatched roof and concluded there was a big risk of the whole house going up in flames. It was filled with beautiful furniture, so they set to and shifted everything to the ground floor and out into the garden. There were a few casualties like the column under the grand piano holding the pedals which was shattered as they trundled it through the french windows. Still smoky but exhilarated, they had most of the furniture out on the lawn and, as things seemed to be under control, drove on into Woodbridge to join the rest of the party for a belated dinner. In the cold dawn of next day they began wondering what they had been up to and their fears were not allayed until the CO had a letter from the owner of the house thanking his officers for what they had done to save his possessions. Apparently, there had been a second incendiary in the roof, the fire brigade flooded the whole house, so everything was soaked and all the furniture on the ground floor would have been ruined but for their hearty efforts.

On 1 August Lieutenant Wright was promoted from the Recce Troop to Captain and Adjutant. His predecessor was Captain "Dad" Green who, at 35, was considered an old man. There had been seven Adjutants of the Regiment since 1940: Tony Hyde, Michael Argyll of the 11th Hussars, who later became a rather controversial judge and whose recollection of his time with the Regiment he summarized as "several wonderful months and tip-top friends. We did all the 'ings'; drinking, gambling, fucking etc!" Next was Robin Miller, an engineer, Jock Smeaton, an accountant, Eric ("Dad") Green and then Wright, followed by Alan Thornton and Donald Mantell. All were men of intelligence. Wright had been at Oxford at the outbreak of war, Argyll was a barrister, Thornton later became a professor at Nottingham University and Mantell a regular Major and a bursar at a large Public School. The job was to do all the staff work of the Regiment and act as something of a buffer between the CO and the junior officers and other ranks.

Captain Wright took over the job at the pre-invasion time and the amount of "admin" eventually grew to a colossal size. Apart from operational matters, he had to deal with personnel, all the loading details and ensuring that everyone knew where they had to be and what they had to do. He was much helped by Major Ellison who had at last been promoted from C Squadron to 2i/c of the Regiment. After Major John Leigh, who had been posted away as too old, for a short time the 2i/c appointment was filled by Major George Turner of the Queen's Bays, who previously had been the CO in command of the Gunnery School at Lulworth for much of the war. Senior regulars were anxious at this period to leave base jobs for fighting units in spite of lack of experience or reduction in rank.

There happened late in October 1943, as the re-equipment with Shermans was about to begin, a disagreement which changed the face of the Regiment somewhat. Captain Wright had not been Adjutant more than a couple of months and, as his gunner in the command tank, was in close contact with the CO. Out on exercises in the Valentines he generated a poor

99

opinion of Williamson even as a tank commander, since he seemed unable to grasp the basic essentials of wireless discipline. A last exercise ended up in the northern half of the Breckland, was tiring and finished with a long trek back to camp in the dark. It had involved much movement and a couple of days with little or no sleep, had rained much of the time and everyone was wet, cold and fed up. Captain Wright was horrified when, as soon as the trek back to camp started in pouring rain, the CO left his tank, got into his staff car and pushed off to bed leaving the rest of them to crawl home in their Valentines. "This," he says, "was too much for me and the others; the Squadron Leaders and I put our heads together afterwards to organize a protest. Major Ellison, then commanding C Squadron, told me to keep out of it as I was too junior and vulnerable." All four Squadron Leaders then formed up to the Brigadier, Errol Prior-Palmer; but he was a dangerous man to cross and, as a regular, regarded Territorials as 'amateurs' with contempt, as he had once informed them before. He sided with the CO and Burstall and Scott (two long-serving Yeomanry Officers) were 'sacked'. Edmund Scott of B Squadron was posted from the ERY which he had joined in 1938 and served with continuously in France and at home till then. He was posted to the RTR and led a Squadron with distinction. He was replaced for a short time by Major Harold Phelps (1st Northamptonshire Yeomanry) often known as the "Lulworth Cove", as he had spent most of his time as an instructor at the Gunnery School at Lulworth. Brian Burstall became a Press-conducting Officer after the invasion of Normandy and frightened the daylights out of his charges by always getting as close as possible to the battle. After the war "Hobo" was reported to have said "he could not understand why the Brigadier had sided with Williamson, as he was obviously in the wrong." However, the Squadron Leaders had lined up to the Brigadier on more than one occasion in the past, so no doubt taxed his patience beyond the limit by then. On 10 November Major Humphrey Philips took over command of A Squadron. He had been in the 5RIDG with the CO and was a friend of his from old days. The CO was not appreciated too much by the junior officers, who had liked and admired the sacked Yeomanry officers. However, the Regiment survived this upheaval and settled down to their tasks to the utmost of their ability.

One remarkable survival from the tales of Hobo as reported afterwards by the QM Bert Medhurst relates to the time when he came along to Rendlesham for an inspection. Bert was a veteran of the Tank Corps in WW1 and had known Hobo from the early days. Anyway, he was introducing the General to his stores staff and Hobo stopped when they came to one small storeman who always had a remarkable greyish-white complexion. "Why is that man so pale, Medhurst?" asked Hobo and Bert made some sort of a show of answering. As he told the story later: "I couldn't tell the General he bashes his Hampton!" One lives and learns – the other common army expression for the practice being "climbing up one's rifle".

In August the Yeomanry had started to collect Shermans in batches from H. R. Owen the big motor distributors on the Great North Road near Hatfield. These were Diesel Sherman IIIs. Whilst training was going on at Fritton on Valentines, one or two squadrons would be on "Shermanization" courses, learning about their strange tanks with new-fangled devices such as power traverse for the turret, a stabilized gun and many other American refinements. "Praise the Lord and bleed the power traverse/ And we'll all stay free" became a watchword, the traverse mechanism being hydraulic.

To help with the conversion, three American civilians from General Motors were attached for several weeks to the Regiment. The senior of these reckoned that he was the equivalent of a colonel in the British Army and had the gall to wear a battledress with badges of rank accordingly. On the first outing with the new tanks he bumped into the regimental staff and received a severe rocket from on high. Ted Wright was even exchanging Christmas cards with one of the other two, Gordon Erstad, until well after the war.

Captain Ernest Clark, the Technical Adjutant, a well-known West End actor in civilian life, led the regimental Concert Party with great gusto and enthusiasm. His lectures at these concerts, on the new tanks, were masterly. He described the turret or fighting compartment as "so called" because of the friendliness that exists between the commander and the gunner. The engine, like the man who ate green plums, is always at the rear. Finally, the tank is American, and therefore WRONG!" It was a vast improvement, however, on its predecessors.

They went up to Castlemartin Ranges in Pembrokeshire for shooting practice, the work on the ranges becoming increasingly realistic, with "battle-practices" using live ammunition.

After the long spell at Rendlesham, the Regiment next moved to a camp further inland at Heveningham Hall near Halesworth still in Suffolk with RHQ in the nearby village of Peasenhall. The original concept had been that the DD tanks would be concentrated with the rest of the specialized armour, the "Funnies", in 79th Armoured Division; but it was later planned that they would be spread more widely in the independent Armoured Brigades which were to support Infantry Divisions in the first landings. The supply of DDs was not great enough for the equipment of more than two regiments in each of these brigades; so the third regiment was required to have its tanks adapted for deep wading (to a depth of 2 metres or 6 feet). 4th/7th Dragoons and 13th/18th Hussars therefore continued training on DDs, but ERY reverted to normal tanks, and all the special amphibious training was wasted. The Heveningham camp had previously been occupied by 4th/7th DG who had moved to Scotland. Morale sank on this news and went even lower when the Yeomanry were told that they were to leave 27 Armoured Brigade and join 33 Armoured Brigade which would not be in the first flight of the impending invasion. There was therefore something of a hiccup in re-equipment, especially of wheeled transport which, with normal wear-and-tear, was becoming inadequate for normal needs. Personnel, however, were nearly up to full mobilization standard and additional drafts were being received, entailing further training to bring everyone up to the required standard. Several changes were made as RSM Moon, a 4th/7th DG Warrant Officer, took over from RSM James who left after failing the DD training. He had been RSM of 2 ERY since 1939 before which he had been a regular in the Queen's Bays. They had exercises all the time, mostly hectic and wet. The Squadrons were also sent off to Orford for battle practice with the new 75mm guns when live HE shells were fired, giving most of them a fright.

Morale, however, remained low and was not improved when orders were at last received in November to move to Fornham near Bury St Edmunds to close up with the Northants Yeomanry and the rest of the 33 Armoured Brigade. The move was being co-ordinated by Major Peter Wiggin, a supernumerary officer from 11th Hussars, like Major Roddy Verelst before him in 1940–41, had severe problems with the shortage of transport.

A few days later Major Wiggin came down to breakfast one morning at the CO's mess and said that during the night he had had a strange dream, in which the move had been cancelled and that the Brigade was to rejoin the 27 Armoured Brigade in Scotland. During the morning a strong rumour to the same effect was running through the NCO's canteen. At lunchtime the CO was called to the phone and told in the greatest secrecy by the Brigadier that this was going to happen. The officers and senior NCOs were all delighted to be destined for the sharp end once again when the invasion happened and it was credibly believed that the rumour in the canteen might have arisen from the 4th/7th DG's previous connections in the village. "Wiggins' Dream", however, may have had a psychic origin.

While all this was going on the powers-that-be decided that armoured regiments with battle-experience in North Africa should be "seeded" into the independent Armoured Brigades destined to support the invasion. So the 4th/7th DG were moved to 8 Armoured Brigade and their place in 27 Armoured Brigade taken by the Staffordshire Yeomanry who had fought at El Alamein and taken part in the landings in Sicily and Italy, They and the 13th/18th Hussars would have DD tanks and the third regiment, the ERY, deep waders. 8th Armoured Brigade would consist of 4th/7th DG, the Notts Yeomanry (Sherwood Rangers) also veterans of El Alamein and 24th Lancers, the first two likewise to have DDs. 8 Armoured Brigade would support 50th Infantry Division in XXX Corps on the right flank and 27 Armoured Brigade 3rd Infantry Division in I Corps on the left.

Chapter 12

INVASION TRAINING

Between Aug 42 & Feb 43	*Americans in Guadalcanal and Australians in New Guinea finally halt southerly expansion of Japs and go over to offensive and by April 43 MacArthur begins drive from south to regain Philippines.*
Aug 42	*Germans reach Caucasus.*
	Fight to secure Stalingrad begins but Russians hold through winter. General Paulus' surrender of 6th Army on 2 February 43 and German thrust to Caucasus withdraws.
13 May	*German remnant in Tunisia surrender, leaving North Africa clear of enemy.*
Early July 1943	*Greatest tank-battle in history fought as Germans try to cut off the Kursk Salient. Attacks held and Russians counter-attack on 12 July. The Germans go over to the defensive and Russians retain the initiative.*
by 30 Sept	*The Russians secure crossings over River Dnieper and continue their advance. By winter the Crimea liberated.*
9/10 July	*Invasion of Sicily (completed 17 August)*
3 Sept	*8th Army cross Straits of Messina and advance up "toe" of Italy.*
	Italian surrender signed.
8/9 Sept	*Salerno landing; Germans reinforce mainland Italy.*
1 Oct	*Naples captured.*
Sept	*Battleship* Tirpitz *disabled by midget submarines in Norwegian fjord.*

Nov	*US Navy under Admiral Halsey start offensive through central Pacific; "island hopping" process begun towards Philippines.*
Dec	*Battleship* Scharnhost *sunk by British squadron under Admiral Fraser off North Cape.*
Feb 1944	*US Navy clear Marshall Islands.*
March	*Japan attacks Imphal and Kohima boxes on the Indian border which hold out successfully until sieges raised in late June.*
June	*US attack Saipan Island (captured 9 July).*
19/20 June	*US Navy win battle of Philippine Sea.*
4 June	*Allies enter Rome: Germans retreat to Gothic Line (Pisa-Rimini) 150 miles north.*
Spring/ Summer & by end July	*Russians assault German centre (Operation Bagration); Most of Poland liberated and the Russians threaten Germany.*
1st August	*Warsaw rising (prematurely) and city destroyed.*

In early February the Yeomanry finally were ordered up to Forres in Nairnshire and on 19 February their Shermans were moved by road-transporters with skeleton crews travelling with the tanks. On 15 February the remaining personnel of the regiment had moved by two troop trains from Suffolk to Scotland and arrived the following day. Their accommodation was in the Lynden Hall Hydro. Lieutenant Tony Mitchell remembers one of the Scottish members of the Regiment saying when he arrived at Perth, "Can ye no smell the air?"

Forres was a small neat town, which was comfortable and friendly. The troops soon found opportunities for socializing. Lieutenant Thornton, himself a Scot, reported some time later that he had been buttonholed by an elder of the Kirk after one regimental dance in the town, who had protested at the allegedly licentious goings on, ending in the telling words, "It was fair like Sodom and Gomorrah!" But the troops all enjoyed themselves and it was later discovered that the elder must really have been jealous as he had been warned off the drink on medical grounds.

Forres was not a soft option. Having rejoined 27 Armoured Brigade, the Yeomanry were given a talk by the Brigadier on the brigade's role in the invasion, and the ERYs in particular. Brigadier Prior Palmer said he was very glad to have them back under his command as he had a high regard for the Regiment, this in spite of earlier confrontations.

Captain Wright continued with the complicated task of mobilization to full scales of equipment, stores and personnel. One intake from the Highland Light Infantry arrived and were soon integrated with the rest. Major Ellison continued to help greatly, as did Captain Medhurst, the Quartermaster. Their task was to calculate the loading of the tanks, spares, provisions, ammunition and the many other sundries required by an armoured regiment about to enter the fighting. At last mobilization began in earnest and masses of new equipment began to arrive.

Exercises in the use of landing craft and invasion tactics generally were carried out, discussed and talked over incessantly. Everyone continued to learn more about the Shermans so that what they had to do in action with the tank became second nature. They fired in their 75mm guns on Tarbatness Ranges and had operational exercises with 27 Armoured Brigade and 3rd British Infantry Division. At this stage the tanks were not waterproofed, so the actual landings from the landing craft had to be assumed and the Regiment joined in the first full-scale exercise in Burghead Bay overland after the first waves of infantry were ashore and the DD tanks had landed. After that waterproofing started, which was a mucky job, the tank-crews having to learn how to apply various grades of putty and other sealants to the correct parts and to erect the massive air-intake chutes so the tanks could wade ashore through a depth of 6 feet in the shallows up on to the beach.

Even with all this training, humour was always in evidence. Lieutenant Stephen Schilizzi was in the orderly room one day when a telephone call came through from the main gate to say that the "Countess of Ayr" was intending to pay a visit of inspection. No one had a *Who's Who* or any knowledge of the lady in question, but they were not to be caught out by failing to pay the correct courtesies. A guard of honour was quickly organized. There were some red faces when the County Surveyor turned up in a little car!

Forres and the beaches nearby faced north, as do those in Normandy; the tides too were similar, so it was an excellent place for rehearsals, although it was still February and March and bitterly cold. On many occasions crews had to sleep out in the open or under the tanks. The feeling amongst the troops was that the invasion proper could not be tougher than this. Captain John Carson, the MO, told the story after the Burghead Bay exercise that he had received one casualty at his RAP in the shape of a half-

106

drowned Pioneer who had been landed in 6 feet of nearly freezing water even though he was only 4' 6" tall.

In the midst of all this activity the Commander of 2nd Army, Lieutenant General Sir Miles Dempsey, came to inspect the Regiment. Captain Wright describes what happened: "The inspection was to take place in the town's park, where a cricket pitch was laid out on a fine flat area of turf. We were much better at tanking than at foot drill and the CO decided the Regiment could achieve a straight line of Squadrons in three ranks only with the aid of marker cords; so for the rehearsal the day before we were all lined up in apple-pie order. Overnight, however, there was a three-inch fall of snow and things looked somewhat tricky. Nevertheless, we all lined up on our markers, which were then reeled in before the Army Commander and Major General Tom Rennie (GOC 3rd British Infantry Division) arrived. After the General made his inspection, we thought we were in the clear, but Dempsey then said to the CO, 'That's fine, Williamson, now let's see them march past!' This threw Tom Williamson into a spin, because he had no idea how to get a complete Regiment in line marching off in column of threes." Captain Wright had known the commands to effect this from is school-days in the OTC, but was unable to intervene! The CO did what could only be described as "call an Order Group" of the Squadron Leaders and describe to them verbally what he wanted them to do. This took quite a bit of time, but eventually the Squadrons got moving in turn past the much amused Generals. The columns trudged along somewhat raggedly in the slushy snow; but Dempsey took it all with great tolerance and observed when it was all over, "That was fine, but it looked a bit like Napoleon's retreat from Moscow." He was not far wrong. What the men on parade said has not been recorded. But it did cause some amusement as the troops seemed to go one pace forward and slide two more paces back in the snow.

In the middle of March Major Hugh Matthews from 3rd County of London Yeomanry was posted to the Regiment and took over B Squadron from Major Phelps (the "Lulworth Cove") who returned to the Northamptonshire Yeomanry. This was part of the policy of larding in-experienced units with officers who had seen action and Major Matthews had had battle experience in the Desert and Italy.

There had been many exercises in the early part of the year, but now at the end of March there was a more realistic one called "Leapyear". The Regiment had been hard at work waterproofing their tanks as this was to be a full-scale dress rehearsal, with them actually wading ashore from the landing craft. Fortunately the work proved successful and none of the tanks actually leaked.

On 1 April an advance party left for a new location at Petworth Park in Sussex. Whilst they were getting things ready, the ERY began water-proofing the tanks over again for Exercise "Fabius" to take place soon after they arrived at Petworth. The various sealing compounds used to shake out after only a relatively short road-march so that waterproofing had to be renewed after each simulated landing. "Fabius" was really the dress rehearsal proper.

The move down from Forres took from 15–21 April. The Shermans were all loaded on transporters and moved by road. Trooper Buckingham was one of the crews that were due to receive the "Firefly", a Sherman with a 17pdr gun rather than the 75mm of the basic tank. These had a crew of four rather than five and one was issued to each troop. They were diverted to Kirkcudbright to practice firing these formidable guns. Trooper Buckingham remembers this well because the first round they fired from his gun they had a flashback and his hair and eyes were singed. Curiously this never happened to him again with all the rounds they fired in Normandy.

The skeleton crews went on the transporters in the same way as they had on the way from Suffolk, while the remainder, other than troops on the wheeled transport, went by train, right through London by some little-used lines which included a halt for tea at Kensington.

The transport – trucks, water lorries, tankers, ambulances and other wheeled vehicles, many by then in need of replacement – all went by road. Lieutenant Mitchell was one of the officers in the road convoy and trav-elled in a Hillman utility. The first leg of the journey was quite spectacular and he thoroughly enjoyed watching the beautiful Highland scenery. By the time they had reached the Lowlands, however, most people were already saddlesore and finding the scenery less attractive. Their first staging camp was Carlisle, where they had a welcome meal, a wash and a bunk. The vehicles were filled up and checked where necessary, so after a night's sleep and a good breakfast they started off again. It took them altogether four days to reach Petworth. This turned out to be a hutted and tented camp in the grounds of Petworth House. "It was," wrote Captain Wright, "an altogether invigorating spot to stay in what turned out to be a fine spring from April onwards."

Now all the missing elements of equipment began to flood in, including brand new trucks and even a few extras such as anti-aircraft tanks (turretless Cromwells with twin 20mm Oerlikon guns) and amphibious jeeps called "Weasels". The Regiment's remaining complement of Fireflies also arrived; so the crews, including Trooper Buckingham, were soon familiar with the gun and the new turret lay-out. A few suggestive names were devised for these, most often suggestive of the long barrels with a muzzle-brake on the end.

Waterproofing had to be done all over again, as well as the fitting of extra stowage which crews thought might help to give a little extra space for luxuries.

The general recollection of this time was the amount of plain manual labour required to waterproof the tanks and the really filthy mess men got into doing it. Fortunately the weather remained warm and sunny, so people were not only fit and well but bronzed too.

All the tanks were sent off in batches to Glasgow to have extra panels of armour welded on by ships' fitters to give extra protection over the more vulnerable areas. There was also a great deal of ingenuity shown to provide additional protection around the turrets. Sergeant Lyon of A Squadron was once asked by the Brigadier on one of his evening tours in his jeep what he was busy with, so the Sergeant demonstrated that with a few metal bars welded to the turret, he could hang another ten track plates around it. It says much for the Brigadier's attitude that Sergeant Lyon's modification was to be applied throughout the Brigade and a Brigade order to this effect was issued the following morning, with the inventor's name quoted too. Such acts were excellent for morale as was the Brigadier's remarkable capacity for learning and remembering people's names. He knew the first name of every officer in his Brigade and all the Warrant Officers and most of the Sergeants by surname, as well as a good number of the Corporals too. This was achieved by sheer hard work as he went round on his periodical inspections.

Briefing about the landing was the main preoccupation of the officers. In the early stages this was all done on dummy maps, with places and names changed. C Squadron Leader, Major Hyde, the one who had been Adjutant in 1940, and who had just rejoined the Regiment after commanding Brigade HQ Squadron, commented on seeing the map of the Caen area covered with bogus names, "They can't fool me; I know that race-course [Carpiquet near Caen]. It is the crookedest race-course in France."

Troopers John Pollock, Eric Armstrong, Glyn Edwards, Reg Brand and Colin Mason had all gravitated to his Squadron at Brigade HQ from the 15th/19th Hussars and found an immediate rapport and respect for their new Squadron Leader. When he was posted to the Regiment, they asked him if they could come with him; he was impressed, and possibly a little flattered, and made arrangements accordingly. So it was at Petworth that the "Famous Five" reported to the ERY. Virtually the first person they saw from the back of the 15cwt bringing them from the station to the camp was Major Hyde himself. Glyn Edwards let out a shout and waved, the Major seeing them gave a huge grin and waved back. They were always known thereafter as "Major Hyde's party".

Having completed waterproofing (again!), from 24 April the Regiment moved by road to its concentration area for Exercise "Fabius" where the final stages of waterproofing had to be completed after the approach-march. Next day they left for the Marshalling Area sorted into craft loads (i.e. the type, number and order in which vehicles were to be reversed onto their landing craft.) They were then sealed into the Marshalling Area for a couple of days so they could complete the waterproofing. The officers spent hours in conference and O Groups. Then on 1 May the vehicles were loaded on to their ships at a "hard" at Gosport; but the exercise was post-poned for a day so they all had to stay aboard the craft. Captain Wright met up with a New Zealand Naval Lieutenant in command of his landing craft naturally called "Kiwi" Choate, who not only promised plenty of gin, but that he would land them as far up the beach as possible both on the exercise and on D-Day itself. "Half-ahead both [engines] to give them a nice shallow wade," was his watchword.

The Regiment landed on 5 May at 1200hrs, having been taken out to sea and "trailing their coats"; but no Germans interrupted them, unlike the Americans on a similar exercise off Slapton Sands in Devon who were attacked by German E Boats with much loss of life. After landing they returned to Petworth and waterproofing had to be done all over again. Final stores arrived and were allocated to bring the Regiment up to full mobi-lization scale on a hectic and frenetic level. They also had to clean their tanks for an inspection of the Brigade by the King and another by General Eisenhower. All Squadrons fired in their guns on the South Downs.

Leave had been granted whilst at Petworth, but after the King's parade the whole camp area was sealed off from the outside world. The tank crews were all experienced in their trade and final practice was the order of the day, as well as the ever-present waterproofing. Tank commanders spent many hours getting to know the members of their crew, their strengths and weaknesses. The crews were getting to know their officers too. There was a final exercise on the South Downs held with the 9th Infantry Brigade which the ERY were to support on the landing. The springs were now tightly wound up, tanks in good mechanical condition, men fit and well, plans worked out to the last detail and equipment of the best.

On 30 May Major Bill Holtby, HQ Squadron Leader, with Sergeant Pond, the Transport Sergeant, and Trooper Jack Windley left camp at 1430 hours to be landed early to prepare for the Regiment's landing and supervise the marking of the route to the de-waterproofing area once the landing had taken place.

After the area was sealed off, the CO had a call from the CO of his old Regiment, Lieutenant Colonel "Hooky" Sangster, asking if he would relieve him of a Belgian Officer who was becoming something of a nuisance with his pleas to get at the Germans at the first possible moment. He had been informed that the Skins, to whom he was attached, were not in the first wave of the assault. Our CO thought that to have a spare French-speaking officer with the Yeomanry would be a useful addition; so Captain Henri Salman of the Belgian Army made his first entry into the ERY. A tall, lean, aesthetic man with a hooked nose and bright blue eyes, a bald dome of a head with white hair cut as it were in a tonsure, duly arrived out of the blue and was welcomed in his Belgian officer's uniform. He was issued with a British officer's uniform and ERY badges and beret in very short order. However, there was then the most tremendous flap. Questions were asked from Brigade and higher up about how he had got to the Regiment, why and how had he found out where we were and so on. It appeared that General Montgomery himself, long suspicious of the security of the "allies", had given orders that there were to be no foreigners in the leading invasion troops. Captain Salman was thereupon ordered to return whence he had come and told forcibly not to go anywhere near the Regiment until the fact of the invasion and the landing area had become public knowledge. In the event it seems he remained glued to a radio and on the afternoon of D-Day turned up at Aldershot where Captain Norman Waller, 2i/c HQ Squadron, was in charge of the rear Echelons, clamouring to be sent over to France with the first available party. He, in fact, arrived with the Regiment in France on 22 June and what later occurred is a story in itself.

The reaction of most of the men to the nearness of D-Day was of excitement, conjecture, determination to finish the job and natural fears which were kept well under the surface. Letters home were written, but now they had to be censored, a most unwelcome but necessary task undertaken by the troop officers. The address was; "APO, then the Army Post Office number, BLA (for British Liberation Army)."

111

On 1 June the ERY rolled slowly out of Petworth to the marshalling area in strictly controlled convoys timed to fit into the larger traffic plan. The tanks were driven straight onto numbered standings on the roads and left under guard outside the wired-in camps. The staff work involved in matching the individual numbers of the vehicles with their own serial numbers painted on the roads was miraculous and craft-loads were made up with vehicles from other units travelling on the same ships. Maps and orders with names in clear were then issued in the sealed camps to all concerned. After two days of waiting they moved out via Fareham and Portsmouth through densely packed streets of half-cheering, half-bewildered people, who gave the men courage, encouragement and tea whenever they stopped and this happened many times. Sergeant Moverley recalled the many and various cups of tea thrust on them, and the kindness and good wishes of the spectators.

They arrived at their hard at Gosport, embarking that afternoon, just as had been practised on Exercise "Fabius". All the planning had gone well, every member of the Regiment was embarked aboard his allotted craft and the tanks secured for the voyage as the landing craft pulled out to their anchorages to await orders to sail.

PART IV

INVASION AND VICTORY

Chapter 13

INVASION OF NORMANDY

At the beginning of June 1944 the Axis powers had lost the initiative on all fronts. In Europe: in the East the Red Army were at the gates of Germany; in the South, the Germans were fighting a dogged retreat up the Italian Peninsula; and in the West the Wehrmacht were expecting invasion at some point on the French coast. In the Far East: the US Navy and Marines had begun the advance island-by-island which was to bring them within striking distance of the main Japanese islands; the US Navy dominated the Jap Navy with overwhelming force; the Japs' southward advance past New Guinea and the Solomons had been held and turned back; and on the Indian-Burmese border the Japanese army had been halted.

The plan for Operation "Overlord" called for near simultaneous landings across the beaches in the Bay of the Seine from the base of the Cotentin (Cherbourg) Peninsula in the west to the mouth of the River Orne below Caen in the east: the Americans on "Utah" and "Omaha" on the right and the British and Canadians on "Gold", "Juno" and "Sword" on the left. The seaborne landings were to be preceded by parachute and glider drops of 82 and 101 US Airborne Divisions behind "Utah" and 6 British Airborne Division about the Orne estuary on the left. XXX Corps on the "Gold" sector went in "One division up" (50th British Infantry Division supported by 8 Armoured Brigade), and I Corps "Two up" (3rd Canadian Infantry Division and 2 Canadian Armoured Brigade on "Juno" and 3rd British Infantry Division and 27 Armoured Brigade on "Sword") on the left of the front. 3rd British Infantry Division had 8th Infantry Brigade forward with 13th/18th Hussars in support with 185 Infantry Brigade and Staffordshire Yeomanry following closely behind and 9 Infantry Brigade and ERY in Reserve.

113

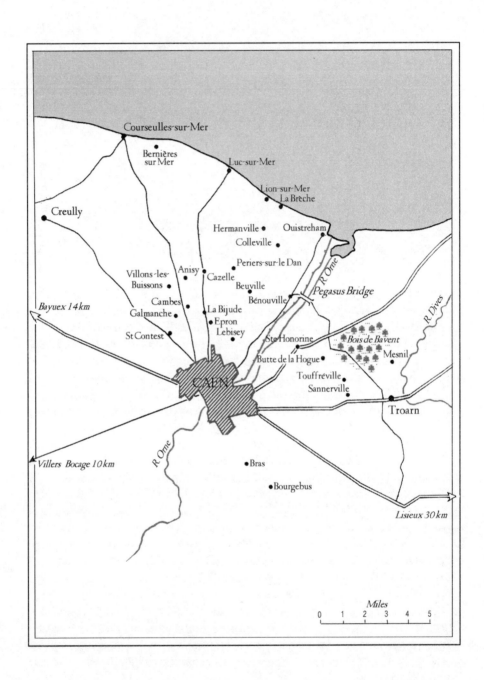

Courseulles-sur-Mer

Bernières sur Mer

Luc-sur-Mer

Lion-sur-Mer
La Brèche

Creully

Hermanville

Ouistreham

Colleville

Periers-sur-le Dan

Anisy

Villons-les-Buissons

Cazelle

Beuville

Bénouville

Pegasus Bridge

R. Orne

R. Dives

Bayuex 14 km

Cambes

Galmanche

La Bijude

Epron

Lebisey

St Contest

Ste Honorine

Bois de Bavent

Mesnil

Butte de la Hogue

CAEN

Touffréville

Sannerville

Troarn

R. Orne

Villers Bocage 10 km

Bras

Bourgebus

Lisieux 30 km

Miles

0   1   2   3   4   5

114

The description of the ERY's participation in the invasion and sub-sequent battles for the first lodgements in France and the enlargement of these into a continuous beachhead is drawn as far as possible from eye-witness accounts of actual experiences. For two months the beachhead was hemmed in by dogged German defences and several major battles were fought in the attempt to break out of the confined area secured in the earlier stages. This first chapter (Ch 13) takes the reader on from the sailing from the Solent on the night of 5/6 June to the first landing early on the after-noon of D-Day itself (6 June) through to the aftermath of the unsuccessful attempt to break out on 18 July (Operation Goodwood) after which ERY left 27 Armoured Brigade, handed over its tanks to the Canadians and waited for 3–4 weeks until the tanks of 144 Regiment RAC in 33 Armoured Brigade became available and the advance was resumed.

As the ERY's vehicles were safely loaded in their allotted LCTs (or LSTs in the case of A Squadron) the landing craft moved out into Spithead and anchored in two columns. The original schedule had been for the assault force to set sail on the afternoon and evening of 4 June so as to arrive off the coast of Normandy at first light on 5 June; but it was blowing hard with rain slicing in from the south-west. The decision was taken by General Eisenhower, the C-in-C, to postpone the landing for 24 hours in hopes of an improvement in the weather. Wireless silence had to be maintained; so "netting" of the Regiment's sets was carried out by the Signals Officer, Lieutenant Alan Thornton, with the use of a portable instrument called a "wave-meter" which he carried round the anchorage in a launch. This ensured that all stations set out tuned to the correct frequency without the need for transmissions. In the event, it was not a howling success and reliable communication was only achieved some time after landing. The 24-hour delay only made waiting more frustrating as there was nothing for the tank crews to do. Many, usually tough and happy fellows, were reduced to a death-wish with seasickness. Others, who were not prone, went on deck to see what the armada they had joined was really like. Mostly the men were trying to find somewhere in which to lie down and sleep, write home, or even eat. Sergeant Colin Brown of the Recce Troop had to look after Trooper Ron Acres who was so sick that "death would be welcome"!

The assembly of ships of all sizes between the mainland and the Isle of Wight reminded one observer of the Athenian expedition setting out for Sicily as told by Thucydides in 415 BC or that of the Gallipoli invasion in 1915 as described by the Australian Alan Moorehead. Trooper Ken

Buckingham, Wireless Operator in A Squadron, was interested to see that his LST was anchored fifty yards from Ryde Pier, which he knew well from family holidays. He mentioned also that he and other members of the troop had had their hair cut very short while waiting. Another sight had been the Wren Officers boarding ships with written orders for the postponement so as to preserve wireless silence. But he too was seasick once they sailed.

After all the additional work he had had to carry out as Adjutant, Captain Wright was quite relieved to get afloat. Both the CO and 2i/c crossed with HQ 9 Infantry Brigade; so he was o/c the vehicles on his LCT, five tanks and a couple of Carriers. He had made friends with the New Zealander commanding the LCT, Lieutenant Choate who was a grand chap, he knew from the rehearsal, inevitably given the nickname "Kiwi", and had been given two undertakings at the end of the warm-up exercise in May:

1. He would land the tanks as near dry-shod as possible with the order "half ahead (engines)" until they grounded;
2. There would be plenty of Export Gordon's Gin on board (with the yellow and red label which the Navy could still get).

Both were amply fulfilled which made the long wait more bearable.

Many of the crews were not so fortunate. There was a great deal of discomfort, men sleeping between tanks, on the engine covers of their own tanks, in the scuppers, on the decks, anywhere to stretch out to sleep, write home, think or while away the time with their mates. A great many were seasick or felt very, very ill. Others weren't and enjoyed, if that is the right word to describe going to assault Hitler's Festung Europa, the sea voyage and sea breeze.

The next morning (5 June), whilst still waiting for the word to go, it became clear to Captain Wright that the Troop Leader of RHQ Troop, Lieutenant David Bellman, was in no fit state to make the crossing, as he had developed carbuncles on his backside and was pretty ill. He was ordered to disembark, which he did very reluctantly. This was done by Kiwi Choate giving the order for the LCT to up anchor and return to the Gosport hard where an ambulance whisked the disconsolate Lieutenant Bellman off to hospital.

For a replacement RHQ Troop Leader Captain Wright picked out Lieutenant Peter Redfern of A Squadron whose troop was due to land a day later than the rest of the Regiment owing to the lack of room in the first "flight" of landing craft and he was delivered with his kit by motor launch to the reanchored LCT within a couple of hours. All that there was to identify him had been the number of his tank and that of the staging camp where he was waiting and Captain Wright was amazed at how little time it had taken to get hold of him. Not surprisingly he was not in the best of tempers at being prised away from his troop which he had trained and led for a long time.

It must never be forgotten that the majority of the men who made up the ERY, junior officers as well as other ranks, were still in their late teens or early twenties. Few were over 25; so there were mixed feelings of excitement, tempered with anticipation and fear of the unknown. Most had never seen a shot fired in anger before.

So they went off to war after years of training and waiting. Only a few such as Major Ellison and Sergeant Bob Coupland had been in the dreadful 1940 campaign, culminating in their escape from Dunkirk. Although none of them said so openly, they must have had pangs of nervousness, but were encouraged by the excellence of the equipment they now had in contrast to the flimsy tanks and carriers they had in 1940.

The forecast for 6 June showed a short break in the bad weather and, after an agony of doubt, the C-in-C gave the order for the invasion to go ahead. So, after waiting the long and uncomfortable twenty-four hours, the fleet set sail, the ERY's flotilla at 1920hrs on 5 June 1944. Captain Wright relates: "Once the decision had been taken, we upped anchor and were timed to arrive on our allotted beach ("Sword") soon after 12 noon. Once our LCTs had sorted themselves out into two columns, I was startled to watch a Royal Navy light cruiser cut clean through the two advancing lines of lumbering landing craft. Thereafter it was a slow plod through the night over a still fairly rough sea, during which, I managed a fair sleep on my lilo on the upper deck. This was helped on the second night on board as we made some considerable inroads into Kiwi Choate's gin, and might have done even better if the unexpected delay had not exhausted the LCT's main fresh-water tank. We had to turn to the reserve, which was fairly old and tasted none too fresh, needing much more gin to mask the flavour."

Others were not so fortunate. Trooper Buckingham was constantly vomiting. Trooper Acres was prostrate. As Sergeant Moverley said, "The ships' rails before long, were festooned with bodies emptying their insides." John Moverley was fortunate; he was not affected, so escaped the misery of *mal de mer*. Food, if and when it was needed, was from the numerous self-heating tins of soup, no doubt supplied by Heinz, together with the omni-present bully beef and dog biscuits.

Slowly, in its rigidly controlled lines, the armada ploughed across towards Normandy. Once securely under way all the troops were told where they were going and genuine maps were issued with proper place names; so at last everyone was let into this well-kept secret. After this briefing, night closed in and where possible the troops slept or dozed; some played cards and some just sat.

Dennis Bell was in the navy and a member of HMS *Force*, a fleet minesweeper. His ship had left the Isle of Wight at midday on 4 June and they began sweeping just south of the island. The flotilla, of which his ship was part, was intercepted by a fast motor launch to be told of the postponement. They returned to Spithead and anchored for the night, then went off again at the same time next day.

"As we swept across the Channel in fairly rough seas but with bright weather, our task was to drop marker buoys flying a brightly coloured flag and with a battery-operated lamp. As dusk fell and the night closed in we looked back on this avenue of lights about a mile apart. We thought how interesting they would be to any enemy aircraft, U Boat, E Boat or even Pocket Battleship that might be passing. However all was well.

"We completed the sweep and dropped anchor to await the start of play. When I came off the bridge after my anchor watch I went into the wheelhouse, sat down on a bench and as I had had very little sleep in the last 48 hours promptly dozed off, only to be wakened up by somebody giving me a clout across the back saying, 'Eh, come above and look at this'. I staggered out on to the 'verandah' half-asleep, and saw a Brooks Special going on ashore. It seems that the bombardment had been going on for some time, so I must have slept through the opening stages of the Invasion. A few minutes later, back at the bridge, just as the first glimmer of day was beginning to show, we heard a dull roar (this was the sound of hundreds of ships' diesel engines) coming from out of the mist to seaward. Although we couldn't see anything, it gradually got louder and louder, until a solid wall of ships of all sizes appeared, and went past us and deployed towards the beaches. I don't know what effect it had on the Germans, but it certainly put the wind up me."

Dennis Bell later became the Hon Secretary of the ERY's Old Comrades Association, so, unknowingly, he was close to those he later called his Comrades.

As they reached the coast the CO and the IO who had been on the 9 Infantry Brigade Command Ship HMS *Locust* returned to the HQ LCT, so he could go ashore with the Yeomanry's tanks. At 0600hrs on 6 June all radios which had been previously netted in on the Regimental wavelength by means of the Wavemeter to preserve radio silence, came on the air. They could then receive the news and the "excitement" of 13th/18th Hussars and the Staffordshire Yeomanry (the two other Regiments in 27 Armoured Brigade) going ashore in their DD tanks, to give the Germans a nasty shock when fully equipped fighting tanks appeared out of the sea to take on the beach defences. They swam ashore and went in to support the first two infantry brigades of 3rd Infantry Division, landing on Sword Beach, just east of Ouistreham. They helped to make good the landing and consolidate a secure lodgement.

The ERY were under command of 9 Infantry Brigade, which was the third and reserve brigade of the 3rd British Infantry Division.

At first light there was a tremendous bombardment from the big ships of the Navy, which was all part of the softening-up process of the enemy positions; as ships carrying the ERY came nearer so the noise became more intense. Aircraft in their hundreds had flown overhead during the night, to drop the first wave of 6th Airborne Division, both parachutists and gliders: bombers roared past to drop bombs on the beach defences, rockets from specially converted landing craft went off in a simultaneous roar to devastate a strip 200 to 300 yards wide. The Royal Artillery fired their field guns from LCTs.

During the early morning of D-Day "We were," as Major Ellison said, "now going very slowly, waiting for reports from the shore for the result of the first landings to see where and when we were wanted. We were timed to touch down at H+5½ or approximately 1230hrs. At 1245 we passed the large landing ships anchored three miles out and prepared to go into France. At 1315hrs we were going well and were about 2,000 yards from the shore when big shells began bursting all around us: some fragments hit the craft and a few minor injuries were sustained. All the crews were in their tanks which were warmed up and ready to land, so no regimental casualties were reported. The Navy were ordered to take the two columns of LCTs out of the firing zone until the big guns from Le Havre, which were making our approaches very warm, could be silenced. The broadsides from HMS *Warspite* fired just as we were passing her were tremendous, but they were pretty effective in silencing the shore batteries."

The about-turn had caused a delay of an hour and a quarter. 9 Infantry Brigade had gone ashore at the right time and felt pretty naked that their tank support was not with them.

Once the shore batteries had been dealt with the tank landing craft ran in to their allotted areas on "Sword Beach" between Lion-sur-Mer and La

Brèche just to the west of Ouistreham. The chaos on the beaches was awful, with dead bodies swirling in the water and blown-up flail tanks which preceded us destroying mines.

Off-loading commenced at approximately 1414hrs and the tanks came ashore, most on their tracks, but A Squadron in their LSTs had first to be trans-shipped on to Rhino Ferries (pontoons linked together and powered by large outboard motors). All then followed regimental signs and white tape laid out for them to mark the beach-exits. This had been done by a small group led by Major Bill Holtby, OC HQ Squadron. He had with him Sergeant Pond, the Transport Sergeant, and Trooper Jack Windley of the Recce Troop. They had embarked with the Infantry from Newhaven and sailed and landed with them so they could put up the markers ready for the Regiment to disembark and follow the exit route. "Soon we neared the shore, our signs etc ready to hand," Trooper Windley recorded. "I remember thinking that if I got ashore first in our little party, I would be able to claim to be the first man in the Regiment ashore on D-Day." Such was the case. "By the exit from the beach we passed a number of bodies with their boots showing from under groundsheets, which was a little off-putting. Following the route we had remembered from studying the mockups, we made our way to the assembly area leaving our signs at appropriate spots on the way. It was somewhat congested at times and having to get our heads down as shells and mortars kept coming our way. We eventually came to the track going inland and seemed to leave the main body of troops. As we passed further down the track there was an open space of about 5 to 6 acres. This was where the tanks would assemble for de-waterproofing. About this time small parties of infantry and an occasional carrier passed us. Major Holtby then said he would go back to the beach, as by then the first of our tanks would be landing, and asked us to check the area for mines. This was not an enjoyable job with only a bayonet to do the job. Fortunately, while we were considering this task, along came a flail tank. I stopped it and asked the commander if he would beat the area which he kindly did! No mines. Good!" Windley was saying to the other two who made up the party that it wasn't all that bad when "Whiz whiz whiz, a crackle" and then he said, "Get down, lads. Some bugger is firing at us". "Minutes later Major Holtby was back and we said, 'Better get down Sir a sniper has just been firing at us'. He assured us that we were dreaming as all the area had been cleared. So feeling proper charlies we got up. No sooner up than it happened again – we all dived down again. I had seen a muzzle flash about 150 yards away. Facing us was a barn and from an open door laying further back were our friendly snipers – but what rotten shots! The tanks arrived minutes later, a 75mm shell was on its way to those snipers who were not going to worry anyone else after that."

Major Holtby, with Sergeant Pond, had an uncomfortable wait on the beach in the open, whilst the Regiment were taken back out to sea, not knowing what had become of them. Captain Wright then records that his friend Kiwi Choate carried out his promise to the letter and came in 'Half ahead both'. "But as we approached the beach there was a lurch followed by a nasty scraping sound. We had gone straight over one of the steel tripod obstacles and had wrecked our propellers. We were all right as the LCT drifted in but he was stuck and had a bad time under the shelling, eventually having to be towed off astern and then all the way back to England. The delay in landing meant that obstacles which were meant to be showing were submerged by the rising tide and several landing craft collided in trying to avoid beach obstacles. Fortunately most of the live shells and anti-tank mines on top of the steel tripods had already been defused by the Sappers before the tide came up. Otherwise it would have been much worse."

On the final approach of one LCT carrying part of B Squadron the commander was uncertain of his depth and didn't want to get stuck in the sand. By this time the ramp was down, "and we were inching forward," wrote Lieutenant George Jenkin. "We were carrying some men of the RUR, and I remember Major Matthews, OC B Squadron, picking on the smallest and ordering him in full kit to attention, facing the beach, followed by 'quick march'. The poor bugger marched off the end of the ramp into the water and disappeared from view. When he surfaced, Hugh commanded, 'Pull him in,' followed by 'Forward a bit, Skipper' to our craft-commander."

Most of the tanks arrived on the beach without mishap, many hearts were in mouths, not only because of the noise of battle, but the personal hazard of getting the individual tanks ashore. Most came off ships and drove straight on to the shore; but some had to wade in water up to six feet and others came in from some distance from LSTs on Rhino ferries. Sergeant Moverley described it. "In the meantime we were sitting in the middle of bedlam. I have never heard such a noise in all my life. At last some action for us; a kind of motorized raft had come up and we had to get onto it. My tank had been selected to lead the way and I didn't like it a bit. The stern of our ship had been lowered like a wooden platform and we moved the tank first on to that. As our ship was going up and down on the waves, so was the raft. I had to judge when the raft would be level with us and then we had to move quick! Any hesitation or wrong guess and we would be going for a swim."

This was how A Squadron got ashore; so they were later than the rest of the Regiment in arriving at the assembly area. In fact all the tanks in the Regiment landed safely. The only casualty was the C Squadron fitters' half-track under Mechanical Sergeant Davis. This was ordered off the LST by a twitchy Naval Officer and plunged into seven feet of sea. All Sergeant Davis' tools, spares and the extra bits and pieces he judged necessary to service the tanks were lost. But Sergeant Davis and his team were not to be thwarted by any naval bod; so they waited until low tide found the half-track some way off shore, salvaged the vehicle and rebuilt the whole machine within three days, hardly pausing for rest. He describes what had happened in his own words: "When we were in sight of the beach, the Commander ordered the ramps to be lowered. I was the last vehicle on so the first one off. I told him I could not go down the ramp with a half-track, because it was not waterproofed. I also asked him to check the depth of the water because there was a measuring pole beside me. He flatly refused and ordered me off. Just then as he dropped the ramp one of the hawsers broke and it fell down unevenly. I drove the half-track down myself because I knew what the consequences were if I did not get out of the way quickly, but the engine stalled when it came into contact with the salt water. I cannot swim, but my normal driver could and he swam to a large troop carrier and was taken back to England in a convoy. After dog-paddling around, I managed to find a foothold. I got fairly up one side of the ramp and the electrician got hold of me at the same time as the ramp was being lifted. I fully expected to be cut in two. By this time the Commander panicked, swung the LCT round and ran over what was left of the half-track. He then took his craft into deep water, so the engineers could repair the cables, and on the next tide he beached the craft and we just walked off, so my losing my vehicle earlier was just unnecessary. We walked up the beach through a mass of dead vehicles, men and other horrors. We saw a half-track way out on the sand, a long way out on its own. We rescued ours after a lot of hard work before we rejoined the Regiment." In *Europe Revisited* Major Ellison wrote, "A small item in a big war, but typical of the undefeated spirit and efficiency of the Yeomanry and especially of those splendid men, the fitters!"

Trooper Buckingham, wireless operator in his tank, after being "Rhinoed" on to the beach came ashore in about three feet of water. They waded up the beach passing men digging foxholes and others guiding both men and equipment as they came ashore. "The atmosphere was frenetic, noisy, unrealistic and an astonishing spectacle." He described the seconds after landing: "Passing between the houses on an exit from the beach we hit a mine, which broke a track and we were stuck there for hours. We could not repair it where we were because of other mines, so we had to wait until another vehicle could pull us back and we could do the repair. While we were there we shelled a nearby house to dispose of a sniper who was causing casualties. We also saw six JU88s make a low level-bombing raid on the landing craft along the beach, scoring hits. They lost three or four aircraft shot down. We could see a line of infantry working their way along the coast road before turning inland. Eventually the second wave of 6 Airborne Division came in overhead. It was quite a sight with the sky full of planes and gliders coming in to land. Some were shot down by the anti-aircraft fire which was intense, and I saw tracer going up much nearer to us than I expected there to be any Germans." After they had been pulled back to repair their track, they caught up with the Regiment and after some hours started to go inland "when we came to a road block. Our infantry had mined the road and were covering it with an anti-tank gun in case of a counter-attack. We pulled back to a position covering the road, cooked a meal and bedded down after a discussion whether to get up at 6 or 7 am!"

The ERY had landed on the extreme left of the 3rd Infantry Division sector just west of Ouistreham, on the River Orne, with Commandos to their left again. The assembly area was just south of Lion-sur-Mer, but was overlooked by a ridge of high ground immediately south again. This was still being attacked by assaulting troops and was by no means clear of the enemy.

The Regiment, however, by following the sign of 27 Armoured Brigade, a seahorse on its tail on a blue background, and the regimental sign of 53 on the yellow and red square background, reached its assembly point and de-waterproofed, ready for whatever support 9 Infantry Brigade required.

The first troop ashore was the Recce Troop in their Stuart tanks, light but fast. They swept down the tracks marked by the Regimental signs and white tapes, arriving at the field shown on the map reference. Lieutenant Stephen Schilizzi, OC Recce Troop, thought it was heavily mined and, not knowing the action taken by Trooper Windley and his flail tank, called up RHQ and a troop of flails arrived to beat up the field. They likewise found nothing although there were still notices proclaiming *Achtung Minen* posted round the area. Lieutenant Schilizzi said, "We learnt later that the

Germans defending the beaches had recently had a surprise visit from Rommel and had hurriedly put up dummy signs to cover up the fact that they had not complied with orders to mine the whole area."

The War Diary states baldly: "1440hrs 6 June 1944. Arrived at Assembly area. Tanks de-waterproofed and took up positions as planned."

The Regiment had touched down on the beaches at 1412hrs and commenced to move to the assembly area around 1420hrs. They had crossed the body-strewn, bullet-swept, tank-brewed-up beach covered with the debris of war, the noise of exploding shells, mortars, tracer bullets, all manner of other offences to the senses such as few had experienced before. Within a short time they were off the beach away from the hold-up of traffic and marching troops, and followed the signs to the assembly area, now clear of mines. Here they blew off the chutes and other waterproofing attachments.

Sergeant Pond, one of those who came ashore with Major Holtby to mark the route, had survived several hours of shelling on the open beach and was standing behind one of the tanks having taken off his steel helmet to mop his brow. At that precise moment the driver of the tank pulled the release lever and down came the welded steel air-vent smack on poor Sergeant Pond's head, giving him a nasty wound which was happily not fatal. This was the Regiment's first casualty of the campaign.

The assembly area was overlooked by high ground immediately to the south. This was still being attacked by the infantry and was by no means clear of the enemy. Shelling of the assembly area started and was heavy. It was soon after they had got rid of the waterproofing gear that B Squadron under Major Hugh Matthews was pushed forward to the flank on the outskirts of Lion-sur-Mer to give protection whilst the Yeomanry waited for orders. There was some desultory small arms and mortar fire and Lieutenant Peter Goodwin was wounded when climbing on to the Squadron Leader's Tank to discuss the situation. Earlier the Squadron Leader had been heard over the regimental net saying, "For Christ sake, Peter, don't you realise this isn't an exercise?" He hadn't even loaded his guns. After he was wounded in the back by shrapnel he had to be evacuated to England.

As 9 Infantry Brigade of 3rd British Infantry Division they had to wait for orders before doing anything much and also for A Squadron, who were landing from their Rhinos which caused delay in landing and getting to the Assembly area. Also they had great difficulty in finding out what if any plan they were meant to carry out owing to the bombing of the Infantry Brigade

HQ, the Brigadier being wounded and several other personnel killed or wounded. But after some hours delay orders began to filter through.

That afternoon was well described by the words "fog of war"; it was a most unpleasant few hours sitting being shelled and not being able to find out, through disrupted communication and casualties at Brigade, where they were supposed to go. At about 1920hrs C Squadron moved forward south towards the ridge of high ground to the SE about 5 miles inland. There they were fired on by a self-propelled gun, the crew of which had spotted the leading tanks. It opened fire, missed with the first shot but hit with the next two. Two of the tank crew were killed. But the flash of the self-propelled gun and the vehicle were in view of the covering troops who opened fire, disposing of the gun on its armoured chassis and two anti-aircraft guns as well. The remainder of the Regiment were still in the assembly area, where they were keeping a sharp lookout to the right of the position where the Germans were putting in small attacks. An unsolved mystery is that no contact was made with some tanks of the 21 Panzer Division who were reported to have reached the sea at Luc-sur-Mer, only a mile or two away, during the afternoon. They apparently retired back inland without meeting the invaders, perhaps luckily for the Yeomanry since they might have been caught in the assembly area before de-waterproofing.

After moving out of the assembly area, our tanks took up a defensive position along the ridge to the south and Brigadier Prior Palmer turned up, urging us to move forward more aggressively, causing Lieutenant Ken Smith of A Squadron to lose his cool a little! Lieutenant Smith, known as "Baldy", was an unusually robust character, having played first class rugby before the war, but he was also slightly deaf. Captain Wright watched the cameo that followed. The Brigadier climbed on the back of Ken's tank to attract his attention, but he was shrouded in his steel helmet and headset. Eventually it got through that there was a somewhat excited officer behind him, but Ken was much preoccupied with his own affairs, giving orders to his tanks on the radio and disinclined to be interfered with. Ted looked on spellbound as Ken carefully took off his helmet turned round and started gibbering at the interrupter, very angry and red in the face, as only Ken Smith could be. To his credit the Brigadier stole softly away.

Then suddenly there was a growing roaring in the sky as wave after wave of aircraft started coming over: Halifaxes, Stirlings, Manchesters, Lancasters and Dakotas, some towing huge Horsa and Hamilcar gliders. They cast off their tows to come down right in front of the ERY's positions.

The aircraft and gliders took considerable damage from flak and small arms fire (some of it uncomfortably close to the regimental position). There was little the Yeomanry could do to help for fear of killing our own side. This proved to be the reserve glider-borne brigade of the 6th Airborne Division arriving to join up with the parachute brigades which had dropped before dawn and made their famous capture of Pegasus Bridge over the River Orne.

When A Squadron arrived they took over from B on the outskirts of Lion-sur-Mer and soon accounted for a German half-track and a scout car. The Regiment was on the exposed right flank of the British sector, 21 Panzer Division's abortive attack coming between them and the Canadians. This was, no doubt, one of several reasons that the objective of the capture of Caen and its airfield at Carpiquet was not achieved on the first day. In fact our furthest objective for D-Day was the open high ground beyond Caen around Bourguebus where Monty expected the armoured forces to "crack about" on the good tank country. It was over two months before these hopes were fulfilled and "good tank country" proved to be good for German 88s too.

Laurie Elvin was a 20-year-old trooper in B Squadron, "Our first action was against dug-in troops, who upset us by scoring a hit on our tank, with the result that we had to bail out under fire. Next day on D+1 we were equipped with a new tank."

The Yeomanry was eventually ordered to move back at 2015hrs through Hermanville and Colleville to a position just south of Colleville, arriving at 2245hrs. Just before deciding on their exact position and as it was just beginning to get dark, the CO and Major Ellison set off on foot to find the exact place for the tanks to harbour. In doing so they found themselves between two lots of infantry, "ours and theirs," said Major Ellison, "both firing tracer bullets at each other – rather a frightening performance, but we emerged unscathed." In this position the ERY drew their tanks up in close laager, guard tanks were stationed and men settled in their tanks or alongside for what was left of the night. There was little chance of sleep as there was constant firing and the enemy was very close. Fortunately no replenishment was needed as none of the tanks had moved far or been heavily engaged. There were no supplies ashore yet anyway; so they lived off what they had. However, there were still happenings. Sergeant Shelton had not arrived at the new location; Lieutenant Mitchell, in the reinforcement squadron still on his LCT, was marvelling at the speed with which the troops were getting off the beach and how quickly the beaches were

126

cleared up, so that later that day and subsequently an orderly and quick landing and exit could take place.

Captain Wright, as Adjutant, still had to keep up with his paper work, then out with his lilo and all too few hours of precious and undisturbed sleep; but it was truly a "long day".

Sergeant Townsend of C Squadron had been landed on the wrong beach, having had a vile crossing. He found himself with his troop being drawn into a convoy of another armoured brigade. He found an RQMS of the 13th/18th Hussars with a number of soft vehicles who seemed to be in the same predicament as himself. After looking at a map, they decided to go north; his troop of tanks escorting the soft vehicles looking for 27 Armoured Brigade. They went some distance "until we came to a village where there was some enemy firing, and some German bullets splattered off the turret of my tank. This was no problem to us but it was dangerous to the soft vehicles. The RQMS decided we should turn and wait for the next day. We therefore laagered outside the village and continued without incident the next day. It seemed the Germans were holding a salient between us and 27 Armoured Brigade, but they must have been withdrawn during the night.

"On arriving at the Regiment, we found them on high ground observing their front so no one took much notice of us, but presumably they were grateful for the arrival of three tanks to complement their strength."

So the longest of "long days" ended and the stragglers were collected in.

Chapter 14

THE BATTLE FOR THE BEACHHEAD

The role of the Yeomanry and its curtailed activities on D-Day were at odds with the original plan, partly because of their late arrival due to the navy having to take evasive action from the Germans guns at Le Havre and the bombing of 9 Brigade HQ and the killing or wounding of the Brigade Staff. It was not for several hours, as has been explained, that they received proper orders on which the CO could direct the movement of his tanks to link up with 9 Infantry Brigade. Quite clearly on D-Day a regiment of tanks on the right flank of the British landing was an excellent reserve should the Germans break through and try to reach the beaches. As it happened the drive of some 21 Panzer Division tanks between the Canadian and British landings previously referred to passed unobserved. On D+1 the Regiment was ordered to support 9 Infantry Brigade in the drive to Caen. It meant reveille at 0400hrs, so no one got much sleep, as German aircraft had been overhead all night and our anti-aircraft guns were adding to the din. The War Diary says, "Quiet undisturbed night", but not many people would agree with that. The CO and the Squadron Leaders first went out on a reconnaissance of the high ground at Periers-sur-le-Dan ridge: they went in tanks as these were the only vehicles available at the time. As a result of this recce C Squadron was sent forward in support of the infantry and arrived at a small area part way up the ridge with a view that enabled them to shoot in the infantry. Sergeant Moverley's job was "to lay down a curtain of fire in front of the infantry as they advanced". His troop were supporting the Royal Ulster Rifles. (2 RUR)

At 1215hrs A and B Squadrons were ordered up prior to supporting the RUR in an attack on Cambes, a small village but one which proved a hard nut to crack from the strategic point of view. Lieutenant George Jenkin describes the attack as follows: "I cannot remember exactly what our orders were, but B was in support of the 2 RUR. This was a regular battalion and

128

had been caught in the West Indies when war broke out, and been unable to get a ship to bring them back. At the start we were back behind the infantry, but sometime after the start I had a message to go forward and help them as they were pinned down by machine-gun fire. We went forward as a troop and came up against a high wall. It was not possible to get over it. (With hindsight I realize that we should have gone up to the wall and pushed it over, but we had never had much built-up area training nor guessed we could use our tanks in such a way.) My next reaction was 'get round' and ordered everyone to circle to the right. Sergeant Tommy Dukes was point tank and led. I forget if I was next or Sergeant Matthews. Tommy found a track which took us into the main street of the village and we realized we had gone into a hornets' nest. The place was swarming with Germans, but clearly we had caught them unawares, some even had mess tins in their hands. I ordered every tank to fire with everything they had and we were firing at houses point blank with our 75s. We attacked in the rear – literally in my case, as I spotted a big fat Boche having a crap and winged him with my .38 (revolver), on target too. A motorcyclist coming round the corner met a hail of bullets. It took me two seconds to realize we had 'walked' into trouble and ordered everyone back. Tommy Dukes had already gone ahead and to my eternal regret took the wrong turning and was hit by enemy tanks coming to join the fray. From now all hell was let loose, and who bagged what I wouldn't care to say. It was only after we had pulled clear of the village, near the railway halt, that I realized Tommy's tank was missing. We were near an RUR anti-tank gun." The remainder of the action was described by Major Ellison: "Lieutenant Jenkin took his troop into the village alone, they were shot at by three Mk IV Specials with the long-barrelled 75mm gun; they set the first on fire and disposed of another. Lieutenant Jenkin still went on; he himself dismounted and manned an infantry anti-tank gun to dispose of the third German tank. In this engagement for the loss of one tank his troop of four destroyed three enemy tanks, one armoured half track, four ammunition lorries and a motor cycle".

This attack lasted from 1500 until 2200hrs and the Germans put down a merciless non-stop barrage from mortars and field guns on our leading troops and tank assembly areas. At 2200hrs the Regiment, with the infantry, were withdrawn to near their start positions, to replenish with petrol and ammunition. Just as it was getting dark German 'Parachutists' were reported as infiltrating into the infantry's lines, but in fact they were the survivors of the crew of one of our brewed-up tanks and the infantry broke into wild firing, a lot of it at nothing in particular. Captain Wright

129

goes on to describe what is recorded in the KOSB's History as "A curious incident". " RHQ Troop were then lined up on the main Caen road along-side a wood and Major Ellison and I had dismounted to stretch our legs. As we were chatting there was a hail of small arms fire from the wood which was occupied by 1 KOSB of 9 Infantry Brigade who were shooting out of it in all directions. We then dived into the ditch where I found myself next to the 2 i/c of 1 KOSB and recognized him from school cricket days in 1931. After a bit the firing died down and we clambered out. Terence Coverdale, the 2 i/c in question, admitted that there was no way in which he could stop the fusillade himself." It was what later was called "friendly fire". Lieutenant Jenkin received an immediate MC for his attack at Cambes.

After Cambes had finally been taken some days later, Lieutenant Jenkin remembered "Captain George Long, the Padre, coming to me early one summer evening and saying, 'George, we have a job to do' and taking me back to Cambes, where we found Tommy's tank which had been hit and brewed up. In the front driver's seat was what remained of Trooper Smith, only his boots and the charred remainder of his legs where he had been sitting. In his seat were further charred remains of his body. It was the same for the rest of the crew. We buried what we found. I've never ever forgotten. They were the only members of my troop killed in the whole campaign as far as I can recall."

Tanks were brought up the line for those knocked out. Trooper Laurie Elvin, who lost his tank on D-Day as had already been recorded, received a new one. "On D+1 we took over our new tank. As gunner, I checked the 75mm main gun: the sights were totally out of true and the recuperator was almost empty. So much for our back-up lads! Of course all our extra gear and personal food stocks were abandoned with our last tank, not to mention our store of cigarettes."

There were many aspects of the fighting on D+1 which affected the Regiment. The main action was the attack on Cambes, in support of the brave 2 RUR. At the same time both A and C Squadrons who were in support on Periers Ridge had a lively time shooting at German tanks and infantry. Trooper Buckingham had a clear memory, as have several others, of A Squadron supporting the RURs in the attack and a vivid picture of the infantry advancing in open order through a cornfield under a heavy barrage from German artillery and mortars. The shells were bursting in amongst them; many fell but the rest kept going. Trooper Buckingham was glad to be in a tank, although they were rocked by several near-misses. The Germans adopted the old First World War technique of mortaring the back of our artillery concentrations on the assumption that the infantry would follow them up as closely as possible. This often aroused accusations that our own gunners were firing short.

At the end of D+1 the Regiment withdrew to its start line, as well as the infantry. Tanks laagered in the open were replenished with fuel and ammunition and the crews managed a little sleep, interrupted by mortaring and shelling. But, it was up again at 0300hrs, and although things were "quieter" by day, they were machine-gunned by the Luftwaffe at first light and returned fire with great enthusiasm; they were shelled and mortared during the day, whilst a plan was drawn up for a full attack on Cambes and Galmanche the following day (D+3).

The respect and admiration the Regiment had for 2 RUR and 1 KSOB was prodigious. They watched them walk in open order through cornfields with spandaus, mortars and artillery raining down a murderous fire upon them. They did not falter at all, but kept plodding steadily on. The tanks of the Regiment gave supporting fire to them at all times, together with the guns of HMS *Warspite* and other naval ships, as well as the Divisional artillery. Tank crews also helped to pick up wounded infantry by raising the hatch on the floor of the tank in the driver's compartment, running the tank over the wounded infantryman and having the co-driver pull him through the hatch, then reversing back and dropping him at the RAP.

Meanwhile reinforcements were being landed and were preparing to join the regiment. On D+2 Lieutenant Mitchell and his tanks came ashore at Berniers-sur-Mer just to the east of Courselles-sur-Mer. Between the time they arrived off the beaches on the evening of D-1, during D-Day, D+1 and most of the morning of D+2 they had had a grandstand view of the invasion. "A continuous stream of landing craft making for the shore, hundreds of aircraft overhead and the massive shelling from the big naval guns of the battleships nearby. When it was our turn to land, the skipper drove his ship straight on to the beach and lowered the ramp so that we were able, as promised, to drive straight on to dry land!" Once ashore, Lieutenant Mitchell described the drive to the RV. "We quickly drove inland, passing all the signs of war, dead cows and other farm animals in the fields, abandoned vehicles and damaged guns, bombed buildings, and small knots of bewildered Frenchmen." Others described how the beaches themselves had been cleared up, with proper signs to follow, taped exits from the beaches and Military Police calmly directing the traffic to places where they were exposed to enemy fire. The dead had been recovered from the sea and the beaches and returned to England; burnt-out, damaged and

131

broken-down vehicles had been collected into dumps waiting for disposal or a chance of repair. There was order now where chaos had existed only a day or two before.

Once at the RV Mitchell and his crew found a place to park the tank and have a meal after they had dug slit trenches. The war was not far away. The noise of battle was everywhere, planes constantly overhead, machine-gun fire from the heavy machine guns of the MG Battalion of the Middlesex Regiment, shells from the Navy and rocket-launchers sending their multi-rockets screaming overhead; mortars coming at them from the German lines and a sound they all learned to hate, the ripping noise of fire of the Spandau MG.

There were quite a number of the Regiment in the LST, including Trooper John Pollock. He later became wireless operator on Lieutenant Donald Mantell's tank. His 21st birthday party had occurred on 5 June as they were coming down the Straits of Dover expecting to be attacked by E boats or other German underwater or surface craft. Having watched the landings "all the hard work had been done by the time we landed, which ensured our orderly and unimpeded landing, so it turned out – but not for me," Pollock related. "I was detailed to hang on to a host of loose gear on the back of the tank as we went down the steep ramp from the jaws of the LST. Trooper Sid Weldon, the driver, fetched the tank far too close to the bulkhead, the turret lock broke and I was trapped between the blanket box at the back of the turret and a rail welded on the side of the tank. Sid was smartly halted, reversed, and I fell in a heap on to the deck. I was lucky, for a severely bruised stomach was the only damage that I suffered according to the diagnosis of the MO at the dressing station."

*   *   *

D+3 (9 June) was a very different day for the ERY. The early morning was spent preparing for battle to come, with such maintenance carried out as was possible, checking fuel and ammunition stocks, having a meal and, what was becoming usual, the Luftwaffe making a visit, which was hotly opposed by our crews. Even as early as D+3 the Regiment had worked out a technique of infantry support which differed from the Infantry Tank tactics in the training manuals. This involved the tanks moving independently and selecting positions from which they could "shoot in the infantry" with observed fire from their 75mm guns and Browning machine guns. It proved most effective and was warmly appreciated by the infantry whom the ERY supported. This was partly because the tanks were not so close to them as to draw enemy fire. This became their standard tactic with both the 3rd British and later the 51st Highland Divisions; but was discouraged a few weeks later by the newly arrived 59th Infantry Division for Operation "Charnwood" who insisted on typical Infantry Tank Drills, to everyone's cost.

The attack on Cambes, the Regiment's objective for that day, was commenced at 1500hrs. A Squadron was on the right to protect that flank and was met by withering anti-tank-gun fire. The battle started off with a massive artillery concentration, shelling the wood in front of Cambes village. Many people have written of the unforgettable sight of the infantry advancing across open countryside through the standing corn. They advanced in open order and fell like flies to German mortar and machine-gun fire. It was the case that even after a heavy pounding by our artillery and the 75mm guns of our tanks, the Germans were still able to offer considerable resistance. Although it was not appreciated at the time, the villages of Cambes, Galmanche, Lebisey and Epron were all linked by underground communications and heavily fortified positions, so reinforcements could be pushed from one place to the other without our shells or mortars doing much damage.

Two troops of A Squadron dashed forward through the infantry with their guns blazing, subduing the Germans temporarily. These tanks led the infantry straight through the wood and into the village of Cambes itself. Of the two troops of tanks which made this dash, Lieutenant David Brooke led the attack in his own tank. He was just returning on orders, after the infantry were established in their new positions, when he was fired on from Galmanche just south-west of Cambes which had also been heavily bombed and shelled previously. When the guns stopped the enemy opened up and two tanks were quickly knocked out and immediately burst into flames. David Brooke was killed in this action and was awarded a Commander-in-Chief's Certificate for Gallantry, the only award for a soldier killed in action other than the VC. Corporal Fellows, the driver of Lieutenant Brooke's tank, drove it until it burst into flames, then pulled out those crew who were wounded, under intense enemy fire, and led them back to safety. He received the MM for his bravery. Each of the leading six tanks fired all their 75mm ammunition.

Replacements were needed which called for the movement of tanks and crews of the Reinforcement Delivery Squadron. Major Hyde, OC C Squadron, had his tank knocked out and several other officers were wounded. Once he had taken over another tank, he wheeled his Squadron westwards to the railway near the woods at Cambes and assisted in the consolidation of the capture of the village by the infantry.

B Squadron were in reserve for this attack and they suffered from enemy artillery and mortar fire; but took no part in the actual attack. They were moved later to the right of the ground overlooking Cambes, where they remained observing until they were withdrawn to harbour. Gradually the bridgehead was more safely secured. More troops landed, but the Yeomanry remained in the front line, their tanks in action a great deal of those long days in early June.

In the midst of all this noise, death and chaos, Captain Wright was struck by the lack of map-reading ability of the CO. As Adjutant, Captain Wright was the gunner in the CO's tank. He was constantly being asked for an exact position; but his only means of viewing was through the gunner's telescopic sight, which had a limited field of vision, or alternatively his periscope, which was no better. This was not easy, so he kept traversing the turret back and forth to give him a wider view. This confused the CO who told him to keep still, which became self-defeating. After a while the CO decided to move out in the tank away from the rest of the RHQ troop to try to see for himself what was going on. They had hardly broken cover before a hail of AP shot was flying at them and he promptly ordered reverse at full speed – zigzagging frantically as they went. Somehow they got back into cover again without being hit or ditched, but it had been a near thing. After that the Colonel was more cautious.

★   ★   ★

Shortly after 0430hrs on D+4 according to the war diary the ERY moved out of its harbour to watch and protect the infantry. B Squadron was on the right between Villons-les-Buissons and Anisy, C Squadron on the left flank near Mesnil, with A in reserve. B Squadron had a "quiet day" observing from the flank. This meant that the tanks were in an area of reasonably high ground amongst apple trees, which tended to pour sharp-tasting cider apples into the turrets and hitting the odd unsuspecting tank crew as the tank was driven slowly under the trees. One driver asked for help from the fitters on coming into harbour, complaining that his "throttle pedal was sticking". The fitter quickly produced a squashed apple which had been causing the trouble. They were concentrating their minds and eyes watching for every move the enemy might make. It was a tiring and not

134

often rewarding day. Usually it was fairly hot, so they had to fight off hoards of midges and flies, as well as get used to the smell of dead animals and other war dead. A recce patrol was sent out to within 250 yards of Galmanche, one of the fortified villages, but no enemy was seen.

C Squadron, on the other hand, observed enemy movement in a wooded area near a little hamlet marked on the map as "Halt", directly south of Cambes. Camouflaged tanks were seen, so a "stonk" or concentration shoot was arranged together with the artillery and put down on this wood. Owing to the density of the foliage, it was not possible to observe the full effect of the fire. No doubt the enemy moved pretty quickly. In fact Sergeant Marris said that, with Lieutenant Rodney Peak in support, he got his 17pdr Sherman to within 1500 yards of an enemy tank and knocked it out. They may have accounted for another one as well.

At a CO's conference that evening they learned that they were to withdraw for a couple of days to take over the area of the Staffordshire Yeomanry. This was east of Périers-sur-le-Dan and Trooper Buckingham remembered that he and his crew caught a chicken, which they had difficulty in killing. They chopped its head off but it ran off with the crew in hot pursuit. There were some Canadians on this side of the building who were very surprised to see a headless chicken leading a British tank crew. Luckily the chicken keeled over so the crew caught up with it and had it for supper.

★   ★   ★

By the end of 10 June (D+4) the initial lodgements of the invaders had been linked up into a continuous beachhead stretching over 60 miles from half way up the Cherbourg Peninsula to a confined bridgehead across the River Orne. On the right, the American landings of the airborne divisions and seaborne forces at Utah beach had gone very much according to plan. At Omaha beach the assault had run into a full Wehrmacht infantry division standing to on D-Day and suffered very severely in securing a lodgement. The British XXX Corps landings on Juno and Sword Beaches had been successful and Bayeux was soon captured by 50th British Infantry Division. On the left, 6th Airborne Division had achieved its prime objective of securing the bridges of the Caen Canal and River Orne and held a bridgehead to the east of the river linking up with the Commandos. 3rd British Infantry Division and the Canadians of I Corps were opposed by the Germans of 21 Panzer, 12 SS Panzer and Panzer Lehr Divisions and failed to penetrate the defensive ring of villages to the north of Caen.

At the more respectable hour of 0700hrs the Regiment moved to its new positions taking over from the Staffordshire Yeomanry. They had received their usual early morning visit from the Luftwaffe, to which they had replied with the .5 Brownings mounted on the tank commanders' cupolas and the Oerlikons of the AA troop. Mortars and shells also fell, but this did not stop them leaving and, on arrival at their new position, carrying out vital maintenance to the tanks. A sharp lookout had to be maintained, however. A Squadron were detailed for this, with C Squadron of 13th/18th Hussars in support. They were withdrawn at dusk. The Regiment therefore got two days' rest and caught up with essential maintenance. Major Ellison records that "up to date most of the men had had fifteen hours sleep or less in the five days since they landed, not including the time spent in the landing craft. We got a slight relief from mortaring at any rate, though we had the odd reminder of shelling at intervals during those days."

When time allowed the tank gunners had practice at the chimneys of the cement works outside Caen used by the Germans as observation posts to observe what was going on in the bridgehead. There were six in all, but none were knocked down by our guns and it took three major RAF raids and most of I Corps artillery before they were finally reduced to the ground.

The 12th June was a "quiet day" with no enemy activity, although B and C Squadrons took up the same positions as A and the 13th/18th Squadron had done the previous day. During the night some bombing of the beach maintenance area occurred, with bombs being dropped on 3rd Division HQ and 27 Armoured Brigade HQ. Bombs were also dropped in the administrative area of the Regiment, damaging four lorries and wounding several men.

It was not all sleep and maintenance, however, since one of the things found was a German food storage dump in a strong-point nearby. The stores were quickly "liberated" and some excellent tinned food found its way into regimental stomachs. Water was quite a problem, as it all had to be chlorinated. Bottled Vichy Water was found with the cache, which helped a little, although Major Ellison was critical of its use by some people for shaving.

So for a few more days there was some real rest until 15 June when the Regiment relieved the Staffordshire Yeomanry and returned to their old positions at the front. They were all geared up for an attack on a corps front but it was cancelled, so they had another "quiet day under the apple trees".

For the next two days all squadrons were watching from their positions, although a stray shell landed in the B Squadron area, killing Lieutenant David Hodgkin and wounding three other troop leaders.

There was much supplementing of rations by the troops. Trooper Buckingham recalls how they were able to dig up potatoes and do some general foraging. Sergeant Colin Brown recalled, "We had to go out nearly every day before daylight in a troop as close to the German lines as possible. We then had to camouflage down and watch. If anything moved we had to radio back to HQ." This was dangerous as the Germans were often listening in and could locate where the transmission was coming from. One day Sergeant Brown watched a German officer and his driver drive up in a Volkswagen car. They parked and went into the woods. "While they were gone I nipped out, stole the car and took it back to base. I hoped to keep it but Intelligence confiscated it."

There were humorous interludes in a deadly serious time of watching, firing at anything that moved, reporting dispositions and keeping as alert as possible. One slip and it could have been fatal. The men kept their nerves and endured the privations stoically.

RHQ had been located round Cazelle (or Mathieu as it is usually now known) and this was to be the springboard for the rest of June This time features in the memories of those who were there: the daily move to positions of observation, under the apple trees of Normandy, the constant looking for targets; some hot and beautiful weather; the awful storm that swept the coast and interrupted the landings; the shells which kept coming over and causing constant casualties, but not so many as expected.

Sergeant Colin Brown of the Recce Troop and very much a free spirit, had the job of going as far forward as he could to keep watch for any flank attack. He and his crew sneaked up to some high ground to get a good position, when he was amazed to stumble on a RN Officer from HMS *Warspite* sending back fire orders to the ship's big guns. Sergeant Brown was staggered that they were there, and able to get there in the first place, but also by the accuracy of the positions which the Observation Officer radioed back to *Warspite*. The 15" guns dropped their shells with precision straight down the village street of Galmanche.

18, 19 and 20 June were spent in detailed reconnaissance of the ground in preparation for a big attack due to take place soon.

There was the usual shelling and mortaring. Trooper Jack Farrell saw his close friend Trooper Braisby take the shovel from their tank parked up the drive leading to the chateau near Cazelle in order to attend to the calls of nature. He trotted off with his shovel and disappeared behind a hedge, dug his hole, all of 50 yards from the tank, trousers down and settled to the job when the shelling started. He did the 50 yards back to the tank, trousers round his ankles, in record time, still clutching his spade. He dived under the tank breathless. This happened three times in quick succession. He gave up in the end, but the rest of the crew thought it very funny. The mild complaint from which many suffered at that time came to be known as "Beachhead Belly".

Many Brigade conferences were held, one in the bunker called Hillman, which had held up the first wave of infantry for some hours on D-Day.

★   ★   ★

On 21 June there was a Squadron Leaders' conference called as orders had at last been received for the big attack, which had been held up by the stubborn resistance of the enemy in the villages round Cambes, Galmanche and Anisy. RHQ was then at a substantial house in Cazelle at a crossroads at the south end of the village with deep cellars which had been reinforced by the Germans for some sort of HQ. Captain Wright was sitting in the front room getting on with the paperwork of the casualty returns with Corporal Williams of the Orderly Room Staff when there was a series of almighty crashes as a concentration of medium artillery shells landed on the house and surroundings. Two of the CO's tank crew, Sergeant Harness and Corporal Emsley, were killed outright and two Squadron Leaders, Majors Hugh Matthews of B Squadron and Tony Hyde of C were wounded, the latter fatally. Shells landed on the MO's half-track, setting it alight. Several people who were sheltering underneath were badly burned as it exploded into flames, and would have been killed had it not been for the quick action of Trooper Windley who, although burnt himself, pulled them to safety. Major Ellison was in an outhouse talking to the Regimental Butcher Private Moody about a large pig which had been killed and was hanging up ready to supplement the rations. A shell hit the roof, killing Moody and filling the pig with shrapnel. Major Ellison was covered with dust but was saved by the pig's hanging carcass. Captain Wright was soon out of his room with Corporal Williams on their way to the reinforced cellar, when Lieutenant David Holbrook standing nearby let out an "Ow", as a shell fragment hit him in the shoulder. Captain Len Cullington diving for cover took a liberal sprinkling of shrapnel in the backside.

The house the CO had chosen for RHQ and the conference had in fact been used by the Germans as an HQ and both it and the crossroads must have been accurately registered by their artillery. The enemy must also have seen the additional comings and goings around the house. The next day a

German officer was captured complete with his map, which showed the area as one of their regular harassing tasks for the artillery. Needless to say, there was a quick move to a new location.

At this stage fighting was taking place throughout the beachhead in the "bocage country", with small fields surrounded by high banks, which made progress with tanks very slow, especially to the west of the Yeomanry area. Also the crews were not trained for this sort of country and casualties occurred as a result.

On 22 June the Regiment heard of the death of Major Hyde from the wounds he had suffered the day before. He had only rejoined the Regiment recently, but his association with it went back to 1940.

Trooper John Pollock had driven Captain Rodney Peak to try to find out where Major Hyde was in hospital. They finally fetched up at Douvres la Deliverande. Waiting for Captain Peak to return, Trooper Pollock "stretched out on the ground by the carrier for the usual nap when the chance was offered. One of the sisters who worked in the hospital asked me where I was wounded. I was able to assure the good lady that for the time being, I was quite all right." Captain Peak returned looking sombre with the sad news to say that Major Hyde was dead; so they returned to the Regiment in silence.

A memorial service was held for the Major in a former German Officers' Mess in the Château at Cazelle. "Those of our party ('Major Hyde's party') who were available at the time, were told to clean up as the CO thought we would like to attend too. There were a number of senior officers present, and one or two were from other regiments. The Service was taken by our Padre, Captain George Long. We were the only non-commissioned ranks there," Trooper Pollock concluded. He had held the Major in the highest regard then and still does to this day.

Captain H. E. E. Salman of the Belgian Army who had tried to get over to France with the Regiment on D-Day, arrived that day and became permanently attached to the Regiment. He was given command of the Recce Troop from Lieutenant Schilizzi who took over as Assistant IO from the wounded Lieutenant Holbrook. It was a fine warm sunny day. Major Ellison had recovered from his shattering experience of the day before and was soon out foraging. He returned with a gross (144) of Camembert cheeses, which he thought might appeal to the Regiment. Demand, however, was minimal: it was hot; flies and 'beachhead belly' cut down the orders for his cheeses. He tried to extend their shelf-life by moving them below ground into the cool. So they were brought into the dugout he shared with Captain Wright and the CO, and, as he was the junior, they were stacked in Captain Wright's bedspace. The dugout had its own smell, as it had received a couple of phosphorus grenades on first clearing. The combination of the smell of phosphorus and ripe Camembert was too much even for Captain Wright's "ostrich-like stomach", so they were finally buried deep underground at a safe distance.

After days of waiting and alteration of plans the attack was ordered for D+22.

There had been some replacement of the Squadron Leaders owing to the casualties: Major Tony Platts promoted in place of Major Matthews in B Squadron, Major Bill Holtby from HQ Squadron to C Squadron with Captain Edward Morley Fletcher promoted Major to replace him in HQ Squadron. The regimental area had been shelled yet again, but from Epron south of La Bijude, without any casualties. Trooper Pollock had been moved from a tank to a carrier and had been kept busy. One task was to round up a troop of tanks at Villons-les-Buissons which had not been in contact for some hours. He had in fact bedded down the carrier for the night. So he went off from Cazelle on the folding paratroop motor-bike kept on the back. It was "lighting up time" when he set off, he remembered, and he was assailed by the fact that it was so quiet, with not a soul to be heard. He went through Anisy, and Villons-les-Buissons and then spotted the tanks. They were neither surprised nor pleased to see him. He threw the bike on the back of a tank, climbed on himself and they shattered the quiet evening as they rumbled back to the harbour.

It was an important attack that was now to be put in. The planning had gone awry because of the tough German resistance on the left flank of the 8 Brigade attack supported by the 13th/18th Hussars, which had to be concluded before the Yeomanry's attack could go in. Our A Squadron moved out to Villons-les-Bussions, but were held there waiting for their infantry. Château-la-Londe had still not been taken by the time C Squadron were ready to move at 0900 hrs, so 1 Troop were ordered to assist in the attack on the château. The Regimental attack went in at 1435 hrs.

Trooper Pollock in his carrier set out with Lieutenant Dick Jackson on reconnaissance. They went in with a company of the RUR. The carrier was placed at the southern edge of Cambes wood. Trooper Pollock went off on foot on "some errand or other". The attack was really starting as he made his way back, so the noise, smoke and smell were intense. He had left the head-set of the radio dangling over the side of the carrier, so that he could go to ground and still use the wireless. The carrier was under constant machine-gun fire. After a time things quietened down and he looked about for Lieutenant Jackson who had stretched himself out on the ground. When the firing stopped Lieutenant Jackson hadn't moved, so Trooper Pollock shook him gently. His head fell back; he had been killed by a mortar fragment which must have sliced through his throat. Trooper Pollock found a medic who said Lieutenant Jackson died when hit. He was a good sort, and like nearly every one else very young. He was a good officer and liked by his troop. He was replaced by Lieutenant Charman, also very young.

The advance started at 1415hrs with the whole of C Squadron supporting the RUR. The Squadron's intention was to occupy the whole area of the buildings of La Bijude. If this was successful the infantry would follow. 1 and 2 Troops were to lead with the remainder of the Squadron in support, supported also by a heavy artillery concentration. The tanks of the two troops moved over the crest of the hill between Cambes and La Bijude. They came under machine-gun and anti-tank fire from the right flank. Immediately the lead tank was blown up and destroyed, but Lieutenant Howitt, the troop leader, didn't hesitate and went straight in to destroy an anti-tank gun, his tank being hit twice in the action, he himself being killed outright and his wireless operator Trooper Armstrong also. The driver, Lance Corporal Frew, brought the badly damaged tank back although it was still on fire.

The frontal assault was tried again without achieving the objective, so a flank attack was then put in from the left, but the Germans could not be budged even with artillery and air support. There were considerable casualties in tanks and crews wounded. Sergeant Fitzmaurice did manage to knock out a MkIV Special. This whole attack lasted two hours: it did relieve the pressure on the 8 Infantry Brigade, which, with the added support of 3 Troop of A Squadron, managed to capture Château-la-Londe on the left. When the Château was cleared several days later; it was found to be a graveyard of knocked-out German tanks and guns. How many of these were caused by the action of C Squadron will never be known.

This was considered a most successful but costly action which earned the personal congratulations of the Divisional Commander to the Regiment, and a Commander-in-Chief's Certificate for Gallantry for Lieutenant Peter Howitt.

They went back to their lines at Cazelle, but received shelling and mortaring throughout the night. The following day A Squadron went out to Villons-les-Buissons and carried out a harassing shoot on the western

141

edge of Galmanche and drew fire in reply. B Squadron did the same on La Bijude. This tended to become a daily occurrence with few casualties but one trooper was killed by mortar fire on 10 June.

Four new officers joined the Regiment on 29 June and replacement tanks and crews arrived.

Meanwhile the Squadrons continued to be on harassing shoots and observation duties. They used to keep hidden in the apple orchards which always showered the crews with hard apples when shrapnel hit the trees.

59th Infantry Division, newly arrived from England, came into the area but were not yet ready to join the battle. The Germans on the other hand had brought up altogether seven Panzer Divisions to the beachhead area, so local attacks had to be postponed whilst the British armour were reinforced and redeployed.

One incident of note was when the RUR told Lieutenant John Scotter of A Squadron that the Germans were trying to recover two disabled heavy tanks. With relish Lieutenant Scotter's troop engaged the two German tanks, set them on fire and dispatched several of the recoverers. The end of June came with the ERY still in the line, carrying out the harassing shoots on both Galmanche and La Bijude.

Early in July the Yeomanry was moved back for three days to Luc-sur-Mer, where baths, a change of clothes and maintenance of tanks made a respite from the constant shelling. Most of the members remember those days with pleasure, swimming in the sea, warm sun, change of clothes, different food, even fresh bread. Hot baths were a happy release from filth.

Trooper Pollock and his friends found an estaminet where they asked for refreshment. They were welcomed in by the proprietress and given white wine. MPs knocked on the door. The lady of the house shooed them away: there would have been trouble as, having just come out of the line, they were in no mood to be dictated to by MPs as soon as they were pulled back. They purchased local cheese which they were forbidden to buy, but stored it in the blanket box of the tank. It was forgotten and soon let them know of its presence with the awful smell. Camembert is still popular even so.

The time of rest was by squadrons, as two had to remain on standby, one on 30 minutes', and the other on two hours' notice.

Chapter 15

ENLARGING THE BEACHHEAD

The first significant enlargement of the beachhead came with the American capture of Cherbourg which was effected by 27 June, although it was a long time later before the port was reopened due to demolitions and mining. Before that the British had made an attempt to pinch out Caen with unsuccessful Divisional attacks – by 51st Highland Division from the Orne bridgehead on Ste Honorine; and 7th Armoured Division which broke out to Villers Bocage, but there met a nest of Tiger tanks which slaughtered the spearhead of 4th County of London Yeomanry. The "Great Storm" of 19–23 June had seriously disrupted unloading, but a more concerted attack by VIII Corps was made over the River Orne (Operation Epsom) between 26 and 30 June during which 11th Armoured Division captured the key feature of Hill 112. The attack was called off prematurely on 30 June and the Armoured Division was withdrawn over the river.

Early in July the British and Canadians on the left began to tackle the stubborn enemy resistance north of Caen and eventually cleared the defences up to the River Orne in Operation "Charnwood" on 8 July and other subsequent costly fighting. The major attempts to break out of the ring followed with the disastrous drive by three armoured divisions east of Caen (Operation Goodwood) on 18 July when 400 tanks were lost and little ground gained. Then on 25 July the US Army launched Operation "Cobra" on the western side of the beachhead which took them to Averanche by 31 July. Meanwhile on their left, where the bocage began in earnest, VIII Corps with 11th Armoured Division leading (Operation "Bluecoat") achieved a breakthrough of six miles towards Caumont and occupied a key ridge four miles further on. The Germans who were trying to counter-attack the American Cobra drive to the west with 9 and 10 SS Panzer Divisions were intercepted and seen off by 11th Armoured Divisions and both these Divisions were withdrawn from the battle, to refit and not to surface again until Arnhem.

Towards the end of the first week in July the Brigadier had given a talk to the officers and all crew commanders about the next operation called

"Charnwood". The Canadians would be on the right flank with 59th Division next and the 3rd British on their left. 27 Armoured Brigade would be supporting 59th Division, which was up to strength but at that time wholly inexperienced. On the evening of 7 July a huge air attack by the heavies of the RAF took place on the enemy defences to the north of Caen as the objective of this attack was the capture of the city. During the day thousands of civilians were seen leaving, having been warned of the impending attack. The waves of aircraft flew over the regimental harbour area at 2130hrs. They dropped 2,700 tons of bombs on their objectives just beyond our infantry positions.

Sergeant Moverley remembered the evacuation of the civilians as he watched through binoculars. He was heartened to see them leave, just as he was glad to see the heavy bombers for the first time which helped the attack and lifted the morale of the forces involved. Whilst preparing to move his troop in, Sergeant Moverley saw that the artillery had moved up beside his troop. Before setting up their guns, the gunners took their bayonets and prodded all the earth of their area. Up popped a heavily armed young German soldier who had been unearthed. Sergeant Moverley never forgot after this to "go hunting before settling down".

Before the ERY moved up for its overnight march to its start line, the air attack started and the place was lit up like a bonfire. Trooper Ken Buckingham and others remembered seeing the bomb bays opening and the bombs actually falling out of the sky.

Orders were given to Squadron Leaders for "Charnwood". They were soon to leave the area in which they had harboured around Cazelle for several weeks, and from where patrols had gone out daily to observe and fire on the enemy. The Squadron areas had been established so that on return from patrol each tank crew knew where to harbour and the "comforts" for the crews were available.

Then came the night move into a wooded area, from which they were to attack, supporting 197 Brigade of 59th Infantry Division, towards Galmanche. A Squadron were at the orchard north-west of Villons-les-Buissons and B Squadron south of Anisy. They had all loaded up with as much ammunition as they could carry and then settled down to get as much sleep as possible. Lieutenant Mitchell of B Squadron was in an area well covered with bracken; and as it was a cold night they were all wearing their greatcoats with their webbing equipment. (Tank crews were supposed to wear webbing across their shoulders attached to their belts in case they had to be pulled out of the tank as a casualty.) Lieutenant Mitchell crawled in

144

under the tank and, as it was a tight fit, lay on his front. On surfacing before the start in the very early morning, his crew turned away from him in disgust. "As it got lighter, I could see what had happened. Some Canadians had occupied our spot before us and they had not been too particular about their sanitary arrangements. I had crawled into one Canadian's private lavatory, and had ground his excrement well and truly into my greatcoat. Fortunately it was not so cold by then, so I took it off and strapped it with my bed roll on the outside of the turret. The last I remember of that great-coat was later seeing it smouldering away together with all my bedding as the tank burnt fiercely after being hit. No doubt that was the best thing that could have happened to it."

Continuing with the lavatorial theme, Lieutenant Mitchell went on, "Later that morning we were to form a square of four tanks to allow the crew in turn to leave the tank through the floor access plates and squat in the middle of the square to perform his task in comparative safety, while mortars and bullets were all flying around us. At least they used to take a shovel with them and buried their offerings before regaining the tank."

Zero hour was 0429hrs. The battle started with B Squadron supporting the untried infantry. They insisted on the attack going in "by the book" i.e. the infantry advancing in front with tank support close behind them in tight formation. The Yeomanry had found this a totally unsafe tactic and had adapted their own method to assist their infantry more effectively, man-oeuvring to give themselves as much protection as possible at the same time by choosing the right ground. The enemy laid down a heavy artillery and mortar attack, devastating the infantry whose control was soon lost and B Squadron was left to rally the remnants before going ahead alone. In spite of very heavy shelling and gun fire they overwhelmed the defences killing a large number of Germans, especially by bouncing delayed action 75mm shells on to their slit trenches. They took the objective of Galmanche and sat there for five hours, but suffered many casualties as a result. Major Platts, the Squadron Leader, was killed by a sniper. Sergeant Bob Coupland was blinded by a phosphorus grenade he had thrown at a slit trench, which was thrown back at him by a quick-witted German. Second Lieutenant Tony Chappell, who had joined the ERY only five days before, was badly wounded in the head and Lieutenant Mitchell was wounded in both knees when his tank was knocked out by the new hand-held rocket weapon, the Panzerfaust, and the rest of his crew killed.

The Brigadier of the infantry had to make a strenuous personal effort to rally his troops to sustain any form of attack and consolidate the gains made by B Squadron tanks. That he did so was greatly to his credit.

A Squadron, with C Squadron in support, went in later that day to attack St Contest to support the 1/7 Warwicks, whilst the Canadians were attacking immediately to their right. There was plenty of ammunition used that day. Major Humphrey Phillips pushed his Squadron practically into St Contest and selected a fold in the ground within two hundred yards of the village, from where his Squadron could pump shells into the Germans without being too exposed themselves. They had no infantry with them by then, but by this bold tactic suffered fewer casualties. The infantry, having suffered heavy casualties, had not advanced with the tanks. The infantry Brigadier had to end his day having as bad a time at St Contest as he had at Galmanche in the morning. He had had his half-track written off and later he had one man killed on one side of him and another wounded on the other by a ricochet. The battle for St Contest was bitterly fought, the enemy counter-attacked with infantry and tanks and threw the Warwicks out of the village. The Brigadier brought up another battalion and the village was finally taken.

The Regiment had achieved most of its objectives, but there was a château at Galmanche which was still occupied by the enemy and the hamlet of Malon also held out.

The Yeomanry moved into harbour near the woods at Villons-les-Buissons at dusk about 2030hrs, having been relieved by the infantry.

C Squadron, with some engineer tanks, destroyed the château at Galmanche early on the second morning of the battle. This was not a healthy task as they had to approach through open country. Major Holtby, however, pushed his tanks through this shelled area and blasted the château to smithereens.

Forty German dead were counted and only twelve prisoners taken. Trooper Les Timms, driver of Sergeant Dry's tank, somehow managed during this action to hop out and dig some new potatoes from the garden for their meal that evening. The 2/8 Staffords consolidated the capture of the château.

An attack was mounted on Malon but it was soon discovered that the enemy had left during the night and the village was then occupied by our own infantry.

A Squadron was then ordered forward to take up an observation role south of St Contest, in case of a counter-attack. It did not take place and our own infantry were now moving on towards Caen. The Regiment had cleared some very difficult ground of inter-connecting villages in bad tank country. Two tanks had been knocked out by fire and two disabled but were recovered. Altogether two officers and eight other ranks had been killed and three wounded. Captain Wright handed over his job of Adjutant to Captain Alan Thornton and was posted to B Squadron, to obtain battle experience as there were a growing number of casualties among the Squadron Leaders.

The Regiment was later ordered back to its harbour at Cazelle and then to Luc-sur-Mer, for a much-needed rest after fifty-four hours of continuous action.

For the first time in six and a half weeks they were, as a Regiment, able to use their messes, billet comfortably and eat reasonably well from their own squadron cookhouses. They bathed, changed clothes, wrote home and relaxed, and of course caught up with the maintenance of their tanks.

Owing to the death of the Squadron Leader of B Squadron, Major Platts, Captain Tom Robinson was promoted Major to command the Squadron in his place, with Captain Wright as his 2 i/c.

They stayed in Luc-sur-Mer until 15 July. During that time some of the Yeomanry had managed to get into Caen to see that the greater part of the city had been reduced to rubble. Sergeant Moverley saw the mess and was told that a full regiment of German tanks was buried under the debris in one street.

On 15 July orders were received to move across country to cross the River Orne by newly built Bailey bridges. This was a change of some importance, as the ERY was to take part in Operation "Goodwood", an attempt to break out from the bridgehead, and draw more German armour to the British part of the line. Three complete armoured divisions and a large amount of other armour besides were required to concentrate in the cramped bridgehead on the eastern side of the River Orne, there to assemble in complete secrecy before pushing through to the south. The Regiment took over the positions of 6th Airborne Division and marvelled at the accuracy of the gliders which had landed so close to the village on D-Day They remained in this area for a day and a half prior to the big attack and met up with the battalion of the Green Howards, which had been formed in 1940 from 2 ERY and some old friendships were renewed. The crews of the tanks were wary of the Commandos in the area who seemed like fully wound up springs. There were a lot of flies and mosquitoes around which didn't help comfort at all.

After crossing the river they moved further east near the village of Le Plein. They started at 1800hrs and it took them six hours to cover six miles. It was dark, no lights were permitted, and the dust created by the dry weather and churned up by the mass of tanks ahead made movement slow and difficult. They finally arrived at the woods at Le Plein where they were to lie up at 0420hrs, but two tanks were blown up by mines on the very edge of the track they had to follow. A camouflage expert showed them how to disguise their vehicles and they settled down to wait for the order to move. There were many conferences and a good deal of reconnaissance of the area in which they were to operate. Of course the enemy had already been alerted to the large movement of armour because of the noise of the engines and the large dust cloud and sent over a heavy bombardment of shells and mortars.

The day of the battle began with a tremendous RAF raid on enemy positions softening them up for the attack; an endless procession of heavy bombers flew over the troops. Morale was high at the sight of these bombers going in and causing trouble for the Germans. The Yeomanry had returned to support its old 9 Infantry Brigade of the 3rd British Division who were on the extreme left flank or shoulder of the planned advance. Their task was to open up the flank and to keep it open at all costs while the three armoured divisions were to move down a corridor to the south and hopefully break out towards Falaise.

Once the battle started the ERY were to occupy an area called Butte de la Hogue which was on high ground, open but, as it turned out, well registered by the German guns. The next objective was to capture the villages of Sannerville and Toufreville also on an open plain, with the small town of Troarn beyond in close country.

A Squadron moved off with the 1 KSOB on the right and B with 2 RUR on the left heading for Troan. They moved clear of the roads and made across country. This created its own dust clouds, which made people even more uncomfortable and dirty with their faces arms and other exposed parts of the body already swollen by constant "dive-bombing" from mosquitoes. The Germans were also joining in.

A Squadron and the KOSB were trying to reach Sannerville. They got into the outskirts of the village without meeting any opposition, but the RAF had bombed the place so thoroughly that it was virtually impossible for tanks to reach the centre. The approach through standing corn was an excellent cover for German anti-tank guns and dug-in tanks. Sergeant Moverley had been sent out at first light to see what was happening; and reported back to his Squadron Leader after his troop had been caught in the middle of an artillery barrage.

Trooper Bernie O'Donoghue was in the tank in which Sergeant Bob Coupland had lost his eyesight at Galmanche: it was now commanded by

148

Sergeant Johnny Larter. They were given orders to engage an enemy tank which was keeping the infantry pinned down. They trundled out of a wood on to a road and between there and where they came out at the corner of the road where they could see what was happening the intercom failed, so there was no communication between the crew. The commander had to shout his orders to Trooper O'Donoghue, the gunner sitting immediately below him, who in turn gave instructions to the driver by shouting. They stopped at the corner. This was the day after the action began and the heavens had opened, making everything a quagmire, with visibility down to practically nothing. They fired a shot, but the smoke from their 17pdr gun obscured their vision even more and, when he could see, he saw not a tank but a dug-in anti-tank gun. A frantic yell to reverse and they ended up barrel-down in a deep ditch.

The rest of B Squadron was delayed in pushing further forward as the Guards Armoured Division was milling about for elbow room to get down the cleared corridor with the other two Armoured Divisions. Many of their vehicles were seen floundering about in the mined area off the cleared part. One of the vehicles seen in this shambles was said to be an Officers' Mess truck.

A Squadron having got to the outskirts of Sannerville, Sergeant Moverley, pushing through the corn, moved on into bad tank country. Enemy infantry with Panzerfausts were causing havoc among the tanks. His tank was knocked out, but he took over another and continued to support the infantry before his second tank too was knocked out and he was badly wounded.

B Squadron was soon in the thickly wooded country of the Bois de Bavent which was difficult for tanks. Troop leaders therefore had to carry out reconnaissance mostly on foot. Lieutenant Chris Moreton was hit and badly wounded. A patrol of the RUR went out to recover him, but were themselves badly machine-gunned, losing several in the gallant attempt. Chris Moreton's grave was later found in a wood nearby when the area had been cleared.

Tanks kept on supporting the infantry as closely as possible with the next objective being Troarn. Just to achieve that objective they had to fight many separate battles against concealed tanks, anti-tank guns and Panzerfausts.

Several ME 109s and other German aircraft flew over the regimental area on Butte de la Hogue and were engaged by as many of the Regiment as possible with no definite result. The day before they had one success in shooting down an ME 109.

B Squadron remained in close contact with the enemy so it was difficult to refuel and re-arm the tanks. However, at 0300hrs on 19 July Major Morley Fletcher, OC HQ Squadron, arrived at their harbour with petrol and ammunition. The attack continued on the 20th with the deluge continuing over them, making the going very difficult. Several tanks were blown up whilst supporting the infantry in their attacks, but no casualties were reported. B Squadron were eventually relieved in their forward positions by C Squadron. Captain Wright had gone off in a scout car to reconnoitre the route and while he was away his tank managed to back into an apple tree containing a hornets' nest. The C Squadron tank which replaced it had a hot welcome, not improved by the German mortar fire when the movement of the tanks was observed!

Captain Wright tells how he used to dig a large cavity and then have his tank drive over it as a shelter and slept well on his lilo. The rest of the crew had comfortable seats on board – all except the tank commander. Others used to come into his personal shelter, including a private from the RUR who said he was a Southern Irishman and when asked what he was doing with the Ulsters said that he had "heard there was a foight on and he wanted to be with the bhoys". They had to be careful with this practice because on wet ground the tank might settle and crush those underneath, as happened in other units.

On 21 July the harbour area on Butte de la Hogue was shelled and Trooper John Pollock, who was out of his tank, had a fierce blow on the wrist. He had no pain but a very badly damaged wrist watch and his left hand was totally useless for a time. Another crew member was also hit in the same way but the injury remained permanent. A few of the RUR had also been caught in the attack, one wounded in the groin. There was a lot of blood but the orderlies were able to assure him that all his tackle was still in place and in working order.

The main battle was faltering and with the heavy rain the going was dreadful. In the middle of this the CO was told that 27 Armoured Brigade was to be broken up. It had been expected to be written off in the assault; but had in fact survived virtually intact so that new dispositions were needed. For the next four days the Squadrons were fighting local actions on the flank of the Armoured Divisions' drive during which several men were wounded but there were no fatalities.

On D+50, 26 July, the ERY was ordered into 2nd Army Reserve. It was a sad day as they had been with the 13th/18th Hussars for nearly four years.

Chapter 16

UNHORSED; THEN RE-EQUIPPED
FOR THE BREAK-OUT

During the time that the Yeomanry were encamped at Creully, the final battles of the Normandy Campaign were fought and won by the Allies. After the "Goodwood" disaster with the loss of four hundred tanks pitted against well-prepared defences in open country and in daylight, three weeks later "Totalise" started well with a set-piece night attack by armour and infantry. This, however, ground to a halt within a few days without achieving the hoped for breakthrough to Falaise. A further set-piece attack, "Tractable", was little more successful; but the American break-out in the west, coupled with relentless air attack and continuous pressure around the "sac" into which the Germans had been driven, including the suicidal Mortain counter-attack, eventually resulted in the final defeat of the enemy in Normandy. From this only about 40,000 resolute men and a score of tanks escaped from the Falaise pocket. Those that got away were largely drawn from the better equipped and fanatical SS Divisions. The pocket was not finally closed until 21 August.

After a stray 88mm shell hit a nearby belt of trees Captain Robin Whitworth the Intelligence Officer was wounded and ended his service with the Yeomanry. The Regiment finally moved back over the Orne and on through the dust to Creully, where they were guided into harbour. It was the first time since D-Day that there was proper messing with the cooks' lorries brought up to the Regiment.

They all arrived at the new location looking very brown, because of the dust and dirt which had replaced the mud. They were glad also to have left the mosquitoes and the stench of dead cattle behind. They had seen during those eight days some of the carnage inflicted on the Armoured Divisions which had taken part in Operation Goodwood.

The site where the Regiment was encamped was just forward of 2nd Army HQ, between woods to the north of the village of Creully, in a pleasant area, with tented messing facilities. General Montgomery's HQ of 21st Army Group was nearby at the château too.

The Yeomanry was to lose its tanks. This was a blow to all ranks, as they had had their Sherman Diesels since well before D-Day. Many alterations, additions and improvements had been carried out to the requirements of the individual crews. There was a week spent in relaxation before the tanks had to be handed over to the Canadians but it was a sad task. The spare stores and equipment which were dug out of the bowels and storage bins of the tanks was amazing, enough rations to keep everyone well fed for a long time and a wonder sometimes that there was room for ammunition. When the tanks were finally delivered to the Canadians they gave full credit to the Regiment for the condition in which they received them. This was part of the rationalization of equipment, so that diesel tanks were concentrated in Canadian army hands while the rest of the armour in I Corps was petrol-driven.

After the tanks had gone they stayed in their comfortable location. The weather was perfect, so games were played and everyone was soon very fit. They fed well and ate good freshly baked bread. What a change from the "Dog biscuits" they had existed on for so long.

They were visited in the camp by the Regiment's former CO, Brigadier Frank Fisher ("Fish"), who was now Brigadier RAC 2nd Army, and who told them that they would not be broken up as a regiment but would join 33 Armoured Brigade with whom they had been for three months in 1943. 13th/18th Hussars went with Brigadier Prior Palmer to 8 Armoured Brigade and fought some famous actions in XXX Corps. The Staffordshire Yeomanry went back to England for training.

Most of the members of the Regiment remember those few weeks as a period of peace and civilization after the maelstrom of all the fighting they had been through since D-Day.

There was one successful Officers' Mess party, where they had been able to invite a number of friends from neighbouring units and their old Brigade. Captain Wright listened with interest to a learned discussion on the "flea line" and where it ran from the Atlantic to the Russian border between Captain Henri Salman, OC Recce Troop, and Peter Murray, the French Liaison Officer with 4th/7th Dragoon Guards from Dunkirk days (really Prince Pierre Murat and a direct descendant of Marshal Murat, one of Napoleon's Marshals). The bar for this function was known as "La Folie Bijude" after the village north of Caen. They were also visited by the press, especially the Yorkshire papers.

Captain Wright was even able to pursue his hobby of geology and found a nice little ammonite in the "upcast from the regimental latrine trench".

The rest could not last and on 11 August a movement order was received that the Regiment would come under command of the newly formed 1 Canadian Army, to replace 148 Regiment RAC in 33 Armoured Brigade who were to receive "Kangaroos", turretless Shermans used as armoured personnel carriers. At 0630hrs 12 August Major Ellison went forward to recce a new regimental harbour in the region of Beuville. The Regiment moved by truck at 1430hrs that day to the open downland on the east side of the Orne near Bras, some four miles from where they had ended the battles some weeks earlier, and the allied advance was now in full swing.

Here they stayed, still in glorious weather, until the early morning of 16 August when they went forward and took over the Shermans Mks I and II from 148 Regiment RAC. These tanks, which had only days before been in action, were lined up ready for handover. Captain Wright gave himself the job of supervising the fitness of the tanks taken over by B Squadron and began logging the daily mechanical state of each tank in the Squadron. These tanks were all claimed by 148 RAC to be "good runners", but a quick check showed that they were not in such good shape, indeed it was quite impossible to start five of the nineteen the Squadron had taken over. Not only were the main batteries totally flat, but the small auxiliary charging engines would not start either.

At Creully the crews had had instruction on the Is and IIs; the Mark IIs had five Chrysler truck engines mounted on a common crank-case. The Sherman Is had aircraft-type air-cooled radial engines. They found the conversion not too difficult as the only differences were the engines and not the layout of the turret or hull compartment.

It had been a big task taking over the tanks, loading them with ammunition, fuel, food, water and the multitude of other items carried on them. The next morning the ERY moved up to join 152 Brigade of 51st Highland Division with whom they worked and supported for much of the remainder of the campaign. The problems of non-runners were not confined to B Squadron, the basic trouble being that their previous operators had never been at longer than 30 minutes' notice to move and so had been unable to carry out proper maintenance.

While the pursuit through northern France and into Belgium was starting, the Regiment, now being part of 33 Armoured Brigade in I Corps under First Canadian Army, were given the less romantic task of clearing the coastal area up to Le Havre where there was still plenty of fighting to

153

do. The area in which the Yeomanry was to operate initially was in fairly thick orchard country, and in the early stages against stubborn resistance. Having taken over their "new tanks", the following morning, 18 August, B Squadron moved up in support of 2 Seaforth Highlanders who had found a track leading to an unblown bridge. The area was split by a series of minor rivers, each a tank obstacle. The Squadron moved up hoping to find the bridge over the River Vie intact. They followed a rough track so that the tanks were noisy, giving warning of their approach. Suddenly there was a loud explosion when the bridge was blown up just as they arrived at the river bank. Major Tom Robinson, the Squadron Leader, climbed out of his tank to search for somewhere to place an assault bridge: he was walking about in the open when he was hit by a burst of machine-gun fire and badly wounded in the back and arm. The approach to the bridge had not only been rough but the infantry had had to cope with German rearguards, the enemy troops supported by at least one assault gun. The weather was also hot and sunny. Up to that time Normandy-based squadrons of the RAF had been concentrating their attentions on the Germans trying to get out of the Falaise pocket further south. On 18 August, however, RAF fighters based in England were let loose to reinforce the Normandy-based ground attack squadrons, the rocket-firing Typhoons being especially effective. The home-based aircraft lacked the experience in identifying friend from foe and, perhaps fortunately, were armed only with 20mm cannon and machine guns – not rockets. With the Seaforths and B Squadron held up in the narrow lane leading to the blown bridge, the Lightnings and Spitfires from midday onwards mistook the attackers for retreating enemy and gave the Highlanders and their supporting tanks no mercy. Perhaps they had misread their maps as the small rivers east of the River Dives would have looked very similar from the air. In spite of the yellow smoke and yellow fabric triangles on the tops of the tanks used as recognition signals, the aircraft took no notice and machine-gunned the stationary vehicles at half-hourly intervals all afternoon. 152 Infantry Brigade HQ came in for heavy attack too and two ambulances were left blazing, several of the supporting gunners' vehicles were written off and the CO's scout car was hit without touching either him or the infantry Brigadier who were standing next to each other nearby. Altogether sixty troops were killed or wounded during the day.

In the middle of all this, a rather battered and dusty Brigadier Jim Cassels of 152 Brigade came up in a scout car to see how 2 Seaforths and B Squadron were getting on. He was very tall and made quite an impression on those who met him. He later commanded the Commonwealth force in Korea and ultimately became Chief of the General Staff.

Captain Wright took over B Squadron after Major Robinson was wounded; but there was little to be done until the infantry could secure a crossing over the river, which was not made any easier by the regular attacks with machine-gun and cannon fire from the air. During one such attack Captain Wright tells how he noticed a line of 20mm cannon shells tracking along the lane a yard from his nose as he took cover under his tank. Later, on diving for the ditch, he wrenched a knee which by the following morning was the size of a football and he had no option except to be evacuated and it took him three frustrating weeks before obtaining release from the tented hospital at Bayeux.

The infantry eventually did manage to get across the River Vie, supported by what was left of B Squadron, even though they had some trouble with a German SP gun which "amused itself by shooting at us and then moving away". What with flat batteries and the inability to start either the main or auxiliary engines, which could operate the power-traverse of the turrets, the Squadron was eventually reduced to only five tanks which were fit for action. Three of the officers from 148 Regiment RAC joined the Yeomanry; at least they knew the tanks.

During the day two tanks were actually lifted off the road by the air attacks, but there were no casualties. It was becoming so dark that the Squadron was recalled to harbour where the transport arrived with fuel, ammunition and mail, and large quantities of yellow smoke canisters and other recognition devices to try to give protection from further "friendly fire".

At 0700hrs 2 and 4 Troops of B Squadron went forward to the positions left the previous night, civilian information having made it clear that no tank crossings were possible. They also had a cat and mouse game with the German SP gun, but with no casualties.

Command of B Squadron was taken over by Captain H. E. E. Salman who was subsequently promoted to Major and led it to the end of hostilities. They were withdrawn to harbour at 1130hrs with A Squadron taking over.

From then on the action began to loosen up and advances could be measured in miles rather than the earlier slogging. At 0615hrs on 20 August, whilst B was back in reserve, A Squadron with 8 Seaforths started a new attack. One tank was soon knocked out by a Panzerfaust team who stepped out of a hedge and fired at close range. Three of the crew were killed, but

155

the infantry dealt quickly and ruthlessly with the opposition. Their first objective was the le Conté cross roads on the road towards Lisieux and they started with the leading company of infantry who were soon held up by heavy machine-gun fire. The enemy was then engaged with fire from both the tanks and the infantry to such good effect that twenty prisoners were taken. Both the infantry and tanks were moving through very close country, which meant that the tanks had to keep largely to roads and tracks. Trooper Buckingham was in the leading tank as they were pushing on after capturing the prisoners. He recalled: "I was keeping a lookout through the periscope, when suddenly a sheet of molten metal blotted out my view. We had been hit, but all bailed out safely and dived into a ditch. I was horrified to realize that we were all alone apart from five riflemen but with no sign of another tank or infantry." They had been knocked out by a 75mm anti-tank gun and nearly everyone else had taken cover. "As we made our way back along the very shallow ditch the Germans fired several rounds in our direction, fortunately exploding in the hedge not close enough to do us any injury. When we came to an opening in a field, I decided to get to the other side of the hedge so as to be able to run along crouched and get out of range more quickly. When I got back on to the road at a safe distance, I met an infantry colonel (the CO of 8 Seaforths). While he questioned me a number of German soldiers came out of the field where we had been in order to surrender, which shook me when I realized the implications. Incidentally I was wearing the asbestos glove used by loaders, which I still have!" He went on to say that at a reunion in 1990 he was very pleased to meet another member of the crew, Trooper Fred Howe, for the first time in forty years. Trooper Howe was the gunner in the crew and one of the first things he said to Buckingham was, "I still don't know how you managed to get out of the tank before me when we were knocked out!" To explain: the loader operator was on the far side of the breach of the main gun from the turret-hatch and therefore had to get around the spent shell bag, under the breach of the gun, climb over the gunner and push past the commander who was at the hatch. He must have moved very fast indeed.

On the way back to get a replacement tank someone found a bottle of Calvados in a barn. It must have been very rough stuff as they all had diarrhoea for seven days afterwards.

The Squadron soon got its own back as 3 Troop destroyed an anti-tank gun, taking three of the crew prisoner. There had been a further hold-up before the crossroads was finally taken. A heavy machine gun had held up the infantry, but the tanks soon silenced it.

The main objective of this advance was the town of Lisieux. The countryside was hilly with many small orchards and wooded slopes: the hills above Lisieux gave the most superb views for miles around. Lovely country and full of greenery, but no good for tanks. The weather was superb, hot and cloudless skies, so there was very little excuse for the Lightnings to strafe the Infantry Brigade HQ for the second time. This time they killed the Brigade Major and many of the staff. Luckily Major Ellison, who was at Brigade HQ at the time, had seen them coming. They had been digging slit trenches and his battledress top was on the scout car. He just managed to shelter under the scout car, but when it was over he emerged to find his battledress top shot to bits.

The advance continued, many prisoners were being taken by the Seaforths and A Squadron; by 1100hrs the infantry had consolidated their position and A Squadron was relieved by C. The same sort of fighting continued and several tanks were lost, but no casualties were reported and they advanced several miles. At the end of the day the Squadron surprised and killed the crew of an anti-tank gun and then came head to head with a German staff car. The officer who was in it immediately jumped out of the car and, drawing his revolver, charged the tank. He was shouting invectives at them, but one shot from the 75mm ended his gallant and fanatical charge. He and his staff car were blown to smithereens.

Early the following morning a counter-attack was launched, but the Seaforths repelled it with A Squadron's support. The enemy lost many dead and wounded together with twenty prisoners during this counter-attack.

B Squadron were sent out next, half under Captain Henri Salman the new Squadron Leader, the other half under Captain Len Cullington, just returned from England having recovered from his wound, as second in command. It was another slow slogging match; sixty enemy being reported in the area; prisoners were taken all day in the line of the advance. The battle then opened up and became more fluid. The Recce Troop of Stuarts, supported by the heavier Shermans, were able to push on and report that most of the road to Lisieux was clear. Captain Salman, as became his usual practice, left his tank and went on in his scout car into Lisieux to find it in the hands of 153 Brigade of the 51st Highland Division except for a few pockets of snipers left in the ruins of that once beautiful town, bombed by the RAF the day before. The driver of Captain Salman's scout car was Trooper Ernest Martin who found driving for Captain Salman for the first time quite a hair-raising experience.

The ERY was now put on two hours' notice, a mobile bath unit arrived

157

and rest and maintenance were the order of the day. Altogether they had four days of this regime in beautiful weather.

A brief passage is included here on Captain H. E. E. Salman.

This most extraordinary man was born in 1905, the son of a Belgian judge. He had one brother who became a priest. Henri graduated from Louvain University with a degree in mathematics, going on to do postgraduate courses in psychology, animal psychology and animal behaviour. He had also studied at the Universities of Berlin, Paris, Oxford and Berkeley, California.

He completed his military training in the Belgian Artillery, attaining the rank of Lieutenant before posting to the Reserve. He was, however, drawn to the religious life, entering a novitiate in either France or Belgium before the Second World War.

At the beginning of the war he was called back to the colours and fought for the Belgian army against the Germans in 1940. Soon after the occupation his brother, the priest, was arrested for his resistance work and shot by the Gestapo. Henri Salman was consumed by an intense hatred of all things German, wanting only revenge. By various means he escaped to England in the late summer of 1940 and joined the small Belgian contingent which had been formed in Britain. After some difficulties with his fellow-countrymen, he eventually joined the Innskilling Dragoon Guards in 9th Armoured Division with the object of going back to Europe to kill Germans at the earliest opportunity.

That is how he contrived to be with the ERY, as they were due to land on D-Day and the "Skins" were not. He showed his commitment to routing the Germans when he took over the Recce Troop. He spoke German fluently as well as English, French and several other European languages besides, so he baffled the Germans on the ground by shouting orders to them to surrender in their own tongue. His appointment to command B Squadron was the summit of his military activities and, as will be seen, his bravery and total disregard of danger brought him the greatest respect and affection of all, especially those of us who served for any time in his Squadron. He was nicknamed "The Monk" by his troops and indeed looked like one. A more detailed account of his life has been written by Ted Wright, but his future exploits will appear at the appropriate time in this narrative.

Chapter 17

THE SEINE, ST VALERY
AND CONFRONTING LE HAVRE

The Regiment, after their four days of rest, largely given up to maintenance and in glorious weather, was ordered with the remainder of the Brigade to help clear the enemy from the loops of the Seine. They were most disappointed that they could not join in the "swan" into northern France and Belgium. The other two regiments in 33 Armoured Brigade were the Northamptonshire Yeomanry and 144 Regiment RAC, later to become 4 RTR.

There were still a large number of Germans in these loops, who had been by-passed by the headlong armoured drive of 2nd British Army to Brussels and Antwerp on the left of the American advance through Central France.

The ERY were ordered to a concentration area near Le Pin in readiness for an attack on one of the loops of the Seine, with the town of Yville-sur-Seine at the neck of the loop and Duclair at the head. To travel from the harbour area near St Pierre-sur-Dives to Le Pin north-east of the mouth of the loop which the ERY was to clear was a revelation. They saw a graveyard of British and German tanks; many dead of both sides. An enormous amount of equipment had been abandoned by the Germans, many a "liberated" vehicle was later driven off by the various regiments; but not for long as a high-level order went forth and most of the vehicles of a "liberated" nature had to be handed in.

They moved through the battle zone and advanced towards St George-du-Vièvre which was in countryside hardly touched by war. The Regiment, as usual, arrived at their concentration area on a Sunday, 27 August. (Nearly all actions and battles seemed to start on a Sunday.)

The advance was to be on a two-squadron front with the Recce Troop leading. The battle for the approaches to Yville was very stiff as the enemy fought hard and fanatically for every inch of ground and for every hour of

159

time to get their remaining forces over the river by ferries, of which eighteen had been established. The Regiment had moved up through Pont Authou in the afternoon and were ready to go through. But, as Major Ellison wrote, "after various orders, counter-orders and disorders, it was decided to stay in the area that night, so, with darkness coming on and mist rising, we moved and spread out to harbour for the night in the open."

Everyone was on the alert and ready at 0630hrs, but nothing happened until 1705hrs, late in the afternoon, when they moved forward a short way and harboured for the night in the open yet again.

The Recce Troop moved out, leading the Regiment, on 29 August, exploring the route forward down the steep hill to Yville. A few enemy were met but they were soon dealt with by machine-gun fire.

Yville is situated in a picturesque area and stands at the gateway to the most beautiful view of this loop in the River Seine.

The Regiment halted on the heights above Yville at dusk and received a most unhealthy reception. There was still fighting at the neck of the loop, which stood on a precipitous road. From the top of the hill the Seine appeared below in a large curve with the left edge immediately below the

160

position where they were waiting. The centre was curling away miles to the east. The assembly point was an orchard on the hill; they had to sit there being mortared for some time. Eventually they moved down a steep zigzag road. B Squadron was leading with orders to push through a burning village below, which was still in enemy hands.

The orders were to find a place where the Regiment could consolidate and harbour for the night. It was intended to advance up the loop at first light. The road down to the village was worse than expected as it snaked through thick woods, with two very steep S-bends on the hill downwards. Through the trees, the fires in the village could be seen, but otherwise it was pitch black and positively eerie.

The Squadron then took a wrong turning in the dark; the road below was blocked, so the remainder were stuck on the hillside all too close together. The zigzags were such that the tanks on one bend were only thirty feet above those on the lower one below. The Germans were having a splendid time shelling them, just missing the doctor's half-track, but fortunately hitting no one. The situation looked very unpleasant as there were still Germans in the village and shells were falling amongst the tanks or screeching over-head, with nobody able to move.

The CO did a good job in personally sorting out the chaos, by moving B Squadron off the road, so that the rest of the Regiment could move slowly forward through the village to a place some two thousand yards beyond. The shelling miraculously stopped, the tanks were formed into a triangle in an open field with guns facing outward and double guards on duty. They were surrounded by enemy positions, but were not attacked. Shells passed constantly overhead, as our own artillery shelled crossing places and roads ahead of the ERY. At around 0200hrs the CO held a conference in the middle of the triangle of tanks and plans were made for the next day. Then a truck came into the triangle, having been through the enemy positions on the way up and delivered mail and newspapers only three days old. This was a welcome bonus for everyone, so the driver and crew of the truck were given lots of praise and thanks.

The ERY were off again at first light the next morning, heading towards Duclair at the head of the loop with A and B Squadrons advancing on either side of the road. The artillery observation officer was with them and as they encountered enemy strong points, he was able to get immediate gun support. "It was a fine sight," as Major Ellison wrote, "to see the whole Regiment tearing across country with an occasional burst of fire from one of the tanks, to silence an enemy position." It was much in the role of a classic armoured regiment's advance, troop supporting troop, going at speed, without supporting infantry. Many prisoners were taken as they passed shelled buildings. Sergeant Colin Brown of the Recce Troop, scouting forward on foot, saw a German going into one of the buildings. He shouted to him to throw out his weapons and come out with his hands above his head, but was horrified when nineteen or twenty Germans surrendered to him as well. He, with another crew-member, then had to march them back to the rear.

Soon they neared the ferry crossing at Duclair; the enemy had got away leaving a confusion of exploding ammunition, with trucks, barns and houses blazing and much abandoned equipment. For the last 300 yards to the ferry the road was one solid mass of enemy vehicles, some intact, some knocked out, plenty of dead Germans, all abandoned by their troops. The scene was one of total destruction, death and chaos. A few prisoners were taken at the ferry and many more came out of the woods and surrendered, as they had not been able to get away over the river to join the general retreat.

The haul in the Seine loop was over 500 vehicles, including ten tanks, a mass of transport of every description, including prams, bicycles, farm and hand carts, every one of them filed with German army equipment. The Regiment gained two half-tracks, some lorries and wireless sets to add to the establishment. Captured cases of brandy did not appear in public, being used to good effect in the officers' and sergeants' messes.

The Yeomanry moved into harbour at 1800hrs, leaving the infantry to deal with the equipment, prisoners and the other spoils of war.

The following morning, 31 August, the Regiment moved out of the loop of the Seine to a position just west of Bourg Achard, where they received orders to advance next day, crossing the Seine at the Bailey bridge at Elbeuf and then going through Rouen to Pavilly, north of the river with the remainder of 33 Armoured Brigade and 51st Highland Division, one of whose special tasks was to liberate St Valery-en-Caux where their predecessors had been cut off and forced to surrender in 1940.

On 1 September the Regiment started to move north of the Seine. A Squadron with 8 Seaforths and the Divisional Recce Regiment (the Derbyshire Yeomanry) moved with the object of reaching the coast and taking Veules-les-Roses, a small town there. This was a long march, but by 1530hrs they reported having reached their objective having met no opposition on the way. A Squadron harboured for the night at Veules-les-Roses just west of St Valery.

The remainder of 51st Highland Division and the rest of 33 Armoured Brigade moved off to harbour at Doudeville, having heard that A Squadron and 8 Seaforths had met no opposition on their way to their objective – a journey of some 85 miles. They also had to cross the Seine at Elbeuf, where there was still only one Class 40 Bailey bridge, so only one tank could cross at a time. Many French people were lining the approach to the bridge, waving and smiling, with children shouting the well-known question *"Cigarettes pour papa?"*

They went through Rouen, poor Rouen which had taken an awful battering from the RAF, but it was noticeable, according to Major Ellison, how damage was worse by the docks and the river area where all the bridges were in the water. Crowds lined the streets, but the tanks could not stop and had to push straight through. The crews saw how ill-clad and strained the children looked in the towns, whereas those in the country around Lisieux, surrounded by excellent farm-land, livestock and poultry, were well fed and healthy. The Yeomanry had had a long day and drive, as they did not arrive at their harbour until the early hours of the morning.

On 2 September A Squadron had the privilege of escorting the leading elements of 51st Division into St Valery unopposed. They stopped just outside the town so the Scotsmen could go in on their own. The Highland Division rejoiced that they had retaken the town where so many of their comrades had been killed or captured in 1940.

As St Valery had been taken unopposed orders were changed: the whole of 33 Armoured Brigade would concentrate prior to moving to the outskirts of Bolbec, coming under command of 49th Division for the attack on Le Havre. A Squadron meanwhile rejoined the Regiment after their excursion to St Valery.

There was still to be no joining in the great "swan" of 2nd Army. So everyone was a little depressed that the Regiment had instead to make a frontal attack on a heavily defended town and seaport, which was by then miles behind the advancing allied forces. But it was necessary to clear good deep-water ports, so that the rapidly advancing armies of the Allies could become less dependent on supply over the beaches and the Mulberry harbour in Normandy.

The ERY moved into and through Bolbec, where British troops had not been before. The town was reported clear and the reception the crews received was almost overwhelming, especially as the column of tanks halted in the centre of the town. Apples, small bottles of Benedictine and other gifts of all descriptions were showered on them. Everybody enjoyed the well-justified tributes.

Trooper Devonshire, who was Major Ellison's wireless operator throughout the campaign, was pretty fed up that they hadn't received much welcome earlier from the French populace and said: "We received a little of this adulation and welcome as we passed through Bolbec en route to Le Havre. I recollect jumping off the tank when we were mobbed and a nice bit of crackling came up and proceeded to give all the crew a smashing kiss. All this was observed by Major Ellison who, with a big grin on his face, had remained standing in the turret." He continued, "The local girls lined the route ahead which bucked us up no end!"

Once through Bolbec they harboured in orchards about four miles from the outskirts of Le Havre. On the way Sergeant Eric Townsend had to get his driver to speed up as they had dropped behind the column, and the Yeomanry was moving very much in convoy. "At that time I was passed by a Brigadier (not ours; I think his name was Waller), who signalled me to stop and climb down. He demanded to know what I had learnt at Bovington about the maximum speed of a tank. I mumbled something about 25mph. He said that I was doing 35mph and told me to put myself under close arrest. I then carried on and on arriving at RHQ decided I should take some kind of action over the incident. I reported to the RSM whose reaction was a quizzical smile. He did, however, take me in front of the CO who had the circumstances explained to him. The look on his face said he would be prepared rather to give me a Mention in Dispatches than the severe reprimand he had to hand out." The Brigadier I had met turned out to be ex-Guards.

*   *   *

On Sunday 3 September B and C Squadrons were supporting the infantry of 49th West Riding Division who were on the left of the I Corps advance along the right bank of the Seine. The north side of the river valley was hilly and well wooded, with deep ravines on the eastern approaches to Le Havre. The immediate objectives were both on the high ground south and south-east of Montvilliers.

B Squadron moved off at 0730hrs, in close support of the infantry to a road running north/south to Montvilliers. They met no opposition up to that point, but as they moved off the road they ran into heavy mortar and shell fire. They nevertheless pushed on and successfully supported the infantry onto their objective on the high ground, where they all dug in.

C Squadron were ready to start at 0700hrs, but eventually did not move until 1345hrs, when they supported two companies of the KOYLI. They had some flail tanks with them of 22nd Dragoons, to clear the minefields known to be in the area. They all achieved their objective, but once on the high ground they too were subjected to heavy mortar and shell fire. At one stage a mobile German anti-tank gun on the left of 3 Troop forced it to withdraw, but it soon regained the ground it had lost.

Whilst B and C Squadrons were engaged in making fairly slow progress on the east side of the River Lezarde, the Divisional Commander ordered the CO to take a force consisting of RHQ, A Squadron, two squadrons of the 49th Recce Regiment with two regiments of field artillery in support, to make towards the coast in the Octeville area. The force was named "Willforce" as Lieutenant Colonel Williamson was in command. They were ordered to take some high ground overlooking the outer defences of Le Havre on the right flank. They moved ten miles without opposition, but on approaching the more open high ground, which was the first objective, they came under heavy fire from artillery and mortars. They stayed on the high ground for the night, holding the ground as a base for future operations.

In order to protect the trapped French civilian population, a truce was called in the afternoon, calling for unconditional surrender of the German garrison; otherwise intensive air bombardment would follow. The terms were refused by the enemy.

British propaganda loud-speakers opened up in the woods near Montvilliers, to try to persuade the Germans of the futility of their position; to tell them that they were well and truly ringed by armour with no chance of escape. This blast of propaganda all went out in the evening with B Squadron harboured nearby. That night was remembered not only for the shells and mortars but for the terrible racket of the loud-speakers.

A Squadron and RHQ also moved into harbour on the high ground near Octeville, but they were not too far as the crow flies, although the hilly and difficult countryside kept them well apart. C Squadron were finally released by their infantry when it was pitch dark, just off the main Le Havre-Lillebonne road.

The following morning, 4 September, B Squadron and their infantry tried to push forward through the minefields and defences surrounding the city, but due to heavy shelling causing many casualties among the infantry, the attack was called off. It was then decided to consolidate and the Squadron harboured in some orchards nearby. Later that day one tank with a 17pdr was ordered to fire at a concrete tower some miles away. Trooper O'Donaghue described the shoot: "We had to shoot at a concrete water tower used by the Germans as an observation post. We went into a farm-yard carrying an artillery officer to range accurately on the target. The only trouble was that the tower was on thin concrete legs. After about twenty shots shooting was stopped. Nothing happened, but next day it fell of its own accord."

A Squadron were sent out to do some probing of the defences, with the 49th Division Recce Regiment. They found they were up against heavily prepared perimeter defences, particularly near Octeville. They succeeded in killing some Germans, and driving all those outside well inside.

Trooper Eric Martin remembered driving Lieutenant Wilfred Crocker, OC Recce Troop, in a very hairy drive to the outskirts of Le Havre and having to move very quickly as some of the big guns in the concrete emplacements began to bear on them.

It was clear that a full corps attack had to be made to capture the well-defended town, so the ERY, with the rest of the Brigade, were pulled back to the area of St Romain where they harboured in apple orchards. The apple crop was tremendous that year, so reversing the tanks under trees laden with apples not only filled the turrets, but the tanks broke many branches. The apple farmers accepted this and were extremely kind to everyone and few tanks were without eggs for breakfast. The water supply locally was unfit for drinking as the French were in the habit of digging latrines to the same depth as their water wells. Cider was the drink and Calvados was distilled from it; so it didn't take long for the locals and our troops to burst into song.

Even so, as soon as the water wagon approached there was a stampede from every direction to fill water containers. The mobile bath unit arrived; there was much maintenance of the tanks and the troops were given all the rest possible.

During this unexpected break Captain Ted Wright came back from hospital, taking over his old position as 2i/c B Squadron, this time under Major Salman who had just been promoted. He was delighted as he had got on well with him in the past. He was even more pleased, as he had his old tank and crew with him.

For the next five days the RAF bombed various parts of Le Havre, causing a great deal of damage to strategic areas. After each raid another ultimatum was dispatched to the enemy. These they ignored; so another dose followed.

On 9 September A and C Squadrons went out on a harassing shoot on known German positions. The five days had been busy times for the officers doing reconnaissance on the ground or studying aerial photographs as well as defence overprints, the latter in great detail.

Civilian evacuees from the town would report where the Germans were, and they, the enemy, were told over the loud-speakers that we knew their exact whereabouts, rubbed in by following up the announcements with accurate artillery bombardment.

Also on 9 September, the Regiment, less B Squadron, moved out to take up position to shoot at various specified targets. It was to be a controlled and concentrated shoot, with ours and the Northamptonshire Yeomanry amounting to some ninety tanks in all. The targets were the fixed defences and German troop concentrations.

B Squadron was to push through gaps made in the extensive minefields and secure a hold within the perimeter. They were amply provided with flail tanks of 1 Lothian and Border Yeomanry to create safe lines for the Squadron to move through. They were to support 2 Seaforths, who with the rest of the Highlanders had by then recovered from two days of typically Scottish celebration in liberating St Valery. During the night of 9/10 September the RAF again attacked using partly anti-personal bombs which exploded just above ground level and left no craters, and also deep penetration bombs to penetrate the concrete blockhouses. It was one of the most accurate bombing raids the Regiment had encountered. When they looked at the area afterwards, everything had been razed to ground level. even the turnip tops!

Preceding this bombing the regimental shoot started at midnight when the ninety Shermans loosed off their guns in one shattering bombardment. This was repeated in successive salvos for about two hours, each tank firing on orders given by the CO. The Navy also took part with their heavy guns and had to retire while the rest with the corps artillery plastered the town all night.

The break-in started at dawn on 11 September. The evening before, B Squadron had moved forward along the edge of a steep ravine. Captain Wright's tank followed a troop of tanks and some flails up a track through a steep wooded area; but the track collapsed after several Shermans had gone by and his tank started to slip. So he dismounted the crew quickly, leaving only the driver and himself aboard, but even then the tank nearly went over a fifty-foot cliff. It had to be pulled out by Technical Adjutant Captain Ernest Clarke with great skill using two Armoured Recovery Vehicles (ARV). It was successfully done but gave them a few nasty moments, in case the tackle gave way. The rest of the Squadron behind them had to find another route up to the start line.

Captain Wright describes the next morning: "Proceedings were opened with a full-scale bombing by the RAF's heavies, designed amongst other things to wreck the massive concrete emplacements with blockbusters."

The "proceedings" on the ground started with a squadron of the 22nd Dragoons and one of the 1 Lothian and Border Yeomanry, using their flail tanks and slowly clearing lanes through the minefields, all of which were covered by enemy anti-tanks guns. On the way through the minefield Captain Wright recognized an old friend in Captain Scott, Technical Adjutant of the Lothians, who told him that fourteen of their flail tanks had been put out of action not so much by anti-tank fire but by the Teller mines which did not go off under the whirling chains of the "Flails" but only when the full weight of the tanks passed over them, the mines having been laid two years before and become corroded in the interval. The two had not met since they had been Troopers together at 51st Training Regiment at Catterick in 1939.

Having cleared the lanes, fascines were laid over an anti-tank ditch, so B Squadron, led by Major Salman, on foot as usual, with 2nd Seaforths soon pushed through the outer defences and "started swanning about" looking for areas to attack. Initially there was some resistance, but the Squadron shot up the opposition from 2000 yards and they quickly surrendered. Major Salman was in his element. Revolver in hand and on foot, in perfect and authoritative German, he ordered the defenders to come out and surrender. He even went into the area of the Doudeville redoubt ahead of both infantry and tanks, and a great many Germans surrendered. His personal tally was several hundred.

With the Squadron Leader way ahead with the infantry, Captain Wright found himself in charge of Squadron HQ and was held up soon after passing the gap in the minefields. One of the surviving strongpoints started some desultory shelling of the area; so he began calling up some artillery support rather than waste probably ineffective 75mm tank ammunition. While doing this he was surprised to see a tall General walking nonchalantly among the shell-bursts. He soon recognized him as General Dempsey, the Commander of 2nd Army himself, not having seen him since Forres days.

Trooper O'Donaghue remembered about Le Havre. "I think it was the only time I really got the wind up. We had to climb up a hill with lots of trees. Having reached the flat top, all we could see were hedges; we were given orders by Sergeant Larter to drive to the end of the hedge and to keep

168

under cover. When we reached the end of the hedge we could see what was in front of us. Jesus! There were gun emplacements; must have been the largest in the world and the guns were pointing straight at us. Before we could do anything someone saw a white flag. They had given up, Thank God! If we'd been hit we would have reached the moon before the Americans!"

They eventually pushed on with the forward platoons of the Seaforths harbouring inside the defences for the night. It had been a "good" day as many hundreds of prisoners were taken, some first shattered by the heavy bombing and then broken by the sight of the tanks moving up and swanning freely around inside the defences, and Major Salman barking orders to them in their own language!

At first light on 12 September the advance continued. A certain amount of opposition was still met, but with Major Salman once again on foot, leading two troops in front of the infantry and calling yet again in German, the enemy poured out in surrender. His battle cry was "Drive them out" and altogether 1,300 prisoners were taken by the Squadron. Trooper O'Donoghue was well into the taking of prisoners. "Trooper Harvey, another of the troop's gunners, and I were out of our tanks searching prisoners for weapons and most other things. Whilst in this process I saw coming towards me a horse-drawn cart, with two Jerry soldiers driving it – nice and slow. Anyway I had them covered and in the cart was a full case of rum; also I think they must have robbed the bank at Le Havre as there were thousands of notes. I got two German flags – I mean real ones; big black and white and red with big swastikas on them – great, until our officer, Lieutenant Donald Hepworth, heard I had them and asked for one. How could I refuse such a pleasant demand? He sent it to his parents who afterwards exhibited it in the foyer of the local cinema. He got a few fags from home and never offered me one."

What Trooper Timms remembers most about Le Havre was the awful sound of the flame-throwers used on the pill boxes near Octeville and the screams of the occupants.

The heavy bombing by both the RAF and guns of the Navy and Army made a big contribution to the surrender which was an open-and-shut business once the infantry and tanks moved in. The justification for this is set out above, plus the fact that the Regiment had no fatal casualties and those of the infantry were far fewer than had been expected.

By mid-afternoon B Squadron were "bowling along a concrete road, the defence of Le Havre effectively over". On their way out Captain Wright looking round with his top half well out of his turret, suddenly saw just ahead of him some telephone wires drooping just above the tank. Either he was going to be caught across the chest and deposited on the ground, or if he ducked he was likely to be strangled. He chose the former and was remorselessly yanked out of the turret, back over the engine compartment and dumped unceremoniously on the road behind. He then chased after the tank, yelling (quite uselessly) to them to stop. Eventually the rest of the crew realized that he was not with them, stopped and he was able to scramble aboard. As he said, "an amusing end to what could have been a disastrous battle". The remainder of the ERY were moved back, not having been required at all.

Chapter 18

IN RESERVE AND THEN ON TO HOLLAND

For nearly a month the Regiment was grounded while great events were taking place to the north. The first great drive by XXX and XII Corps into Belgium had been held by hastily gathered but brave and seasoned defenders, mostly parachute units under General Student, who had made good use of a few days' breathing space while the attack was delayed when it outran its supplies. When the offensive was resumed the defence proved tougher than expected, but great efforts were made to reach the jumping-off point for the launching of the airborne landing of the Anglo-American I Airborne Corps with whom XXX Corps with only a single road available were set to link up and relieve the lightly armed airborne troops. After bruising fighting, crossings over the River Maas at Grave and the River Waal at Nijmegen were captured. The 1st British Airborne Division held one end of the "Bridge Too Far" over the Lower Rhine at Arnhem, but were eventually overwhelmed before support could reach them in time. 21st Army Group's attempt to end the war by the end of 1944 failed and northern Holland had to endure another winter of famine before liberation came in the Spring of 1945. The survivors of 1st Airborne Division, just over 2,000 of the 10,000 dropped, were evacuated on the night of 25–26 September across the Lower Rhine.

B Squadron and the Highlanders having broken the crust of the defences, the road to Le Havre was clear and 49th Division moved in on the left along the River Seine, with 51st Division cleaning up on the right. The town, and particularly the whole dock area, was a mass of mines, booby traps and rubble. The concrete emplacements were massive, but had been thrown about like nine-pins. It was still a hazardous place to be since the local resistance were having a field-day letting off their guns at anyone and anything. Altogether over 11,000 prisoners were taken, of which 1,350 were captured by B Squadron alone.

It will be remembered that the Regiment had landed at these very docks in 1940, and had been among the prime troops in liberating it. It was now unrecognizable from five years before. None of those veterans who had landed in 1940 recognized the town at all, even the Rue des Galleons which had been obliterated. However, a stock of champagne had been freed amongst vast stores of food for consumption by the German garrison. The British soldiers of all ranks did it justice! At least a million bottles of champagne were captured much of which was sent to hospitals.

After Le Havre was captured the Yeomanry settled down at Gerville on the coast north of the town, between Étretat and Fécamp. Fécamp was a town well known for the Benedictine Monastery, which distilled the excellent liqueur of the same name. A quick dash was made to Fécamp to collect some of the stock left by the Germans before the Highlanders could get all of it, but ours was purchased from the good monks! Shortly after their arrival, the 51st Highland Division arranged a special "Beating of the Retreat" at St Valery with pipes and drums in honour of their predecessors. Trooper Buckingham took the opportunity to be present. "The massed pipes and drums of those famous regiments gave a stirring, yet moving, performance, which was a privilege to witness."

Now concentrated at Gerville together with the remainder of the Brigade, the ERY settled down to a routine of squadron parades, maintenance, baths, swimming and games. Other things were happening as well. Captains Norman Waller and Len Cullington had the inspirational idea of taking a jeep and trailer to Rheims to see what champagne they could buy before the Americans had it all. Off they went, with suitable subscriptions from the officers. They ran down Charles Heidsieck himself who said how delighted he was to meet some British instead of Americans, whom he described as "Les Primitives" or "Les Barbares"! (He was a great Anglophile!) The jeep and trailer were filled to capacity. Our two Captains declined an invitation to dinner with M Heidsieck, but had a night out on the town instead. When they came to pay with "invasion francs" next morning they were refused as Heidsieck was quite happy to accept a cheque drawn on an English bank. It is not recorded if it was ever even cashed.

Whilst at Gerville the Curé of the village invited the CO, Major Ellison, the Adjutant and Major Salman, to dinner with the Mayor and the Chef de Resistance. His speech after dinner showed the welcome and gratitude of the French in this part of France.

Major Ellison took the opportunity to visit Ivry la Bataille, after four years absence, to collect the Regimental band instruments, which had had to be abandoned there in 1940. They had been left in a factory and the key was handed to the Mayor. Major Ellison was stunned to find the factory empty;

North
Sea

Ijselmeer

HOLLAND

Neder Rijn Arnhem

Waal

Nijmegen

Rhine

s'Hertogenbosch

Vught

Helvoirt

Xanten

Oudenbosch

Boxtel

Schundel

St Oedenrode

Maas

Tilburg

Eindhoven

Venlo

Turnhout

Roermond

GERMANY

Antwerp

Dilson

Roer

BELGIUM

Liège

Meuse

Namur

Ciney

Miles

0   10   20   30

173

it had been occupied by SS troops and some of the instruments had been sent off to Germany. But the Mayor, Monsieur Thirburville, had taken as many as he could from under the noses of the Germans and stored them in a loft in his own factory and was delighted to hand them back. He had some of the Fife and Forfar Yeomanry's as well. Had he been caught, he would undoubtedly have been shot.

During their stay of several weeks stuck at Gerville, the Regiment were able to hold several dances, which were extremely popular; not least the food that was provided. When the food arrived, usually sandwiches, it was seized on by the locals and as soon as a soldier hove in sight carrying a plate he was almost felled to the ground in the rush, the plate going for the pro-verbial "ball of chalk" leaving the less fussy contestants to scramble for the remnants.

Captain Wright made an unsuccessful foray to the chalk cliffs to look for more fossils but on the way back found a large number of wild mushrooms, only to lose half when he was chased by an aggressive bull on his way across the field. That ensured the full digestion of the excellent dinner he had had with Major Ellison and several others the previous evening at Étretat on a magnificent turbot. Then on 20 September he was deputed to take thirty 3-tonner trucks on secondment to boost the supply-run up into Belgium. The whole of I Corps were grounded in the Le Havre area, as well as 33 Armoured Brigade, so all available transport was needed to support the main army thrust north. As an officer in a fighting squadron, he much resented this job and grumbled, feeling that the duty should fall to Captain Waller in HQ Squadron, but to no avail. He went off with a jeep and another for his assistant, Lieutenant M. A. Knight, and the trusty 3-tonners. After a few experiments they developed a first-class convoy discipline, an espirit de corps was established and the transport was kept in the best state of repair possible. But they had to rectify the short-cuts the makers had taken to turn out the lorries for the invasion from the factory as fast as they could. The trucks proved to have short-life engines which were prone to give up the ghost with the big mileages involved. They did, however, manage to contribute to the build up of what became enormous store-dumps and they all felt that they had achieved some worthwhile success.

Of the many experiences they had, Captain Wright remembered that, returning from Belgium on one trip, they took a wrong turning near Mons. The road soon became narrower and narrower until it petered out in a grassy and overgrown track. Looking for somewhere to turn the convoy round at the end of this they came to a small hamlet somewhere near Cambrai. On asking where they were in rather broken French, Lieutenant Knight discovered that the convoy was the first and only military the locals had seen from either side since 1940 when a small unit of the Wermacht blundered into the hamlet too. So much for the German occupation.

Many members of the Regiment went into Fécamp and tried, amongst other things, the Benedictine liqueur which was even better cut with brandy. Trooper Buckingham said it taught him to appreciate liqueurs! As opposed to that, Trooper O'Donaghue remembered that many of his Squadron preferred beer to liqueur and also visited the "houses of pleasure". Basically everyone was able to relax from the noise, smells and sights of battle, calm ragged nerves, get physically fit, maintain their tanks and feel human. The weather was patchy with overcast closing in after some hot days.

C Squadron's football team won the Brigade football competition.

The local French were soon foraging in the empty transport lines, looking for anything that had been thrown out.

On 2 October everything suddenly started up again. The CO was told that the ERY would be moving to Holland to help clear the Scheldt estuary. By 2000hrs it was all called off, so everyone relaxed again. But not for long because the lorried transport, the detachment having only very recently returned, left on 13 October for Holland.

The tanks were loaded on to transporters and left on 14 October arriving at Herentals in Belgium south of the Dutch border the next day. Trooper Buckingham's transporter had broken down before crossing into Belgium; so they had to finish the journey on their own tracks. They spent the night in a village and went into the local estaminet for a drink, where they soon met up with the local French. Singing was started by the French and was replied to by an English song. It soon became a great sing-song, with everyone thoroughly enjoying themselves.

In Belgium there were grapes and other appetising produce for sale in all the shops and on the roadside. The crews were given a warm welcome by the Belgians, with many of them being given hospitality and some home comforts. They stopped in Herentals for two days then moved on to Holland, to Eindhoven, the town where the large Philips electrical factory seemed to own everything in the vicinity.

There was some interchange between the regiments in the Brigade, as our A Squadron relieved B Squadron of 144 RAC on guard duty. On 18 October the ERY moved to St Oedenrode north of Eindhoven into a wooded concentration area. Here they linked up with 152 Brigade of the 51st Division for future operations to start clearing the area south of the River Maas. As it was by then mid-October, it was becoming duller, and the ground was flat and depressing. It also became wetter and wetter, making the land sodden and everything else too, so the small fields with ugly wire surrounding them soon became quagmires.

To make matters worse, a Major Sullivan arrived at the Regiment on 20 October. He was from the 14th/20th Hussars, had never been in action and was a regular from Home Forces. Ostensibly, it emerged that he was to take over B Squadron, as Major Salman was officially only on attachment to the Regiment from the Belgian Army in which he still held the rank of Captain. To us he was promoted to Major in command of B Squadron, wore our Regimental badges and British Army uniform and a Major's crown. His leadership of both the Recce Troop and B Squadron had been outstanding and his bravery undoubted. The CO, who seemed to have an excellent instinct for this sort of situation, sent Major Sullivan off to A Squadron to get a taste of action.

He was sent with a scout car on patrol on 23 October with the intention that he should find the position of the forward troops, in the direction of St Michael's Gestal, but he was soon reported missing. He had apparently succeeded in driving straight into an outpost of the German defenders, got his scout car ditched in trying to withdraw, was wounded in the hand trying to get his pivot-mounted machine gun into action, was captured, but later escaped. That was the last the Regiment heard of him. Major Salman was not disturbed and B Squadron breathed a sigh of relief.

During the night of 22 Oct, the Regiment having moved up into their concentration area, half of A Squadron under Captain Len Cullington supporting 5 Camerons and C Squadron moving off with 2 Seaforths. The other half of A Squadron, under Major Phillips, was with 5 Seaforths. Information was very scrappy about the enemy, but it was thought they were thin on the ground. They were expected to use all manner of demolition and other devices to delay the advance.

The objective was to advance towards the Boxtel-s'Hertogenbosch road. The battle started with a heavy artillery bombardment; A Squadron soon took some prisoners, but they also lost two tanks on mines, without injury to either crew. The infantry were rushed on to their objectives in Kangaroos. Six were attached to each troop; it was the first such attack with infantry carried into action with the tanks. The fighting here was most unpleasant. It was flat country, so the whole area was bullet-swept, each stream or canal had to be forced, with German mines and anti-tank guns at every crossing aimed to shoot down the road which was the only means of approach, the land being flooded too so that the tanks were silhouetted. Still the advance continued with the Regiment making for the gap between the small industrial town of Schundel and Boxtel to the west of Tilburg.

The advance continued to clear a way up to the Maas. 1 Troop A Squadron "recovered" an American pilot from the village of Kateren, who had been shot down and crashed there three weeks before. He had been hidden by the brave Dutch farmers who knew that if they were caught hiding an allied airman they would be shot. This area was soon known to have harboured many such airmen, some of whose hiding places were the height of ingenuity.

The following day the advance was due to continue, but a reconnaissance of the next water obstacle by the CO and A Squadron Leader was interrupted by a machine gun opening up at them from the opposite bank and the two senior officers had to take an undignified dive into a ditch full of water to escape.

The assault crossing nonetheless went ahead during which one of the tank commanders, Sergeant George Dry, was shot in the head. He had been with the Regiment since before the war. He died instantly. Trooper Timms, his driver, recalled, "the most dreadful thing was losing George Dry with a gaping head wound".

Later in the day the crossing was carried successfully.

At night the Regiment was able to harbour around barns and farmhouses. The weather was terrible as it grew colder and very, very wet. Most of these billets were taken over from the Germans who left them smelly and unpleasant. All the furniture and household goods they had not looted and removed had been hacked, broken and abused. Some of their personal habits were foul too: "worse than animals" was the general opinion.

The Squadrons not being used in these attacks were kept back in dripping woods. Captain Wright remembers the dreary skirl of the bagpipes, played each evening to lift the spirits of the Highlanders. They had the opposite effect on Englishmen.

On the evening of 24 October the CO called an emergency conference when he told his officers that ERY had to break off action in support of the Highlanders and the following day move to the area of s'Hertogenbosch and come under command of 53rd Welsh Division. This meant pulling out of their river and canal-hopping actions. At 0600hrs the following morning the ERY moved off in a westerly drive entailing a road march of 25 miles, as most of the bridges were blown. B Squadron, with 1 East Lancs, were immediately rushed in to the southern end of the town; on the way they just had time to pick up Major Salman who had been at the CO's Order Group. They were to support 158 Brigade who were already in the middle of a heavy battle in the city. The tank in which Trooper O'Donaghue was gunner broke down on the way and had to follow on its own in the dark. "Most eerie," he remarked.

s'Hertogenbosch is surrounded by canals and old fortifications dating from the 15th Century, so there were several bridges to be won. The Squadron pushed round the southern rampart, crossed a canal-bridge at the intersection of three canals and joined up with their infantry. It was the first time the Regiment had been involved in street fighting and they were engaged now because the powers-that-be thought that Shermans working with infantry were better able to cope with street fighting than the thinner-skinned Cromwells of 5 Royal Inniskilling Dragoon Guards. The Regiment, however, thought the reason a pretty thin one.

B Squadron were teamed up with a very competent unit, the 1 East Lancs, and one troop was with each of the leading companies of infantry. Fortunately the infantry had suffered few casualties as they crossed the first few bridges. The town being surrounded by water, the only approach on the east side was along the ramparts on the southern edge. This route heading clockwise round the ramparts was actually suggested by the CO. The water meadows on the left flank were flooded and impassable; so the left flank was protected and the attackers only had to concern themselves with the right flank and what was ahead of them. Self-propelled anti-tank guns opened up as soon as any tanks poked their noses round a corner or bend; so artillery was called for to silence them. Captain Wright found that the supporting battery commander was an old friend from his Oxford days.

The infantry then continued their advance, but came under concentrated fire from a big yellow building which turned out to be the Palace of Justice (or Law Courts). Major Salman had hardly been in his tank during the action and spent his time out with the leading infantry clearing buildings, carrying only his revolver. He used to shout at the Germans in their own language, as he had done at Le Havre, ordering them to surrender. If they didn't, he shot them.

When the Law Courts needed to be cleared, the "Intrepid Belge", as Major Salman was called by both the Infantry and the Artillery, jockeyed two of Lieutenant John Davies' tanks into position. These proceeded to plaster the building with high explosive. Major Salman then led the infantry in on foot and cleared the building of the enemy floor by floor. As it caught fire twenty prisoners came out with their hands up.

Once the Law Courts were well and truly burning the advance continued to the next bridge, when again heavy fire was met, causing some casualties to the infantry. Now tanks went in on their own with machine guns and 75s blazing away and silenced the strong point. A few yards short of the next bridge, the supporting troop was met by a self-propelled anti-tank gun, which opened up at close range. Lieutenant Davies in the leading tank was hit and his tank brewed up. All his crew got out except for the driver who was wounded. Lieutenant Davies managed to pull him out of the tank and dragged him to safety, whilst another tank of his troop gave effective covering fire. The light was now failing and the Squadron was over half way round the southern perimeter; so they pulled back five hundred yards and laagered for the night on the wide rampart.

At the same time that B Squadron was moving on the southern perimeter, C Squadron to their right was supporting 1/5 Welch Regiment and having a similar battle through the middle of the town, more difficult because not only were they in streets with tall buildings on either side, but civilians kept crossing over and not keeping clear of the fighting. Sergeant Townsend recalled how difficult it was when civilians were looking down from the windows of the upper floors of the buildings and the Germans were taking advantage of this by mixing with the civilians and lobbing grenades on to the tops of the tank turrets. It was further impossible to elevate the guns far enough to reach the windows. They did, however, manage to keep up the advance and capture several blocks of buildings, hitting quite a number of the defenders and taking prisoners in the process. They had finally cleared the main street through the town, so at last light they too pulled back to harbour.

The next day two troops of C Squadron moved out at 0900hrs in support of 1/5 Welch Regiment and gave heavy covering fire against the buildings and enemy positions on the far side of the canal forming the main water-barrier to the west. The infantry stormed over the Wilhelmina Bridge and established a bridgehead beyond. Things got very hot after that. Sergeant Morrell was held up badly in the wreckage of a building. He had a nasty time as an SP anti-tank gun crew spotted him and were gradually shooting pieces off the corner of the building so they could get a clear shot at him. However, the other tanks in the troop were able to bring a great deal of fire to bear on the opposition; so the building-entangled Sherman was able to make its escape.

179

There were several more anti-tank guns covering the bridge and they were making things so hot that the Squadron had to pull back. One of the Troop Leaders, Second Lieutenant C. W. Laing, was shot in the head by a sniper and later died of his wounds. He had led his troop well in most unpleasant conditions and their effort was a big factor in the clearing of this part of the city.

Meanwhile, B Squadron were still at the southern end of the canal supporting 1 East Lancs. They were in a position to be able to attack the enemy from the rear and take some of the pressure off C Squadron. This was successfully achieved, more prisoners being taken and Major Salman again leading the tanks and infantry on foot. The main road bridge on the exit road to the south-west had been half demolished. The area was swept by machine-gun fire, artillery and an SP anti-tank gun which was also lurking about. The infantry had secured a toe-hold on the far side of the bridge, but there was no means of getting vehicles across until the bridge could be replaced. "We hung about waiting for an assault bridge (on a Churchill chassis) to be brought up. It took about a couple of hours before we got the message that 'Holdfast's erection' as it was coded on the radio was on its way. When it did arrive it was festooned with all the town's tram-wires!" reported Captain Wright. The bridge was duly deposited across the canal, so B Squadron were able to work their way up to one of the main roundabouts and many more prisoners were taken. Flame-throwing Crocodiles were also used in support against strongpoints. As it became too dark for the tanks to see effectively, they moved once more back into harbour. Trooper Laurie Elvin thought how strange it was that they seemed to have lodgings for the night, went out fighting all day and returned to the lodgings the following night. "Like a regular job!" he thought. It was also his twenty-first birthday.

At about 0715 the next day, 27 October, two troops of C Squadron moved up to support 7 Royal Welch Fusiliers when a counter-attack was launched by the enemy. The Germans sent in about a hundred infantry, one tank and a self-propelled gun. C Squadron found the gun and destroyed it, so the Germans thought better of pressing on and withdrew.

Although the main attack had to be postponed to clear the rest of the town up to the full length of the eastern bank of the canal, this did eventually go in at noon. The objective was reached by 1545hrs that afternoon and C Squadron had taken over a hundred more prisoners.

Off they went again at 1630hrs and captured some of the town's commercial area and the peninsula beyond the town itself.

180

B Squadron were directed to support the infantry in an attack on a large barracks in the commercial part near Vught. This was to be a large-scale battalion attack with the divisional 25pdrs and Medium artillery from Corps plus flame throwers as well. Major Henri Salman pleaded with the CO of the infantry that the Germans had already left, so there was no point in damaging good buildings or "Winter Billets" as he used to put it. He even offered to go in on foot to prove the point, but his offer was refused. So artillery and flame throwers made no small mess of the buildings with a tremendous clatter as the tiles came down. The infantry went in un-opposed, proving Major Salman's reading of the battle to be right as usual. As soon as they went into the buildings, the Germans who had evidently been watching the bombardment from the other side of the Maas, and guessing what would happen, promptly plastered them with gunfire from the north side of the river which caused unnecessary infantry casualties.

That night a young Second Lieutenant Paul Mace arrived at B Squadron, having been brought up from rear echelon in the morning. "I was sent up to the Squadron after they harboured that night and went to join George Jenkin's No 4 Troop. Although welcomed with polite indifference, I was no doubt thought a liability rather than an asset at that moment."

"The following morning, 28 October, I was given a tank to command and told to follow the Squadron Leader, whom I had met the previous evening. He had asked the minimum of questions and I had been given a billet in which to sleep. He promptly set off down a street on foot, with me following along behind. He turned and shouted, 'Come along, Pol; this way'. We worked our way up the street with some buildings on either side and he went into a doorway whilst I halted the tank and looked for any Germans. My gunner had explained what was happening and what we had to do. Out of the building Major Salman had gone into came a load of Germans with their hands in the air. We covered them with our guns, but the infantry then took charge of them, and we trundled on up the street. Later that day we were withdrawn. I think we fired the machine gun once and the 75mm once also. I know that I was glad the British Army wore khaki uniforms. I think I was more scared of showing that I was scared than I was of the enemy! This ended our battle for s'Hertogenbosch."

The battle there was recorded by war photographers; Lieutenant Jenkin's tank was shown arriving at the town and in another, later printed in the national press, of a father dragging his two small daughters along a road using Sergeant Rose's tank as protection. When, in 1984, the city of s'Hertogenbosch celebrated the 50th anniversary of their liberation Ted

Wright and a party of the Regiment were there and he was introduced to the family including one of the little girls, by then middle-aged. The father seen in the photograph was dead, but his widow was present. She, pregnant at the time of the photograph, had been following her husband with another of the children. As they made their way across the open, they were escorted all the way by one of the ERY scout cars to protect them from the hail of small arms fire. This was driven by Corporal Frank Hodgson whom Ted was proud to introduce to the family in 1984 as he was in the ERY party as well.

The praise of 1 East Lancs and 158 Brigade was tremendous for the performance of the ERY and Major Salman, "our Intrepid Belge", in particular. He was awarded an immediate DSO for his bravery at Le Havre and s'Hertogenbosch. It says much for the Yeomanry's adaptability that they had driven straight into action on 25 October supporting a formation they had never met before and clicked instantly.

One recollection of Trooper O'Donoghue of this battle was, "Funny people, the Dutch". He wrote, "We were parked down a side turning when not actually in action, and on Sunday the Dutch people came round looking at the tanks, all dressed in their best Sunday clothes, and the men smoking big green cigars."

This had been a hard battle and a first experience of street fighting. The crews were glad of a rest the following day, although for some days more the German artillery bombarded the area. It was a sad sight to see the defending garrison's dead horses lining the main street into the city, killed by shellfire. Most of the Wehrmacht's infantry divisions depended entirely on horse-drawn transport. The locals were not above supplementing their rations by some butchery on the dead horses.

The Yeomanry moved out on 30 October to support 71 Brigade of the Welch Division to the area around Helviort. But nothing came of this except extensive reconnaissance. They came back under 33 Armoured Brigade on 31 October, and remained in the area of s'Hertogenbosch sending patrols to the Maas to round up stragglers of "Muffs" as the Dutch called the Germans, who might still be lurking in the area.

After that the weather turned foul again with pouring rain which never seemed to stop; the low-lying, flat countryside was waterlogged and depressing. Any tank off the road had to flounder through thick, glutinous mud. As no one ever seemed to be dry, it was difficult to keep warm. "I have hated rain ever since! You never forget the smell of wet serge nor of slightly oiled wet metal, the soaked tarpaulins and the slippery touch of the hands on machinery," Second Lieutenant Mace commented with feeling.

On 3 November the ERY were then put on notice to support their old friends 51st Highland Division again in an attack on the Aftwaterings Canal. Moving up to the Canal, Sergeant Morrell's tank hit a mine and brewed up straight away. It was burnt out, but all the crew escaped. He remembered that the bins were full of sardines which the chaps disliked and used for bartering with the locals. "We could smell them frying for a long time after."

More canal crossings were undertaken between 3 and 23 November and were carried out in terrible weather, with the countryside all but impassable; the mud churned up must have been as bad as anything in the First World War.

During that time B Squadron did an interesting controlled shoot. They were lined up facing the enemy on a white tape laid down for accuracy. Each tank commander had had to synchronize his watch and at the appointed time the Squadron had to fire as one. Each salvo from twenty 75mm guns made a spectacular noise and a number of these were loosed off; but then the order was given "Up one turn, left one turn — FIRE." This was a touch introduced by Major Salman from his days in the Belgian artillery, and the idea was to cause havoc to any rear headquarters, particularly generals who might by pure chance have been lurking about behind the German lines. The impression was that we probably only stirred up a lot of mud. It had been an interesting shoot nonetheless.

A Squadron on one of these crossings were given the task of towing boats down to the canal so the infantry could make the crossing, all bridges having been blown. The tanks, artillery and "Crocodiles" (flame throwing Churchills) brought down a large concentration of fire, so that the infantry were able to cross without difficulty and establish a bridgehead on the other side.

"I personally saw a flame thrower in action," writes Second Lieutenant Mace, "when we were trying to clear one pill box. The noise of the 'woosh' of the squirt of burning fuel was furious. The jet of flame went straight through the embrasure of the pill box. I heard, even through my headset and all the noise of the guns, engines and other turmoil, the screams of the occupants of that pill box as they were ignited. We shot them as they came out all on fire. It was not a pleasant sight."

He goes on with some more personal reminiscences. "That night we harboured in a farm; the crews were in a comfortable barn. Outside it still poured with rain. We had been out to check our troop's tanks. Some of us went into the barn to see all was comfortable. We opened the door, no words were spoken – only the sound of the glorious music of Beethoven's Violin Concerto coming from the wireless. Everyone was just taken up with the magic of this sound. What a contrast to the sounds of the day!

"I also remember supporting the Seaforths on a canal crossing and being ordered to do a shoot on a farmhouse across the canal. We fired a great deal of HE with fuses set to airburst. When it was over I was talking to Lieutenant Jenkin; he said, 'That was good shooting (praise indeed!), if you meant it!' Deflated! I also remember having to get out of the tank to relieve myself as we had thrown overboard all the shell cases usually used for that purpose. I felt very naked, especially as at that point the Germans started air-bursting our position. I was back in that tank with the hatch closed very quickly!

"We were next sent down to the Venlo-Roermond district where we did the same job of canal-hopping. The good people of this part of Holland were very religious, poor and kept their animals under the same roof as the family. The wife would often be seen squatting, relieving herself in nearly any part of the property, not batting an eyelid if we came across her. They were brave these people; we saw many escape-chambers, used by the RAF during the occupation, constructed in small haystacks. We crossed the Nederwert canal as one of the last of this round of operations, and a press photographer took our troop as it was crossing. I can even recognize myself in the tank just about to come off the bridge. I remember seeing this photographer and asking my gunner if he thought he was a panzer-faust operator. 'Nar, he's a war-photographer!' He was nearly a dead one."

On that action the Regiment acquired a Stuart tank which the Germans had captured earlier when they overran an American formation and had used as a listening post. It was concealed in a haystack inside the perimeter of what became the infantry Battalion HQ. It was the latest model with twin Cadillac engines in first class order and it was taken on the strength of the Recce Troop with great alacrity. Unlike their other Stuarts which had air-cooled radial engines, this one was water-cooled which resulted in slight embarrassment later.

On 20 November the ERY were pulled out of line and moved by transporter through Eindhoven via Rosendaal to a small town called Oudenbosch where they were destined to spend nearly a month. This was a remarkable town near the estuary of the Maas. For a church it had a magnificent 1/7th scale replica of St Peter's, Rome, together with a monastery in which the Yeomanry were housed. This building was modern in that it had central heating, and was well equipped with baths and lavatories, in stark contrast to the primitive farms and homesteads of the area in which we had been operating for the past month.

The Yeomanry were billeted in the Monastic School, where there were separate messes and curtained-off cells to sleep in. One of the bathrooms on the lower ground floor actually had at least twelve large baths in it, and plenty of hot water too.

All troops were well looked after; the cooks produced some good food with the rations available plus some extras in the shape of chickens and other items which bartering produced. Fresh bread was perhaps one of the luxuries remembered best. It was, of course, a relief for all to be under a proper roof and not out in the constant rain all the time. The tanks were given a thorough overhaul, many of them being stripped right down to replace worn components. It was expected that the ERY would be in these billets for at least a month, with Christmas there too.

There was a large assembly room with a stage in the monastery and at least one regimental dance was organized and very well attended. The very junior officers were ordered to act as unofficial "chuckers out" should anything get out of hand. There was nearly the same scramble by the locals for sandwiches as had happened at dances at Fécamp, but it was all good-humoured.

We were taught how to prepare for the new SVDS (Super Velocity Discarding Sabot) ammunition for the 17pdr Fireflies which we were told could even penetrate a Royal Tiger tank. Everyone was a little sceptical!

There were local leave arrangements to Antwerp, so there could be some rest and a change of climate; to go to the clubs set up by the Welfare services, or the cinema to see the latest films. Antwerp was in "Doodle Bug Alley" and the V1s and V2s were sometimes targeted on the city, so it was not always restful.

Second Lieutenant Mace recalls: "One did land on 16 December and three of the Regiment were killed. Second Lieutenant Keith Loughlin and I were on day leave, but in charge of the party and had to identify the three who had been killed, after we had spent some time helping to clear casualties from the wreckage."

Several people had interesting experiences whilst in Oudenbosch. Trooper Laurie Elvin was in his bed half-asleep when suddenly he thought he was dying – he saw just above him floating in the air a glowing crucifix which was becoming brighter all the time. He was so startled that he woke completely and saw on the wall above his head that there was in fact a crucifix – a luminous one!

Trooper O'Donoghue spent his time off getting to know some of the local Dutch people. His recollection was that the Dutch would give anything for "French Letters" as condoms were called in those days. He did a good trade, he said.

Lieutenant Schilizzi, the Intelligence Officer, recalled the generosity of the monks. "Many of us, including me, made use of the talents of the Artist Brother, and I still have a pencil sketch he made of me, for which I paid him in chocolate – his great solace, as he said he was a chronic insomniac."

The Brothers were kindness itself to the Regiment and helped look after them extremely well.

There was a parade one day before the Brigadier and another later before the Divisional Commander, and it was then that Major Salman's DSO was announced. B Squadron were very proud of him and his exploits.

There was also a visit from an ENSA team playing Noel Coward's *Blithe Spirit*. This had been organized by Major Ellison who knew Ambrosine Phillpots, the leading lady. She was married to a colleague of his in his peace-time job. As he knew Ambrosine personally, he had asked her if there was any possibility of them coming to front-line troops like us and giving a performance. They had a Sunday free in their busy schedule and arranged two shows for the whole of the Brigade. Emlyn Williams was in the male lead.

At dinner after the performances Lieutenant Schilizzi sat next to Ambrosine who took his name and his parents' telephone number. When she returned to England, she phoned his parents to say she had met Stephen and that all was well with him.

The top stars in the theatre always came to the front-line troops and their kindness in conveying messages to the families at home was much appreciated. All of us who saw the play loved it, including the Brothers, who asked for a copy of the script. They roared at all the jokes and were much amused at the subject of the play.

Another story told by Second Lieutenant Mace goes: "A day or so after the *Blithe Spirit* performance, I was sent off with a section of 3-tonners and the "Coal Brother" to Aachen to collect coke and coal. This was to be our contribution to heating the Monastery over Christmas. There was some skirmishing on the way but it didn't stop us, nor did the terrible weather, blizzards of snow. We collected the fuel and struggled back to Oudenbosch; but found no Regiment. There I met Captain Ken Smith who was in charge of the rear party consisting of the soft vehicles. He told me to get ours un-loaded and then join the Regiment myself as quickly as possible. Unloading was swiftly carried out by many willing Brothers. Once the trucks were empty of coal we refilled them with supplies and went on down to where the Regiment was, somewhere between Brussels and Louvain. It was a nightmare of a journey."

Chapter 19

THE BATTLE OF THE BULGE

The "Battle of the Bulge" came as a total surprise to the Allies. In great secrecy the Germans had refitted their armoured reserves and formed a new Army Group B consisting of three Armies; 6 SS Panzer, 5 Panzer and a holding army, 7, of four infantry divisions. On two roads through the wooded and hilly Ardennes, they had attacked at the junction of the 1st and 3rd US Armies on a sector thought to be impenetrable and weakly held by a few US divisions resting from action elsewhere. Thick fog prevented the Allied air forces from flying and a quick breakthrough was achieved. Field Marshal Montgomery took command of all Allied forces north of the Bulge and moved his only reserve, XXX Corps, to block the way to Brussels and Antwerp, reinforced by formations rushed over from Britain. The first attack began on 16 December, but the Americans held the shoulders of the Salient with great gallantry, especially at Bastogne, and once the fog had cleared so that aircraft could fly, the advance soon ran out of steam. By 27 December Field Marshal Montgomery actually sent General Horrocks, the Commander of XXX Corps, back home to rest before the next big battle for which his Corps had to plan. 51st Highlanders and 53rd Welsh Divisions with 33 Armoured Brigade under command, were moved alongside the US 1 Army to reinforce the action to drive in the northern flank of the attack. Orders were that 52nd Welsh Division had to fight until exhausted, when 51st Highland Division would take over. 33 Armoured Brigade would support each Division in turn.

At 1830hrs on 19 December there was a CO's conference at Oudenbosch and the Regiment was ordered to be ready to leave at first light on 20 December. This meant that all the Christmas preparations were abandoned or at least put in limbo and many of the luxuries we had gathered were pilfered from our transport in turn. Tanks had to be filled up with fuel and ammunition and the equipment of the crews loaded back on board. It was hard work and few people had much sleep that night. Anyone who did get some was up again by 0500hrs.

The Brothers from the Monastery all got up to see the ERY depart and many had tears running down their cheeks as the tanks rumbled out. It had been an unforgettable time for all spent with the Brothers under the roof of the Monastic School of St Louis in Oudenbosch.

The advance party found an area south of Louvain allocated to the Regiment. There were some tanks left behind as they were off the road or had engines stripped down. Sergeant Davis, one of the Sergeant Mechanics, was ordered to have all 'dead' vehicles fit as soon as possible and to take them all to a place called Braybos. The convoy included the three German half-tracks collected in the loop of the Seine and likewise the CO's caravan.

The CO, who had been attending Brigade conferences, gave his officers as much information as possible. The Germans had broken through the American lines in the hilly country of the Ardennes and had pushed further into Belgium than was thought possible or expected. Maps had been captured showing intended routes through Namur, Dinant and sweeping on to Antwerp and the sea. 33 Armoured Brigade was to be part of XXX Corps whose job was to block the head of the penetration while the

Americans were closing in on the shoulders and sides of the thrust. At first there was in fact nothing to stop the Germans between Brussels and the head of the thrust except 33 Armoured Brigade, the first formation to join the corps. For some time to come, we were told, there was little help to be had, either British or Allied, so we were to act as an independent armoured regiment covering the crossings over the River Dyle just south of Brussels. 53rd Welsh Division was being hurried down to join the make-shift XXX Corps with 6th Airborne Division and 29 Armoured Brigade who were brought over from England.

The Regiment arrived on 20 Dec at 1800hrs well after dark into laager just south of Louvain. The tanks had moved on their tracks for about 120 miles in bitterly cold, snowy weather. The crews had, some time before, been issued with new tank suits. These consisted of a one-piece overall garment, dun coloured with rubber under linen and a khaki felt inner lining. There were many zips and pockets. It kept one reasonably warm; but the temperature dropped well below zero and then the cold seeped in every-where; so all manner of clothing was used to keep the crews warm. It didn't help as most of the tanks were air-cooled with large fans sucking air down through the turret, and out through the vents at the rear to clear the fumes from the guns; so the turret was a constant "draft corridor". Winter in the Ardennes was the coldest weather the Shermans had yet encountered. Rumours flooded in: German paratroops were reported everywhere; and Germans in captured American uniforms and jeeps were supposed to be swanning about causing mayhem in the rear areas. Fortunately the ERY did not actually meet any, but everyone had to be on their guard just in case. The crews were housed in small farms near the road, with the tanks tucked in by the farm buildings. It was especially cold doing a stint of guard-duty during the night.

Second Lieutenant Mace goes on: "The Regiment was in this situation over Christmas. All the Christmas dinner was back in B Echelon, while we were on 'compo' rations. We did manage to scrounge a chicken for our troop which was cooked up with the perennial bully beef and tinned veg-etables on our tommy cookers. We ate it in the tanks out of our mess tins with tea and dried milk. We had been ordered to keep on the regimental net rather than the usual Squadron net, as we were on an hours notice to move; but in our troop we all listened to Vera Lynn and the King's Speech. Even so it was not a festive season for us, although the fog had gone, the sky was clear and at last we saw our aircraft going over to blast Jerry as hard as possible, which lifted our spirits somewhat. All our guns

190

were kept loaded, no one approached without being checked thoroughly; there were constant guards and it was truly cold. We were only about twenty miles from Brussels, and we heard later that the Staff there were having large and uproarious parties. Fortunately we did not know about this at the time. Shades of the Duchess of Richmond's Ball before Waterloo in 1815!

"We stayed in this position until 28 December, when B Squadron were ordered south towards the Ardennes. We moved off at 0730hrs, but it was terrible going. There had been a slight thaw and then the ground froze hard so the roads were like a skating rink. As the Squadron moved south, they saw many vehicles in the ditches which had crashed out of control. The tanks went gingerly along, it was full credit to the drivers that they made any progress at all. I did get stuck on a tank trap and had to be pulled off by an ARV. I managed to catch up with the Squadron but it was a difficult march. I had hit the tank trap right in the middle of the field where the battle of Waterloo had been fought! It was dark when we reached our harbour at Philippeville. This was good tank country; so reconnaissance was carried out, as German tanks were expected. All the 17pdr Fireflies had been issued with the new Sabot ammunition."

Lance Corporal Read summed up the Ardennes: "I remember staying in a house with no windows, no doors, no heating, everything covered in frozen snow and ice. The water supply came from a small stream nearby. To get water, one had to go down a steep bank with a canvas bucket and an axe to break the ice which was 9–12" thick. The way was to chop a hole large enough to drop the bucket into the water below. I didn't mind the work as it was the only way to get warm. It didn't take long and we soon had the little petrol stove going full blast for a hot drink. As regards keeping warm, we had on as many woollies as possible plus cap comforters, otherwise ears would be nipped. We wore rubber boots for better grip. I wore fisherman's stockings inside, also inner soles of compressed furry material, so my feet were never cold. Needless to say, we never removed our clothes for days and it was a long time before we could have a good hot shower."

Sergeant Townsend had slept on the floor of a laboratory at Louvain University before the journey south, before experiencing the intense cold as they went into the Ardennes, to say nothing of the difficulty of guiding his troop along the icy roads.

Trooper Buckingham and many others remembered the hazardous journeys up steep slippery slopes, and coming down the other side, where the weight of the tank created its own momentum. Many a tank nearly slid

191

off the side down the steep ravines on the side of some of the roads. Somehow none were lost in this way. Shermans had rubber treads on their tracks which gave no grip at all on the icy roads. But within forty-eight hours we were all issued with bolt-on, steel "spuds" and these proved most effective in biting through the ice. Many German tanks were seen in the villages below in the valley where they had slid over the side, with the bodies of the crews thrown out and crushed as they crashed off the road to end up in the valley below.

B Squadron was pushed nearer the action. On the way to the town of Hotton they saw the Americans of 4 US Armoured Division move into position to attack the flank of the bulge exchanging rude gestures between the crews as they passed. However, stopping at one of their cookhouses the Squadron were given a very good meal of roast chicken, roast potatoes, vegetables, freshly baked white bread, butter and real coffee. How the Yanks could feed their troops like this in such forward positions, while the British were existing on bully beef and biscuits, no one knew.

Once down in the Ardennes, the Regiment was back with 53rd Welsh Division and early in January B Squadron were on the far left of the line, with the River Ourthe on the left flank and the Americans on the other side of the river. The Squadron was harboured in the little town of Hotton. This was the furthest the Germans had reached in their thrust in this sector. The Squadron was ready to support 6 Royal Welch Fusiliers. It was going to be a tricky operation getting the tanks up the steep roads just outside Hotton, but luckily the operation was cancelled.

Both A and C Squadrons were moved up to support their respective infantry battalions, but it was impossible to take the tanks into positions where useful support could be given. B Squadron moved out of Hotton and met some of the units of 6th British Airborne Division who were pushing forward as well. Amongst them Second Lieutenant Mace saw an old school friend who was a medical orderly. "He had just come back from a patrol behind the lines 'to try to capture Field Marshal von Rundstedt', or so they said. John joined the Armoured Corps with me, going through the training, then deciding that he could not kill men, as he had a Quaker background. He suffered great humiliation but eventually showed his great courage by joining the Airborne forces, training as a medical orderly, and later dropping at the Rhine crossing."

Second Lieutenant Mace continued, "At Hotton both Sergeant Davis and I remembered seeing burnt-out German tanks by the bridge, the crews had had several women in them. I was physically sick at the sight of them.

I have from that moment on always been against British women being involved in front-line battles, especially in tanks."

In Hotton they managed to find some shelter from the cold, most of the houses having large chimneys with a space between the chimney and the wall where hams were hung for smoking.

B Squadron spent several days in Hotton and several reconnaissances were carried out, taking tanks into the surrounding hills. By this time the "spuds" came into their own as with these on the tracks the tanks could get a grip and move easily on the icy surfaces.

"On one of these recces Major Salman took us on foot right to the edge of a forest, high above a wide valley. There we could see German tanks lumbering along the valley, until they suddenly stopped, the crews dismounted and started digging in frantically. 'Run out of fuel,' said Major Salman. The rocket-firing fighters were called up and soon dealt with them. By this time 51st Highland Division had taken over from the 53rd Welsh Division and we were back with our old friends again. I remember taking my tank up a steep mountain track into a wood overlooking the river on my left. There was a Highlander in a slit trench which he had laboriously dug in the rock-hard frozen ground. He wore everything he could but was still cold. We offered him tea, which he accepted, and a chance of shelter in the tank out of the biting wind. 'I wouldna get in one of those fucking things if ye gave me £1,000.' I could only reply that I wouldn't like his job myself either.

"On 10 January 1945 B Squadron were supporting the 2nd Seaforths and occupied the village of Halleux not far from La Roche. We were shelled quite heavily. One large one exploded right by the front of my tank and I remember no more." So ended Second Lieutenant Mace's effective stay with the Regiment.

A Squadron passed through B and captured Rondchamps, where they were also heavily shelled and lost a tank on a mine but they took several prisoners.

On 11 January C Squadron moved with their infantry to Velmont, which was on a high ridge on the main La Roche to St Hubert road, but no sooner had they shown their noses at a crossroads than a great deal of shellfire crashed on them. They had to stay there for some hours being shelled and mortared all the time. Even so their transport came up to replenish them with fuel and ammunition.

A Squadron were also in the same village and received similar treatment. Fortunately a large number of the shells were duds so did no damage, otherwise casualties would have been much higher, for the infantry particularly.

These two Squadrons pushed on to Mierchamps and found the bridge blown. The conditions were terrible with hairpin bends to negotiate, even without the weather and the Germans. Buffalo amphibians had to be used to bring up petrol and ammunition.

The Recce Troop was with the advance Squadron; so, as soon as the new bridge was erected by the Sappers, they were across and scouting on the other side of the river and up to the hills beyond. It was again a freezing cold night, the more so as they couldn't get back to harbour and had to stay out all night.

Trooper Ernie Martin, now a Stuart tank driver, remembered his tank commander, Second Lieutenant Loughlin, battening down the hatch, and the crew drinking their rum ration to keep warm. They had very little to eat.

The following morning they were again able to get their Stuarts started with the exception of the water-cooled model captured in Holland and now resplendent with the regimental signs. Second Lieutenant Loughlin went to check on the other tanks he had and told the crew to unthaw it. They did so by lighting a fire under the engine compartment and the whole machine caught fire and was burnt out.

As it was officially not on the strength, nothing too much was said, but the section leader was blamed as the officer responsible. Captain Wright saw the brewed-up tank on the main Corps axis and well behind Corps HQ still bearing the regimental signs and was puzzled as there had never been any action there which might account for the casualty. He heard the true story later.

Captain Peter Consett, now commanding the Recce Troop, had heard tank engines, but saw nothing so they moved out cautiously. Then they saw several Germans running into a house. He, Second Lieutenant Loughlin and their troop-sergeant, Sergeant Townsend, called on the Germans to surrender. They fired a deal of bullets at the house and ten prisoners came out. As the prisoners marched back a German light tank came on the scene, behind the prisoners and escort. The German commander, an officer, stuck his head out of the turret, not realizing what was happening, and beckoned the Germans back. Captain Consett also "did some beckoning in the opposite direction". The German, understanding his position, took the hint, closed his turret and reversed back at speed, which was a great relief for the Recce Troop.

In the meanwhile 3 Troop C Squadron went forward with their infantry into Erneuville, the next village to Mierchamps. A machine gun opened fire and the tanks quickly put it out of action, but then a nest of three Spandaus opened up as soon as the infantry patrol, a small one, were well into the village and this cut them off from their unit. Lieutenant Bulford immediately charged straight down the village street with his troop of Shermans abreast, knocked out the Spandaus and rescued the patrol. Many Germans were killed. C Squadron was ordered to remain in the village all that day and Germans kept coming out of the woods to give themselves up. They were grey with fatigue, cold, frost-bitten, unshaven and demoralized. They had only eaten looted food or roots as no rations had been brought up to them.

Major Holtby, OC C Squadron, captured several half-tracks, completely intact, fully loaded with men and ammunition, but out of fuel. A sight Sergeant Davis remembered was the infantry bringing in the prisoners. They had made the Germans remove their braces and run through the deep snow. The local ladies, seeing the spectacle, brought out buckets of potato peelings and all sorts of rubbish, ran alongside the prisoners pelting them with swill. Although the weather was extremely cold the prisoners were steaming.

14 January was a day of "reshuffling". The infantry patrols going south linked up with the Americans. ERY was now pulled back as the area of their responsibility was clear of enemy.

There was still some shelling and two men were wounded; but apart from some anti-personal bombs dropped, no enemy counter-attacks took place. There was also one casualty in 152 Brigade HQ – a new staff officer, who had only arrived that day, had never been in the front line before and was supposed to be observing what the Ardennes battle was like after it was already virtually over. He received a parcel of anti-personal fragments in the backside and his new posting was soon ended.

For three more days the Regiment stayed in this cold area, before receiving orders to move. Just at that time the weather gave a hint of improvement. A signal came from Brigade: "General thaw expected". Corporal Danny Daniel, the RHQ senior clerk, wrote, "One of our clerks, seeing the signal, dashed out of the office shouting 'More bloody bullshit. Some General Thaw is coming to inspect us'."

Chapter 20

BUFFALOS AND THE RHINE CROSSING

Before 21st Army Group could force a crossing over the Rhine it was necessary to fight one of the fiercest battles they had undertaken in the whole campaign in NW Europe, the Reichswald Forest operation, code-named VERITABLE. This was conducted initially by XXX Corps and preparation for this was the reason for General Montgomery ordering General Horrocks back home for rest while his Corps was still in action in the Ardennes. The attack was made from Nijmegen southwards down the corridor between the Rivers Maas and Rhine where much of the defences were part of the Siegfried Line. The already wet ground was further flooded by the defenders so that the going was frequently confined to the limited roads, where it was difficult to deploy tanks and often amphibians had to be used. II Canadian Corps and XII Corps were later involved and XXX Corps alone was reinforced to a strength of 200,000 men. The attack went in on 8 Febuary and with all reserves of infantry drawn into the bitter fighting it took over a month before the western bank of the Rhine was finally cleared at great cost in casualties to the British and Canadian attackers.

Further afield, the allies fought a tough winter campaign in Italy against a resolute defence in difficult country. In a Norwegian fjord the battleship Tirpitz *had been sunk by RAF bombs in November. The armies in Burma ground on towards Mandalay and the Akyab peninsula was at last gained early in January. In October 1944 American ground forces invaded the Philippines and by the New Year had occupied the island of Leyte. More importantly the US navy won their greatest victory at sea on 24/25 October at Leyte Gulf which put the Japanese Navy effectively out of the war. In mid-Pacific the Americans took one more step towards domination of the Japanese main islands with the capture of Iwojima between February and March 1945. The Russians meanwhile continued their drive to regain occupied territory on the eastern frontiers of Germany. British intervention in Greece saved that country from a Communist coup. In the New Year the Red Army began their onslaught from western Poland which was to lead them to Berlin itself.*

On 17 January, after a couple more days of horrible conditions in houses with no windows, still freezing weather where tools froze into the hands and everyone was cold, uncomfortable and weary, the Regiment was informed that the Brigade would cease to be under command of the Highland Division. Major Ellison, the 2i/c, in either a jeep or a scout car, came round in place of the CO with a cheery word and plenty of encouragement. He was much respected by all ranks.

The ERY was moved back a few miles. The journey was hazardous, getting tanks down the hills they had laboriously climbed some days earlier. It was accomplished eventually and having passed through La Roche, recently liberated by 144 Regiment RAC with terrible damage to a lovely town, the regiment harboured at Hampteau.

One of the things about Hotton came out later. Some of the Regiment who had been killed in the 1940 campaign were buried in a war cemetery there; but the 1944/5 Regiment knew nothing about this until the war was over.

The Yeomanry also heard that they were to lay up their tanks and to prepare to become a "Buffalo" unit for a special operation – the Rhine Crossing. The Buffalo was an amphibious vehicle, officially known as "Landing Vehicle Tracked" or "LVT". For the next few days the tanks were prepared for laying up in Brussels. All the "luxuries" were taken off them, ie tank cookers, pots and pans, bivouac sheets and items the crew could not trust to other peoples' care. Again the amount of food and accumulated rations found in bins under turret-floors was incredible. There were some good meals brewed whilst waiting for transport. The Regiment moved by squadrons to the railhead at Ciney, a further hazardous journey for tanks and crews. Captain Wright, having missed most of the Ardennes battles, being on leave in the UK, now took charge of B Squadron's move. It was a difficult job as B Squadron were the last in the Brigade to load and there was a shortage of chains to secure the tanks to the railway "flats" all painted with the notice "Not to be loaded with AFVs" (Armoured Fighting Vehicles) and even then, once secured, one of the tanks still chained to the top of its "flat" without any warning toppled over on to the snow leaving a pair of bogies on the line. After much persuasion and diplomatic pleading, the Squadron managed to get all its tanks loaded up and left them under guard while the crews went back to their billets in the town. They marched down before daylight next morning to be met by the disconsolate guard with the news that the whole train with its cargo of tanks had gone off – even leaving the guards' breakfasts cooking on the side of the wagons. The Americans in charge of the railway station rarely showed their faces but spent their time in a nice warm waiting-room heated by a roaring stove. What had happened was that the Belgian train-crew arrived with an engine during the night, hooked the two lengths of train together and pulled off on to the main line under the noses of our guard and then disappeared into the dark, leaving one of their own train-crew behind as well. The B Squadron crews were therefore left stuck in Ciney with only their overnight kit, the rest being stowed in the tanks, including such items as revolvers and ammunition. Captain Wright had some anxious hours waiting for his old friend the Adjutant, Captain Alan Thornton, to turn up at Ciney so that he could beg some transport to reunite his crews with their tanks. He later heard that the train had stopped as soon as it reached open country and some locals swarmed aboard and looted whatever they fancied – rations and pistols mostly. Eventually it was all sorted out and fortunately nothing more was said about the matter, luckily for Captain Wright. But he had a pretty red face over the loss of nineteen tanks. Altogether it took fourteen days to get the Regiment's tanks safely laid up in Brussels.

The personnel were taken by road to Dilsen, just a mile from the banks of the River Maas. The country was still covered with snow which was gradually melting and leaving everything slushy and wet, muddy and unpleasant. The river level was very high as the Germans had opened the dams on the River Roer, a tributary upstream, to add to the effects of the thaw.

On 31 January the Yeomanry had a belated Christmas Dinner, with a half-day off to enjoy it. Just to make the point that the war was still close, Buffalos started to arrive as well. Eventually ninety-eight of them were sent instead of the sixty-one laid-up Shermans, the Regiment's normal compliment. The crews, therefore, had to be changed around and people trained as drivers who had never been in a tank, let alone driven one. This part of the Maas was being overflown by flying bombs at the time. Lance Corporal Read remembered one landing soon after they arrived at Dilsen and injuring several of the men.

Once training proper began it was intense, with little rest. The track-plates of the Buffalos had surfaces like deep scoops which were the means of propulsion through the water as well as land. The hull was something like a landing-craft, with slab slides and an open top, and the machine was driven by a Chrysler engine and had a Browning .5MG or a 20mm Oerlikon as armament. Some Buffalos had front-loading ramps and others slab bows. The former took light vehicles, the latter the infantry.

They had to work hard to master the art of steering these "craft" in water, and especially how to land them on the banks of the fast-flowing river.

Trooper O'Donoghue described it: "When in the water, to get ashore on to the banks which were quite steep and very slippery, you had to come obliquely into the bank with the run of the river (flowing at about 5 to 6 knots) and if you missed the first time, as many did, the current would catch the tail of the vehicle and you would swing round and round and maybe round again. You hit the bank hard to the 'pleasure' of the NCOs and officers; but you landed more by luck than by judgement."

Exercises continued day and night. Lieutenant Jenkin was detailed with his Troop to carry out a different role from that of the remainder of the Regiment. He had to cross the Rhine early to guide the DD tanks and lay fascines for them on the shore. He and his Troop did their training on the Maas with 10 RTR (of 79th Armoured Division) so he was not so much involved with the remainder of the ERY.

In B Squadron Major Salman was once again looking up his old associates in Brussels and Captain Wright was left in charge. His story highlights some of the problems of the new-fangled vehicles, especially the technique of bringing them into the bank from a swiftly running river. He explained: "The culmination of our training was a night exercise on a stretch of river just upstream from a site where Canadian engineers were struggling to build a Class 40 Bailey Bridge. They had stretched a steel cable across the river to protect their construction work from anything floating downstream. Below them again the east bank was enemy-controlled. We had all been messing about along the banks for most of a dreary day, which was followed by a long wait until dark. Having worked out a timetable and ever mindful of the chaps' well-being, I sent B Squadron, in their Buffalos, back to Dilsen, a mile away over the sodden water-meadows, for a hot meal before the night exercise began. To my acute embarrassment, they failed to get back in time, some not at all, so that we failed to participate, while A and C Squadrons, who stayed forward, operated according to schedule. All, however, had 'to pass out' with a launching and landing at night. I was assigned to someone else's Buffalo for my trip in charge. With an unfamiliar crew and not in the best of spirits after the earlier foul-up, I headed the Buffalo too much square-on for a good landing, so we were sent spinning into the middle of the river. [According to Trooper Geoff Harding, who was driving, the throttle linkage had snapped.] Before we could regain control, which involved getting the beast answering to the steering, then easing it back against the current, I suddenly saw the Canadians' cable. It just, but only just, passed over the corner of the hull. Had it hooked under the hull we would have capsized. We slithered along under it losing all our radio antennae in the process. When we picked ourselves up off the floor, we were first swept against a bunch of timber piles, happily strong enough to stand the pressure of a Buffalo against them. The only way ashore was by walking along planks insecurely fastened to the piling. We managed it without anyone falling in, aided by a few pretty angry Canadians who were having quite enough trouble with floods without runaway amphibians knocking their bridge about."

They were luckier than one Buffalo in A Squadron which turned over on a steep bank trapping three of the crew under water who were drowned in spite of the gallant efforts of Corporal Brignell to save them.

These two incidents apart, the Regiment passed its tests, completed its exercises, carried the infantry on some of them and were told that their crossing-places on the Rhine would be only two and not three for which they had trained. A and C Squadrons were the obvious choices, with the remaining troops of B Squadron coming under their control.

Lieutenant Jenkin and his troop with 10 RTR trained hard for their special role. The difference with his Buffalos was that they had to carry "fascines," great rolls of chestnut-paling. These were to be dropped on the top of the bank on the German side of the river, and then the Buffalos had to reverse back into the water, laying the fencing to form a trackway. The idea was that DD tanks would then have a secure grip for their tracks as they came out of the water.

They spent the whole of February and March learning how to do the job. Major General Hobart (Hobo), the Divisional Commander, came to the Maas to see how they were getting on. He asked what angle of entrance to the water they took from the bank. "Cocky-like," said George, "I said, 'Well, you put the vehicle at a slight angle to the water and slide in'. 'Slight,' bellowed Hobo. 'Be precise, boy'. I was to use the expression 'Be precise' many times in my future career!"

Several officers were given unusual jobs to do. Lieutenant Stephen Schillizzi was trained in the use of special navigational aids. Lieutenant Keith Loughlin was a Bank Control Officer and he had to learn to control vehicles in and out of the river. Captain Wright was left with the remnants of B Squadron to organize the maintenance and rest areas. Captain

Consett, having once been a Naval Officer, was made Navigation Officer.

Dilsen had hardly been touched by the war. It came as quite a shock when the Regiment descended on the inhabitants. They tried to organize a dance or two. The local Priest banned them; so Major Ellison had to go to the Burgomaster before the locals could be allowed to come, closely chaperoned by their mothers. There was the usual scramble for the food the cooks provided.

Some flying bombs landed around the regimental lines. After Corporal Brignall had tried to rescue his comrades from the upturned Buffalo, he was sent back to his billet for a rest. A flying bomb landed and exploded thirty yards away from his billet, he and his bed were dumped one floor down, but he was only shaken and otherwise unhurt. On the edge of the large crater a goat was tethered; all it did was to carry on munching.

So the build-up continued, from the early days in the still water of the learning-canal, then to the River Maas with its fast current including the exercises with infantry, and finally a day and night exercise with engineers, infantry and the full organization put to the test.

On 17 March preparations were made for the move. Recce parties left for the concentration area in the Hochwald Forest. The CO and Squadron Leaders had all been to the Xanten position to reconnoitre the area. The whole length of the west bank of the Rhine was covered by a thick smokescreen. This made extensive walking in the open in front of the infantry on the banks of the river itself less hazardous.

On 18 March the Buffalos were all loaded onto transporters timed to arrive at the Hochwald Forest early the next morning. There was a camouflage officer from XII Corps who directed and supervised the concealment of the LVTs. The crews bivouacked beside their vehicles in the woods. As the weather had turned warmer, the land was drying out and the warmth was welcome to the troops. The Luftwaffe were active most nights, dropping flares, with one landing in the regimental lines. The Germans also sprayed the area with cannon fire whilst on photographic reconnaissance. Fortunately no casualties were caused to our people. The crew commanders all had to walk every inch of the approach, crawling by day and night in front of the smoke screen.

All civilians had been moved out of the houses overlooking the river, which were already badly damaged by the ferocious fighting between the Allies and especially the German Parachute Army of the defenders, by that time protecting home soil. Allied bombing had added to the destruction.

Bank officers were assigned to inspect and walk the area of their responsibility. Lieutenant Loughlin: "My task as a Bank Officer was to make a reconnaissance over the river side of the Inner Bund (flood dykes), initially to locate a suitable entrance towards the water's edge for our Buffalos. Our first task was activated on 20th in daylight. Under cover of the intensive smoke screen, Corporal Fellows, a trooper and myself, adequately armed, made our way over the Bund, checking the immediate position in front and locating any unusual features. Our first obstacle was to recce a German bunker nearby. It was most essential to ensure that the objective was unoccupied bearing in mind the incident of the night before when three German frogmen were caught, having slipped over the Rhine with demolition explosives."

Lieutenant Jenkin, working independently, wrote, "On the big day we were to set off at H minus 2. The Royal Engineers were to blow a gap in the Bund as it was too steep to go over. This was followed by an artillery barrage, much heavier even than the famous one at El Alamein. Then we set off, with searchlights blinding the enemy, across that long waste of land, until we found the Rhine. It seemed enormous. I was scared, I assure you. We then had to 'sail' across and, aided by the searchlights and 'artificial moonlight', find the exact place which photographs had shown as suitable. How we did it I've no idea, but we did! We made a successful landing and laid the fascines perfectly. Then, armed with only our Brownings, we waited for the DD tanks to arrive and hoped the Germans had not seen us. As first light came, we had a grandstand view of the 6th Airborne Division dropping. If I recall correctly, one chap landed near us and we surprised him. Fortunately he took no action – probably by now we had a brew of tea going and offered him a mug. We successfully brought ashore the whole of 10 RTR with their DDs, although some loads were more awkward than others. Once they had landed, we returned across the Rhine and I found Lieutenant Colonel Williamson with Hobo, GOC 79th Armoured Division and made my report. Hobo told Tom to see 'he gets (me) something for this' . . . I never did!"

Trooper Tuke, also in 4 Troop B Squadron, who was a gunner in one of the Buffalos wrote: "Thinking that there might be land-mines on the other side, I packed as many sandbags under and around my seat. It's a wonder the damn thing didn't sink. Regarding the crossing, the two things I vividly remember:

1.   The Alamein type barrage, which Field Marshal Montgomery arranged at 0600hrs the morning of the main crossing; very impressive,

all types of field guns, wheel to wheel along a three-mile stretch of the river bank; and

2.   The very impressive number of gliders (hundreds upon hundreds) being towed, some being hit, sending jeeps, anti-tank guns and personnel tumbling to earth."

There had been great activity before the day of the crossing. Routes the Buffalos were to follow had to be clearly marked with tapes and lighted; assembly areas zoned, wirelesses tuned in on both regimental and administrative nets. A maintenance area had to be prepared, with ammunition, fuel and food as well as a rest-area for the crews. Then the Buffalos themselves, which had been hidden for several days in the Forest, were brought out in the order of march, moved to their assigned routes, all behind the great smokescreen.

The Regiment was to transport the assault in two waves. On the left was A Squadron, with C on the right. The Beach or Bank Officers had to complete their final reconnaissance. Lieutenant Loughlin's account runs, "Full of trepidation our little party set forth on the night of 23 March, equipped with our consignment of coloured lamps. We made our way out to the Bund. Moving through the gap blown by the Royal Engineers, we took up our position on the appointed start point. We could see the black line of the far bank of the Rhine clearly visible between the sweep of the broad, fast-moving water. Prior to lighting our 'green for go' lamps we were, from 2000hrs, subjected to the terrifying sound of the barrage of guns, fortunately directed over our heads at the enemy. This massive load of explosives fell 800 to 1,000 yards to our front on the opposite bank.

"Apart from the deafening noise of the guns, the skies were lit up with a new incandescent light fired by tanks. Sited on the top of the outer Bund provided a panorama of the great moment of the assault units launching off across the Rhine. Clearly seen in the light, the tanks on the Bund were subjected to a considerable amount of enemy fire and one tank was brewed up.

"In the meantime the lamps were lit and the passage of the Regiment's Buffalos went according to plan with a great sigh of relief on our part."

So at 0045hrs the assaulting Buffalos started forward and at 0207 the leading troops entered the water and went across in a perfect line to disgorge their infantry at the points planned. There was some difficulty in getting back off the bank, once the infantry had been put ashore, because of the deep and glutinous mud. It took some skilful manoeuvring to unstick all the Buffalos before they could start back across the river. Some of the infantry were immediately involved in heavy fighting with German Paratroops. Where possible, support was given with the .5 Brownings on the Buffalos. However, there was such intense artillery fire that there was little need for our machine-gun support as well.

Sergeant Ernest Cone had a harrowing time getting his troop back as they were stuck in the mud on the far side; but, with a great deal of courage, he got them off.

After the assault troops were carried over, A and C Squadrons started a regular ferry service. This service proved vital, continuing day and night, to such an extent that once the opposite bank had been cleared, it was only necessary for a driver alone to do the trip. Oh his return he handed over to another driver, so that the men could be rested and fed for their next trip. The Buffalos had to be loaded with stores once the infantry had been landed. When prisoners were brought back, armed guards were needed.

After a couple of days, however, the Buffalos were ordered to halt their ferry services because they brought so much water ashore with their tracks that the landing-places became an impassable quagmire. By then the first bridges were ready in any case.

Sergeant Brown was a bit scared at the first crossing. Trooper Buckingham: "Of the actual crossing I remember the tremendous gun barrage, as we made our way, loaded with infantry, towards the bank. Our troop went into the river upstream of the rest, in order to achieve a simultaneous landing on the other side. It was quite eerie floating downstream in the 'artificial moonlight', nervously watching the bank for any reaction. I remembered to sing 'Sailing down the river on a Sunday afternoon', but not very loudly. Luckily we had no opposition to disturb those thoughts or my solo. After the attack, we took turns in ferrying reinforcements and supplies, although there was the occasional shell landing nearby. In the afternoon a German jet fighter whistled its way along the river."

Trooper Donald Foster of RHQ troop remembered that the Padre held a service the night before the crossing. Sergeant Green remembered crossing the river altogether forty-seven times, taking personnel out and prisoners back.

Sergeant Townsend had been on leave in UK and returned the day before the assault. "There was a bit of shelling on my arrival, but nothing intense. The following day was very fine and we all lived in our Buffalos, ready for the plunge into the Rhine. As it was so warm, I dozed off, only to wake up later to find the Regiment had disappeared across the river. I later joined them, but nobody appeared to notice my absence."

Sergeant Rawlins of C Squadron had been wounded back in Normandy when Lieutenant Howitt had been killed, but arrived back about six weeks before the crossing.

Lance Corporal Read, the Technical Storeman, remembers a vast American artillery gun, known as a 'Long Tom'. When it moved, everyone and everything had to move also to allow it a clear passage. The wheels and tyres were much bigger than a man. It passed by the regimental area with two men running in front shouting, 'Get out of the way'. It was a monster and added mightily to the noise of the barrage.

Sergeant Morrell of C Squadron reckoned the crossing was easier than expected. "I met my brother-in-law who had piloted a glider with the Airborne. He took a letter home, which I had been writing to my wife."

Captain Wright: "The only interference we had in the maintenance area was a little mortaring, which cost our only casualty, Sergeant Theobald, wounded in the leg." Captain Wright next saw Sergeant Theobald in 1950. "Jane, my wife, and I were on our way back from our honeymoon, having been met at Northolt with our car by Tom Robinson, who had commanded B Squadron before being wounded. We lost our way near Harrow in the small hours. There was one lone figure standing at a bus stop; so we pulled in to ask for directions. Tom put his head out of the passenger's window and who should we see but the familiar face of Sergeant Theobald of B Squadron! It's a small world!"

To conclude the Battle of the Rhine, the CO received a letter from Lieutenant General Ritchie, commanding XII Corps:

"I am writing to thank you for the magnificent way in which you and your Regiment carried out all that was asked of you, and it was a lot, in connection with the crossing of the Rhine. This task was no easy one, and I feel sure that when the history comes to be written, it will be looked upon as a great achievement. I cannot help thinking that it will rank high in the annals of your Regiment. I shall be glad if you will pass on to all those under your command the high appreciation and admiration of those of 12 Corps."

Chapter 21

AFTER THE RHINE

At 1900hrs on 25 March the ferry closed down. Seventy-four crossings had been completed on the actual assault and another 637 on the ferry service. All but one of the Buffalos, which was broken down on the opposite bank, were pulled out and restored to their original harbour areas. Three further days were spent in the Hochwald Forest doing maintenance and resting. On 20 March the Regiment moved further back to comfortable billets, taking over farm houses and farms.

Trooper O'Donoghue, as usual, had a stroke of luck. "After the crossing we were sleeping in German farms. While looking around this place in the cellar, I found a small zinc bath full of pig's dripping! Can you imagine – Dripping! AND there was a field full of spuds! The lads had chips for ever! Two tank cookers, one each end of the bath and away we went! I think in that short time we put on weight."

On 31 March the Buffalos were handed over to be transported to another unit. Trooper Buckingham had a nasty experience loading a Buffalo on to a transporter, with its paddle-shaped tracks overhanging the ramp up which we had to back the vehicle and the bed of the transporter as well. "At the top, instead of dropping gently on to the transporter," he reported, "it swung sideways out of line. I stopped and just hung there. It was decided to carry on in hope and luckily it swung back just sufficiently to land square on to the transporter."

The ERY was to go back to its tanks and form a Yeomanry Brigade with the Northamptonshire Yeomanry and the Staffordshire Yeomanry. They collected their Shermans from Brussels and were told they were going to join in the operation of "cracking about over the North German Plain" as Field Marsal Montgomery described the last part of the campaign. Orders were received to move to Bocholt. Major Ellison went off to arrange billets, but the order was cancelled. They eventually moved to Dongen, the tanks being transported at night from Nijmegen. The move was completed by 15 April: it was clear that the Brigade was to be part of a mobile reserve to contain the Germans still holding out in the north of Holland after the Arnhem set-back. It was also to be available if required to go on into Germany, but the immediate task was to counter and destroy any penetration by enemy patrols over the River Maas. The long front was held by an Anti-tank regiment, 2 Belgian Infantry Battalion and 33 Armoured Brigade. Emphasis was put on "good turn-out, and general cleanliness of the men, their billets and their vehicles". The general feeling was "back to the bullshit days!"

Some made good use of their time. Trooper Buckingham was billeted at s'Gravenaar. "Two of us were billeted on an old Dutch couple who were retired. They made us very welcome, and taught us how to play bridge, later inviting friends to come in and play with us. The occasional night spent acting as infantry was the only serious matter to occupy our time."

Later in April orders came that 33 Armoured Brigade were to revert to Buffalos for crossing the major rivers up in Germany, but that one regiment was to retain its tanks, and, as Major Ellison wrote, "to our great relief, it was decided that we should be that regiment."

The ERY, therefore, had to take over the task previously allotted to the whole brigade, with the help of a Dutch Volunteer Battalion, the Anti-tank regiment and a Heavy Artillery regiment, all under command of Lieutenant Colonel Williamson, so that the makeshift formation was named "Willforce". The CO immediately moved into the house that had been Brigade Headquarters.

One or two German patrols came over the river, but no incidents were reported. Trooper Buckingham commented: "We did take the tanks for a shooting practice on one occasion. Targets had been set up on the Bund, and I remember the Troop Officer commenting on our few hits. Fred, the gunner, had put the range up so that some of the rounds went across the river, to give the Germans a surprise."

At the end of April it was clear that the Dutch in the north of Holland were starving, so talks were conducted with the Germans about feeding them. Bomber Command aircraft were seen on our front dropping supplies at one time; and a temporary truce was agreed on 2 May so that barges loaded with food at Oosterhout could pass across our front. A mined bridge had to be cleared of explosives. As negotiations had to be conducted with the Germans, Major Salman carried them out in their own language and in his usual robust fashion. Observing officers were posted with wireless sets to report on the conduct of the Germans in the removal of mines and others obstacles. No further fire came from the German side, and on 4 May news was received that the German forces in north-west Germany, Holland and Denmark had surrendered.

At 0800hrs on 5 May there was a cease-fire on the regimental front to allow transport of food to the starving Dutch population. During the negotiations Major Salman spotted Prince Bernhard of the Netherlands taking photographs from his car in the background of the proceedings.

Later on that same day, 5 May, Captain Ken Smith met some German officers who refused to believe that the truce was permanent – some eight Germans who had deserted to the Belgians and had no idea that a truce was being negotiated, let alone in being.

Ultimately on 8 May 1945 the unconditional surrender of all the German forces in Europe was concluded. Hitler was dead and many of his gang with him.

On the Sunday there was a church service conducted by the Padre, Rev George Long, when the Regiment gave thanks for coming safely through the ordeal of the last eleven months. They remembered their dead comrades too, with sincerity at the loss of their old friends.

Trooper Buckingham said, "Once it was over, the relief we felt was enormous and was followed by dancing and singing with the Dutch in the village street. We got Very pistols out from the tanks and had an impromptu firework display with the different coloured flares."

Rest and sport filled the days after the end of the fighting. The CO tried to bring in one of his friends from his old regiment to take over as 2i/c from Major Ellison, but he failed in the attempt. Major Percy Legard, the officer in question, was a fine sportsman, but had failed to pass the Senior Officer Course to make him superior to Major Ellison; so stayed and became instead a "spare major". He once asked Major Ellison for something to do, so he was sent off with a 3-tonner to Hamburg to collect as much gin and spirits etc as he could lay his hands on before the NAAFI took over supplies. Major Legard did this so well that Major Ellison was able to sell it to the Officers' and Sergeants' Messes and the result financed the publication of *Europe Revisited* which he planned to write (and did). Once written and printed, everyone who served in the Regiment should have had a free copy.

There were official victory celebrations; the CO was even given the freedom of the village. At the end of May education took on importance for post-war life after demobilization. The Education Officer was Captain Wright, with Lieutenant Stephen Schilizzi (a school-teacher in peace-time) as his Chief Instructor. Then at the end of May the Regiment became part of 4 Armoured Brigade and on 11 June the move was started up into Germany to Laboe near Kiel.

Chapter 22

VICTORY AND PEACE

The German surrender took place on 8 May 1945 and the war in Europe was over. Germany was divided into four Zones of Occupation: American, British, French and Russian. The long process of repatriation of POWs, forced labour and displaced persons took a long time, the last being the most difficult. During this time the war against the Japs continued. The outer islands were one by one reduced or by-passed, Okinawa captured by the end of June 1945 proving the most costly operation. Mainland Japan had been within bombing range since the capture of Saipan and in March Tokyo itself was fire-bombed. By July 60% of Japan's major cities had been destroyed. In Burma 14th British Army captured Rangoon on 2 May 1945 and preparations were put in train for the invasion of Malaya and the liberation of Singapore. But the need for the dreaded invasion of the Japanese home islands was overtaken by the dropping of atomic bombs; first on Hiroshima on 6 August, and three days later on Nagasaki. Japan's resistance collapsed and the formal surrender took place on 2 September 1945. The Second World War was over.

Laboe was a small harbour-town on the Baltic to the north-east of Kiel. Most of the houses were in reasonable shape, so all personnel had good billets, with Germans to look after their comforts. They finally arrived on 14 June and took over the duties of policing the area where surrendered service personnel from the northern German forces concentrated in a large enclave between two river-estuaries. They took over from the Grenadier Guards of 6 Guards Tank Brigade who were to give up their tanks and resume their old infantry role as part of the Berlin garrison. The Guards had established command posts along the boundary, using troops from a surrendered Panzer Division to do the actual guard duties. These men were reissued with their own small arms and ordered to keep discipline with force if necessary – which they proved quite ready to do. The only presence of the Supervising Power was a troop of tanks at each crossing point where

210

main roads led into the enclave. The Germans were doing a first-rate job, keeping in those who wanted to get out and keeping out those who may have wanted to get in, to the point of shooting their own people if the need arose. For the Yeomen the war was over and they would have been far too tender-hearted for that.

Near Laboe there was a magnificent memorial to those in the U Boat command in the First World War. It was a large dominating tower in the shape of a U Boat Conning Tower. There was a museum inside giving the history of the German Navy, with a diorama of the Battle of Jutland from the German viewpoint and exhibiting many model German ships as well as British. The display had already been partly vandalized and Trooper Harding, an inveterate collector, "collected" several of the models for himself.

Quartered around Laboe, the troops usually paid for comforts with cigarettes, which had become the usual currency in post-war Germany at that time.

Sergeant Brown looked after the stocking of food and drink in the Sergeants' Mess. When he was on Guard Duty one night, taking with him the keys of the storeroom, the Mess ran out of drink. There was a great uproar and the Regimental Sergeant Major ordered him off guard duty to open the store. Colin Brown never did another Guard Duty.

Trooper Buckingham spent his off-duty time that summer on the beach nearby swimming and relaxing from the hell of the campaign. He swam a good deal and, when winter came, played rugby football.

The Regiment had "acquired" two inshore minesweepers and called them *Hull* and *Humber*. Many interesting excursions took place in them.

Having organized the frontier-guard duties, it was all comfortably restful. There were as many as 750,000 men in the enclave at its peak and, after a while, some of them became restive. They started a little mischief like forgetting who were the victors. Snap patrols with tanks had the desired effect of showing the flag. Who better to command one of these patrols than the Regiment's ace German-speaker, Major Salman? "I went on one of these patrols", Captain Wright recollected. "Major Salman was completely in his element. We would go to whatever HQ each 'camp' might have, usually in one of the farms scattered about the countryside, and require to see the officer in charge. The contrast was an interesting one. At one end of the scale was an obviously dedicated Fregattenkapitän (Commander) from the German Navy in Kiel, with about 1,500 men under his care, with limited resources, doing a great job very effectively with no more clothes than those he stood up in. The opposite extreme was another camp. We started with the Orderly Room Sergeant who tried to bluff his way until it was made crystal-clear that we required the boss and quick. The boss eventually turned up in Panzer black uniform, with pink facings and the badges of an Oberst (full colonel), with a handsome young Adjutant in tow, expecting to overawe our party. It took only a few seconds of Major Salman's German to put him in his place. We then started a tour of his camp with which he was plainly unfamiliar. It was neither clean nor were the latrines as hygienic as they should have been. After the tour he received the full range of the Major's invective."

Trooper Laurie Elvin never forget going with Major Salman to quell a riot of ex-Wermacht troops – just the two of them. Major Salman's presence did all the quelling that was needed. He also remembered going on escort duty on a ship taking a flotilla of boats to Sweenemünde in the Russian zone, as part of the repatriation scheme. "The storm we sailed through coming back, made me appreciate being a tank man."

There was one troublesome camp containing about six hundred Ukrainians and Russians who had been enrolled in the German army and surrendered with them. There appeared to have been an agitator among them from outside the enclave. Every day they used to parade with their kit at the camp gate expecting and demanding transport to take them back to Russia. To begin with they would return to their bivouacs; but after some days they firmly announced their intention to leave, which they said was their right. One morning the Sergeant in charge of the tank picket rang the Orderly Room to say that these people were marching in column up the road towards the post. The Duty Officer confirmed orders that if they crossed the border of the enclave the tanks should open fire. Fortunately two scouts from the party were marching ahead of the main body to test the opposition. The Sergeant hauled them up onto the turret of his tank and showed them that his machine guns were loaded and aimed down the road and making it quite clear in sign language that if the column came on he would open fire. The scouts returned and the column quietly retired. A very nasty incident was avoided by the diplomacy of Sergeant Lyon of A Squadron. It was announced the next morning that the heads of state of the Big Four had just started the Potsdam Conference. Some officers speculated that the incident had been orchestrated. If it had gone wrong it would have been jam for Soviet propaganda!

Officers and other ranks with sufficiently long service in prospect before demobilization began to go on postings to the Far East where the war against the Japs still continued, which didn't do a great deal for morale. The older ones and longest serving were starting to be released too. In the meantime "peace-time soldiering" was the order of the day with the maximum of sporting activities, entertainments and education courses, the last with much emphasis on "Current Affairs" to get people used to becoming civilians again.

It was a lovely summer in 1945 and a lot of cricket was played. Some, like Sergeant Fitzmaurice, went boar-hunting, some sunbathed and others fished. In the autumn football and rugby started to great effect. In August the war in the Far East finished, a service of thanksgiving was held by the Padre and the Regiment was given a holiday. Leave was organized by rota and demob began to start in earnest.

After nearly six years' service Major Ellison was demobbed and left the Regiment in September, to the great regret of those who remained. He was succeeded by Major Creagh Gibson MC from the CO's old Regiment (where else?). "Creagh was in fact an East Yorkshireman and a very good chap," said Captain Wright. "I first met him when he was 2 i/c of the organizers of the demonstration of tanks to Winston Churchill in 1941."

The regimental football team, with several Hull City players among them, swept all before them. One of them, Sergeant Jack Rawlins, even had an England trial after he was demobbed. The Rugby Union side, as four years before, benefited from several Hull and Hull Kingston Rovers League players in the Regiment as well.

Christmas was a most enjoyable time, starting with the usual football match between officers and sergeants. It began with a rugby ball but finished more or less in an orthodox fashion with a round one. Christmas dinners were, as customary in peacetime, served to the rest of the Regiment by the officers and sergeants. What a contrast to the previous Christmas when the celebrations had been overtaken by the Ardennes affair.

Some officers started to be posted to other regiments, including Major Salman who, according to the War Diary, "left the Regiment on being recalled to the Belgian Army". Captain Wright went to a staff job at 21st Army Group and the Regiment began the unwinding process. In January 1946 it was announced that the ERY was among those to be disbanded in the spring.

By January 1946 Captain Wright had become a Major and GSO2 Personnel in the RAC Branch at Rhine Army HQ and was responsible for all aspects of RAC postings. He took the night sleeper to Kiel for a visit to the Regiment to see if there was anything to be done to ease the blow. He was duly met by *Hull* (or *Humber*) and cruised out to Laboe. It soon became clear that whatever was left of the ERY did not mind what happened to them as long as they stayed together for what time was left to them before demobilization or posting. Not least was the problem of the regimental football team who had reached the final of the Rhine Army Cup to be played in a few weeks time in Berlin. So he had what he thought was a brilliant idea: "Why not move the whole outfit to another territorial regiment which was not due to be disbanded and had about the right number of survivors to accommodate the influx?" So he went back to HQ and lit on 3/4 County of London Yeomanry, also in 4 Armoured Brigade and of about the right size. So it was arranged and the ERY put away their Foxes and moved lock-and-stock to the CLY. It should have worked out all right, but he heard later that psychologically it was a disaster because the two parts didn't mix at all, but stayed rigidly in opposing camps. But there was one bonus that came out of it: the regimental football team stayed together, put their Foxes up again (as did the supporters) and went to Berlin to play in the final. Some of the team even postponed their demob dates so that they could play. Alas, the ERY lost to a Signal Regiment, at 1600 strong nearly four times the size of the Yeomanry. But it showed a fine regimental spirit just the same.

The ERY was finally disbanded on 7 March 1946. That was the last entry in the War Diary saying "Disbandonment completed". Those remaining had been posted to the 3/4 County of London Yeomanry, with Lieutenant Colonel Williamson as CO.

Without doubt this was a regiment that had done its utmost at carrying out hazardous duties during the Second World War. It should be recognized as attaining a high place in the annals of the Royal Armoured Corps and the Army. Monty himself on his farewell tour of Rhine Army HQ, when recognizing the fox on Major Wright's beret, commended the ERY. Brigadier Rex de Winton, BRAC in the Branch, also passed on to Major Wright the word that Brigadier Mike Carver of 4 Armoured Brigade (later Field Marshal Lord Carver) had told him that the ERY was one of the best, if not the best, armoured regiment that he had come across. So much for a "bunch of amateurs".

⋆   ⋆   ⋆

Territorials Again

On 12 March 1947 Lieutenant Colonel Ellison MC was entrusted with the re-forming of the Regiment in the TA, based in the East Riding of

Yorkshire. His appointment was for three years. It was quite a job starting from scratch, but he had the most loyal support from those who had served with the Regiment in the War, such as Tom Robinson, Len Cullington and others, plus several such as Roger Waterhouse and Nick Wilmot-Smith MC, who had been Prisoners of War for the long years from 1940–45. 3 Dragoon Guards (Carabiniers) provided a regular Training Major, Adjutant and a Quartermaster. With this nucleus the Regiment was rebuilt and equipped with a few Comet tanks. Camps were held yearly and many of those who had fought in the war rejoined and passed on their experience to others who came along. It was, truth to tell, a little like an Old Comrades Association when in camp at Hornsea. They had two brewers in the Regiment, who went early each day, but were on parade at 0600hrs, with the day's supply of beer for the troops.

Victor had to retire in September 1950. Meanwhile the Regiment had had a moving Memorial Service in their newly built barracks at Endyke Lane, Hull on 8 May 1949. A Book of Remembrance was written up with the names of all those who had died in the Regiment in the Second World war. It is now kept in Beverley Minster.

After Lieutenant Colonel Ellison left, Lieutenant Colonel Tony Phillips DSO, lately of the King's Dragoon Guards, took command. He became a keen Yeoman in the spirit of the Regiment.

The East Riding Yeomanry as a regiment in the Territorial Army was finally disbanded in 1966 and was combined with the two other Yorkshire Territorial armoured units, the Yorkshire Dragoons and the Yorkshire Hussars, to form the Yorkshire Yeomanry. The other two regiments paid the ERY the compliment of incorporating both the Fox and the "Forrard" motto prominently in the new badge. Each of the founding units provided a squadron, but the Territorial Army continued to be run down and the Yorkshire Yeomanry was absorbed into the Queen's Own Yeomanry which covered much of the north of England. What had been a full Regiment – or even two for a short time in 1939–40 – became part of the "York Squadron" of the QOY and as this story closes further cuts are being made in the TA and the Hull barracks are being shut down.

But the motto is still
Forrard!

215

APPENDICES

Appendix I

SETTING THE RECORD STRAIGHT

After his release from prison camp and return to England in May 1945, Lieutenant Colonel Douglas Thompson DSO MC TD, who had commanded the Regiment in 1940, handed to Lieutenant General Sir Ronald Adam, who had commanded III Corps in that campaign, the War Diary complied by himself and his officers in the difficult circumstances of the POW life. This Diary is the basis of the narrative set out in this story of the 1940 Campaign.

In 1950 Lieutenant Colonel Thompson, with two former senior officers from the ERY, made a tour of the French countryside the Regiment had covered during the advance and withdrawal of the British forces in May 1940. They had with them a copy of 1 Armoured Recce Brigade War Diary which Lieutenant Colonel Thompson thought was a moderately accurate record of the movements of the Brigade. However, two passages alarmed him so much that he wrote to Brigadier H. B. Latham at the Historical Section of the Cabinet Office to have the official war Brigade Diary amended and the Regiment's actions properly recorded.

Two statements from the Diary are as follows:

(a) an entry from 29 May at 0800 hrs that the ERY had "received a message from 48 Div by an armoured car, very much delayed, giving them the option to withdraw to a line SE of Bergues or hold on where they were [in Cassel]. Later a wireless message was received to withdraw on the night of 29/30 May across country crossing the canal between Hondschone and Buiscamp [northwards towards Dunkirk]."

(b) May 29 2100hrs. ". . . meanwhile at Cassel the ERY had destroyed

216

their vehicles and machine guns in the tanks and the withdrawal from Cassel began."

In his letter to Brigadier Latham Lieutenant Colonel Thompson denies completely that he had received any message as set out on (a) and that (b) was wrong also. It was set out that the information in (b) had been supplied by four survivors of 145 Brigade HQ who had reached Dunkirk and their story was accepted as the fate of the ERY.

At the conclusion of his letter Lieutenant Colonel Thompson says, "It is my personal opinion that the statements above, and the last one in particular, had a detrimental effect (i) on the morale of the survivors of the Regiment who reached England, and for example (ii) on the Honorary Colonel (Colonel the Hon G. G. Wilson CMG DSO TD) who did not, like others in a similar capacity, write to the survivors of his Regiment in captivity expressing appreciation for their work, and (iii) on the relatives of the next-of-kin of those killed or made prisoner."

In his reply Brigadier Latham gave details of the officers who had written up a "diary in October 1940 at Witham Essex". None of these officers were with the Yeomanry at Cassel, so Lieutenant Colonel Thompson sent Brigadier Latham a copy of the War Diary mentioned in the first paragraph of this Appendix. "It was," Brigadier Latham replied, "the most interesting Diary and to me the first coherent account of the last few hours in Cassel that I have seen so far."

He took a copy of the Diary to the Official Historian of the 1940 campaign, Major L. F. Ellis, who also was most interested and assured him that no mention would be made of "destroying vehicles etc".

A copy of the correspondence and the "Real War Diary" were to be attached to the records to correct the statements and show that the Regiment had fought to the end, conducting itself to the highest standards of the British Army.

Appendix 2

ROLL OF HONOUR OF THOSE MEMBERS
OF THE ERY KILLED IN ACTION IN
THE SECOND WORLD WAR

Major	A J	Fitzwilliam Hyde
Major	A	Platts
Major	G M	Radcliffe
Captain	D	Hall
Captain	T E B	Sissons
Lieutenant	D J	Brooke
Lieutenant	D J	Hodsman
Lieutenant	P G F	Howitt
Lieutenant	R G	Jackson
Lieutenant	C V	Moreton
Lieutenant	A F C	Wickstead
2/Lieutenant	L T	Brabrook
2/Lieutenant	J F	Cockin
2/Lieutenant	P M	Cockin
2/Lieutenant	R L	Hudson
2/Lieutenant	C W	Laing
TSM	T W	Arbon
Sergeant	G	Dry
Sergeant	L	Harness
Sergeant	H	Lysons
Sergeant	T	Whiteside
L/Sergeant	T A	Duke
Corporal	T M le B	Brodgen
Corporal	J	Cooper
Corporal	A	Elmsley
Corporal	C	Garner
Corporal	G T	Hoyler

Rank	Initials	Surname
Corporal	J	Jack
Corporal	P D	Neesham
Corporal	J E	Pickard
Corporal	R	Smith
Corporal	J G	Spencer
Corporal	L N	Wilkes
L/Corporal	G J A	Allen
L/Corporal	F W J	Arnold
L/Corporal	B G D	Ball
L/Corporal	K A	Bellamy
L/Corporal	L C	Chick
L/Corporal	A	Cox
L/Corporal	J	Dunn
L/Corporal	R	Gibson
L/Corporal	C J	Hayes
L/Corporal	R W	Hodgson
L/Corporal	H	Hotchkin
L/Corporal	F	Overton
L/Corporal	D	Whiteside
Trooper	E S J	Armstrong
Trooper	W	Bailey
Trooper	K	Baker
Trooper	J	Barton
Trooper	S G	Barton
Trooper	S H	Batty
Trooper	G A	Bathurst
Trooper	R	Beautement
Trooper	D	Bird
Trooper	H	Brown
Trooper	G E	Clarke
Trooper	R	Cochrane
Trooper	J R	Coney
Trooper	M	Finnegan
Trooper	S	Foden
Trooper	R	Giles
Trooper	J P	Glover
Trooper	R	Green
Trooper	W A	Grant
Trooper	R	Grunwell
Trooper	G W	Harper

Trooper	H	Hill
Trooper	PP	Hodkinson
Trooper	G A	Jackson
Trooper	H	Jackson
Trooper	W	Lloyd
Trooper	R	Longhurst
Trooper	J G	Macdonald
Trooper	H	Marshall
Trooper	A J C	May
Trooper	J E	Mouser
Private (ACC)	R	Moody
Trooper	R	Norris
Trooper	H	O'Brien
Trooper	W	Ostler
Trooper	J	Park
Trooper	G A	Payne
Trooper	E H	Pocklington
Trooper	B	Redmayne
Trooper	T M	Shortt
Trooper	G	Smallwood
Trooper	J	Smith
Trooper	W A	Stead
Trooper	L	Steel
Trooper	L F	Talbot
Trooper	J	Thomson
Trooper	A	Todd
Trooper	W G	Tomkinson
Trooper	C	Tubbs
Trooper	C E	Wales
Trooper	F	Walker
Trooper	W	Wells
Trooper	W A	Welton
Trooper	E	West
Trooper	J	Whyte
Trooper	A	Wilson
Trooper	K	Wingate
Trooper	E B	Wiseman
Trooper	R F	Witt
Trooper	J F	Wolfe

Appendix 3

DECORATIONS FOR BRAVERY 1940

Distinguished Service Order

Major	Horace Maylin Vipan	Wright

Distinguished Conduct Medal

SQMS	William Henry	Smelt

Military Cross

Lieutenant	Charles Nicholas	Wilmot-Smith
Major	John	Burns (RAMC)
Lieutenant	Victor Charles	Ellison

Military Medal

Corporal	John Joseph	Brown
Corporal	Edward	Scott
Trooper	John Joseph	Bell
TSM	Austin Cyril	Robson

Mentioned in Dispatches

Major	John	Hodgson
Major	Geoffrey	Radcliffe
Lieutnant (QM)	Martin	Mulchinock
Lieutenant	Thomas	Carmichael
Lieutenant	Harold	Hopper
Lieutenant	Michael	Trevor
Lieutenant	Roger	Waterhouse
SSM		Hester

Appendix 4

HONOURS AND AWARDS – NWE CAMPAIGN

Bar to Distinguished Service Order

Lieutenant Colonel	T C	Williamson DSO

Distinguished Service Order

Major	H E E	Salman

Member of the British Empire

Captain	B G	Medhurst

Military Cross

Major	H F H	Philips
Major	W F	Holtby
Major	T F	Robinson
Captain	E W	Clark
Captain	P G	Clemence
Captain	G A O	Jenkin
Lieutenant	A C	Bulford
Lieutenant	E J	Scotter

French Croix De Guerre

Captain	A H	Thornton (with Gilt Star)
Lance Corporal	J	Albison (with Bronze Star)

Military Medal

Sergeant	E	Bean

Sergeant	S R	Jubb (now Lieut)
Sergeant	E W	Cone
Sergeant	M	Fitzmaurice
Sergeant	F	McBain
Sergeant	B	Matthews
Sergeant	J H	Moverley
Corporal	J	Felllows
Lance Corporal	A E	Adams

Mentioned in Dispatches

Lieutenant Colonel	T C	Williamson DSO
Major	E	Morley-Fletcher TD
Captain	P G	Clemence MC
Captain	Hon J H W	Lowther
Captain	G R F	Peak
Lieutenant	J H	Davies
Lieutenant	D R	Mantell
Lieutenant	E J	Scotter
SSM	J C	Morris
Sergeant	R	Coupland
Sergeant	W H	Morrell
Corporal	G T	Boughton
Corporal	H	Clucas
Lance Corporal	R	Green
Lance Corporal	H J	Jackson
Trooper	P J	Blankney
Trooper	G J	Bolton
Trooper	R	Dunn
Trooper	G H	King
Trooper	K C	Simpkins

Commmader-in-Chief's Certificates

For Gallantry

Lieutenant	D	Brooke (Posthumous Award)
Lieutenant	P G	Howitt (Posthumous Award)
Staff Sergeant	C B	Neil (REME)
Sergeant	J G	Rose
Sergeant	M R J	Yuille

Sergeant	H	Walters
Lance Sergeant	J W	Lever
Lance Corporal	A C	Moore
Lance Corporal	K	Robinson
Lance Corporal	F E	Sandford
For Good Service		
SSM	F W	Parker
SQMS	H	Morris
Sergeant	J	Dent
Sergeant	M E	East
Corporal	J B	Priestley
Lance Corporal	E	Harvey
Signalman	L	Monk (R Sigs attached)

Ranks as held when awards gained

Appendix 5

BATTLE HONOURS

FIRST WORLD WAR

1917	Palestine	Gaza
		El Mugbir
		Nebi Samwill
	Egypt 1915–1917	
	Palestine 1917 –1918	
1918	France	
	October	Selle
	November	Valenciennes
	November	Sambre
	France and Flanders	1914–18

SECOND WORLD WAR

1940		
23–29/5/40	France	St Omer
		La Bassée
27/5/40	France	Cassel
1940–1942		N W Europe
6/6/44		Normandy Landing
9/6/44		Cambes
9–18/7/44		Caen
18–23/7/44		Bourguebus Ridge
18–20/8/44		La Vie Crossing
21–23/8/44		Lisieux
28–30/8/44		Fôret de Bretonne

20/10–2/11/44		Lower Maas
14/11–3/12/44		Venlo Pocket
3–14/1/45		The Ourthe
25/3–1/4/45		The Rhine
6/6/44–5/5/45	NW Europe 1944–45	

INDEX

227

229